The Cinematic Rebirths of FRANKENSTEIN

Universal, Hammer, and Beyond

Caroline Joan ("Kay") S. Picart

PRAEGER

Westport, Connecticut
London

Library of Congress Cataloging-in-Publication Data

Picart, Caroline Joan, 1966–
    The cinematic rebirths of Frankenstein : Universal, Hammer, and beyond / Caroline
Joan ("Kay") S. Picart.
        p. cm.
    Includes bibliographical references and index.
    ISBN 0–275–97363–8
        1. Frankenstein films—History and criticism.   I. Title.
    PN1995.9.F8 P52   2002
    791.43'651—dc21   2001021186

British Library Cataloguing in Publication Data is available.

Library of Congress Catalog Card Number: 2001021186
ISBN: 0–275–97363–8

First published in 2002

Praeger Publishers, 88 Post Road West, Westport, CT 06881
An imprint of Greenwood Publishing Group, Inc.
www.praeger.com

Printed in the United States of America

∞™

The paper used in this book complies with the
Permanent Paper Standard issued by the National
Information Standards Organization (Z39.48–1984).

10 9 8 7 6 5 4 3 2 1

Copyright Acknowledgments

The author and publisher gratefully acknowledge permission to reprint the following
material:

Parts of Chapter 1 and Chapter 2, section 2, "Creating the Monstrous: Karloff as Cinematic
Archetype," were published in an earlier article, Caroline Joan S. Picart, "James Whale's
(Mis)Reading of Mary Shelley's *Frankenstein*." *Critical Studies in Mass Communication* 15
(1998): 382–404. Copyright by the National Communication Association, 1998. Reproduced
by permission of the publisher. Some of the language in Chapter 1 on Dionysus and Baubo
appeared earlier in Caroline Joan S. Picart, *Resentment and the "Feminine" in Nietzsche's
Politico-Aesthetics*. State College, Pennsylvania: The Pennsylvania State University Press,
1999. Part of Chapter 5 was published as Caroline Joan S. Picart, "Visualizing the Monstrous
in Frankenstein Films." *Pacific Coast Philology*. 35.1 (2000): 17–34.

To Mom and Dad, who have always encouraged my penchant for stories
and imaginative forays,
and to Ray Fleming and Tom Benson, who have nurtured and pruned
my passion for Romanticism and Film.

Contents

Illustrations

Preface

I thank the Academy of Motion Picture Arts and Sciences for the camera-ready photographs that appear in this book. I also wish to thank the University of Wisconsin–Eau Claire Office of Research for a grant that enabled me to collaborate with an outstanding group of graduate and undergraduate students comprised of Keith Woodward, Elizabeth McDermott, Andrew Swant, and Kelly Smith in integrating my research with teaching. I gratefully acknowledge the support I received through a large research grant from St. Lawrence University in order to bring this, and another book, *The Frankenstein Film Sourcebook*, to completion.

To all those who have critically engaged with my work, I owe a debt of gratitude. In particular, I wish to thank Ray Fleming and Tom Benson, whose brilliance, kindness, and enthusiastic and unflagging support have been invaluable in my venturing beyond the disciplinary boundary of the strictly "philosophical." Jan Rushing and Tom Frentz, as well, have been an inspiration in their meticulous and constructive commentary, as well as collegiality and good humor, in their remarks on sections of prior versions of this material. Looking at how much of my life has entailed sojourning forth these past few years, I am suddenly deeply aware of and grateful for friends at the Department of Philosophy, University of Wisconsin–Eau Claire: Jim Brummer, Ron Koshoshek, Dick Behling, Richard DeGrood, Ned Beach, Kathleen Hathaway, Lisa Wersal, Marty Webb, Lori Rowlett, Jonathan Paradise, Joanne Erickson, and Joyce Hageness, as well as at the Department of Philosophy, St. Lawrence University: Grant Cornwell, Baylor Johnson, and Laura Rediehs. I also wish to thank my new colleagues at the English Department and the Humanities Program at Florida State University, and, in specific, Hunt Hawkins and Leon Golden for their kind and enthusiastic support as I have transitioned into a new environment, as well as a broader, interdisciplinary milieu.

Finally I wish to thank Eric Levy, whose wit, humor, and efficiency place him among the most pleasant and effective editors I have had the opportunity to work with. Yet the deepest and most unsayable thanks go to both the Picart and Houck families, for their continuing support and love. Ultimately I wish to thank my husband, Davis, for the joy, intimacy, and challenge of sharing and enabling, among many other things, a communion of embodied minds and spirits.

Introduction

The ubiquity and endurance of the Frankenstein myth has resulted in its widespread popularization, producing a spate of diverse films. Films on Frankenstein, or that have a Frankenstein-related story, are usually classed purely as horror films, yet the flexibility of the narrative has spawned other types of progeny, such as musical horror-comedy (*The Rocky Horror Picture Show*); outrageous horror parody that verges on sadomasochistic porn (*Flesh for Frankenstein*), and science fiction dystopias (*Blade Runner*). The diversification and domestication of the narrative has also birthed a complex spectrum of television shows, toys, and video games.

Thus, some methodological choices require explanation at the very outset. First, given the proliferation of various *Frankenstein*ian films and related media, I have chosen to limit the scope of this study to the Universal Studio film series (1931–1945), the Hammer Studio series (1957–1974), and two poststudio interpretations, Allied Artists' *Frankenstein 1970* (1958) and TriStar Pictures' *Mary Shelley's Frankenstein* (1994). My choices were dictated partially by pragmatic considerations, such as the availability of scripts, production history documents, and video reconstructions of these films, all of which served as primary texts. In addition, I chose these films because there is a considerable amount of intertextuality—visual, thematic, technical, plot-wise—that bind these films into a rich and complex fabric.

Second, I have chosen to limit my survey of films to those that constitute a traditional appropriation of the Frankensteinian myth. Other genre offshoots—such as comedic, science fiction, horror, animation, and even porn versions—constitute a multiplicity of other deformations of the myth, and fall outside the purview of the project.

Third, this study is not concerned with proving Mary Shelley's feminist intentions or in making the novel (in its 1818 and 1831 editions) the "original" in relation to which the films constitute a blasphemous descent. What I aim to show is that the evolving Frankensteinian story, understood as a myth (i.e., a recurring and ever-malleable narrative that both reveals and conceals primordial sites of fascination and repulsion—such as demarcations of the "masculine" from the "feminine" or the "natural" from the "artificial"), is part of a larger mythic unfolding. In earlier converging myths (such as those of Dionysus and Baubo), patriarchal and matriarchal mythemes originally coexisted in a tense and creative agon. Traditional *Frankenstein*ian films, which have become the repository of this mythic unfolding, hide and unconceal this continuing tension, despite the overt dominance of patriarchal myths over matriarchal myths.

Finally, the project is essentially a genealogical one, which means that it is less concerned with rating or debating which films are more successful than others, or in finding a "solution" to the dilemma of the Ego's generation of its shadows. Rather its aim is to excavate how the Frankensteinian myth evolves through these films, involving several sources of information, such as the evolving scripts and screen treatments, censorship issues, critical and popular reception, publicity gimmicks, and the final artifacts. This is because I am convinced that the Frankensteinian myth, embodied in film, does not nevertheless stay locked into the ahistorical vacuum of its celluloid medium. The Frankensteinian myth, as an expression and dispersion of cultural aspirations and traumas concerning gender and technology, takes form, precisely within the context of this complex and often messy process that involves commercial and public considerations, as well as private artistic visions. Thus, whenever the requisite material was available, I have attempted to trace the continuities and disruptions across various primary source documents in relation to the final film, with an eye to how the Frankensteinian narrative, with its strained hyperbolization of the myth of male self-birthing, ironically reveals its dark underside. This attention to genealogy is a fundamental hallmark of the methodology I use.

CHAPTER 1

Envisaging the Monstrous

... film versions of *Frankenstein* implicitly remind us that filmmaking itself is a Frankensteinian exercise in artificial reproduction.
—James A.W. Heffernan, "Looking at the Monster: Frankenstein and Film"

MYTHS OF CREATION AND DESTRUCTION

The stunning rise of James Whale's 1931 version of *Frankenstein*[1] from its initial image as "a grisly, blood-soaked example of exploitative filmmaking"[2] to the status of a classic whose "sensitive craftsmanship and relentlessly macabre tone still set horror movie standards, even after decades and noisome parodies and splatter-film overkill"[3] has resulted in numerous attempts to account for this phenomenon.

Many of the critical approaches that address the question of Whale's *Frankenstein*'s filmic longevity fall under the headings of the technical and the thematic.[4] As a general overview, most of the technical approaches draw attention to Karloff's acting or Whale's directing, or a combination of the two, in conjunction with Pierce's makeup skills.[5] The thematic approaches range from the film's fidelity to its Romantic roots; its ability to tap into prevailing cultural adolescent identification with monstrous feelings of alienation and entrapment; its fulfillment of the need for rituals of initiation; its re-creation of the symbols of its European literary background; to its ability to mirror the anxieties that haunted the thirties and its reconstruction as a parody of the Resurrection.[6] Yet the endurance of the celluloid transformations of the Frankenstein narrative certainly transcends the boundaries of Whale's icon-producing film.

Still from *Frankenstein* appears courtesy of the Academy of Motion Picture Arts and Sciences. Universal, 1931.

I view the question of these filmic rebirths through the prism of how gender is continually constructed, deconstructed, and reconstructed. In particular I trace a shifting (though nonlinear) emphasis from bodily reproduction (female) to technological production (male) in the reenvisaging of Shelley's novel into film. Such an approach necessitates an examination of what lies at the heart of Shelley's Romantic tale: the critique of the masculine attempt at *parthenogenesis* or male self-birthing. This study is also an attempt to examine how this essentially Dionysian and Promethean myth, European and Romantic in origin, is transmuted, in some cases, such as in James Whale's and Terence Fisher's movies, into a modern version that parodies the Resurrection as one of its central motifs. Furthermore, it is an attempt to excavate the traces of the covering over of the myth of Baubo—the refractory image of woman as whore, mother, and goddess of disruptive humor and sexual energy. The twofold motion of hyperbolizing the Dionysian myth, and muting or eradicating the myth of Baubo, is crucial to doing a genealogy of the filmic (d)evolutions of the Frankensteinian narrative.

Briefly summarized, the essential strands I weave together that are crucial to a filmic genealogy of the evolving Frankenstein film narrative are the myths of Prometheus, Dionysus, and Baubo. This is not to say that these are the only myths that may be used as theoretical lenses to interpret the evolution of Frankensteinian films but that their conjunction-rupture is a particularly fruitful one, as I show. I now embark on a brief review of these myths so that the cinematic allusion to, and overlaying of, these archetypal mythemes will be self-evident as we proceed. Prometheus is known as the "savior of mankind." Not only did he steal and bestow the gift of fire upon men,[7] but he also tricked Zeus into choosing the bones disguised in fat, rather than the meat, wrapped in hide and covered by entrails, as the proper sacrifice to the gods. Thenceforth, only bones and fat were sacrificed while men kept the meat for themselves. In retaliation, Zeus sent men the "gift" of Pandora, who, like Eve (and supposedly, all women), unleashed evil unto them. Prometheus's punishment lay in being chained to a rock on the Caucasus Mountains, where an eagle would tear at his liver during the day; Prometheus's liver grew back nightly, concentrating the unending torment. The Promethean myth is significant insofar as Shelley subtitled her novel, *The Modern Prometheus*. This subtitle conjoins the messianic character of Victor's attempt to win over death as an aspiring savior of humankind, with his "modernity"—which comes to stand for his fallenness from the state of nature and his obsessive desire to "penetrate into the secrets of nature." Like Prometheus, Victor attempts to steal a dangerous secret—the knowledge of how to bestow life; like Prometheus, Victor is punished through the deaths of all whom he held dear, prior to his own descent into obsessive pursuit of the creature, and his eventual wretched death. Yet Victor never quite rises to the classical nobility of the heroic Prometheus;

his quest remains a quest for the quest itself, that is, a self-absorbed and narcissistic attempt to overcome all that resists his attempt at thoroughgoing control.

Preliminarily sketched, the intersecting myths of Dionysus and Baubo are competing myths of reproductive power. Dionysus's birth from the thigh of Zeus, as a son born from the thigh of his father, over the dead body of his mother, Semele, is a patriarchal myth that appropriates the female power of birthing. In contrast, Baubo's successful cajoling of Demeter, from the realms of grieving, anger, and despair over her daughter's rape and abduction (in which both Zeus and Dionysus are implicated) to scandalous laughter and a joyful reassertion of female reproductive power, is matriarchal. Unlike the Promethean myth, which has been a site for continuous critical and genealogical commentary, little or no connection has been made relating the myths of Dionysus and Baubo to the changing Frankensteinian filmic narrative. What has usually been thematically centrally located is the desire to usurp the place of God, which is an interpretation of *Frankenstein* that became popular largely because of *Presumption!*, a moralistic play based on Shelley's novel that harnessed the ambivalences of the original. In my view, the evolving Frankensteinian narrative is more principally about power and gender. This means that one of its central concerns is the dynamic dislocation and momentary congealing of the porous borders separating the "masculine" from the "feminine"; the "human" and "superhuman" from the "bestial" and "subhuman"; and the "natural" from the "artificial" or "mechanical." The bulk of this book is precisely geared toward substantiating that connection and showing how an examination of the myths of Dionysus and Baubo may illuminate how the Frankenstein cinematic narrative/s, which themselves have achieved mythic status, struggle with similar issues of gender and power. Like the mythemes of Dionysus and Baubo, which are malleable and nonlinear, the Frankensteinian narrative, as transmuted through film, has been constantly reenvisaged and retold.

To perform this genealogy of disruptive links and lacunae—ricocheting across the porous borders of myth/s and film/s in relation to the novel—it is wise to retrace briefly a simple (and perhaps necessarily oversimplified) plotline of Shelley's *Frankenstein*. The purpose of this summary is to serve as a general point of reference in relation to filmic versions. I realize that there are differences between the 1818 and 1831 versions of the novel, which I reference only when these are relevant, as I do briefly in Chapter 2. The fulcrum of this critical commentary lies neither in an analysis of Mary Shelley's biography and her intentions,[8] nor in the intricacies of the details of the 1818 and 1831 novels, however rich these areas are, but in tracing how the Frankensteinian myth has earlier mythic correlates (e.g., the intertwining stories of Dionysus and Baubo), whose creative agon points to an earlier coexistence of matriarchal and patriarchal myths. The

Frankensteinian narrative, which unconceals the tension between these two types of myths, in the traditional films progressively (though with much ambivalent strain) suppresses matriarchal myths in favor of patriarchal myths. Insofar as myths are eternally rewritten, there is no "original" from which to gauge motives or intents; there are only dynamic genealogies, whose silences are as significant as the "noise" they generate.

To begin a rough synopsis: Robert Walton, an explorer relentlessly determined to find a path to the North Pole, writes to his sister Margaret (Walton) Saville of his adventures. The story unfolds as a multiply framed tale, with Margaret W. Saville's (whose initials are the same as *Frankenstein*'s author) readership forming the outermost layer; Robert Walton's voice forming the next; Victor Frankenstein's embedded within; and, finally, the creature's account forming the innermost layer. Walton writes of his burning ambition to withstand the torments of the deadly weather in order to forge a passage to the North Pole, and thus join the exalted ranks of those who have improved the lot of humankind through bravery; yet he also writes of his loneliness and isolation. Serendipitously, Walton and his crew come across the strange sight of a disheveled man using a dogsled to chase after an apparition that, briefly glimpsed, resembles a human form and yet is gigantic in its proportions. The ice cracks; the giant disappears, and they manage to save the strange man, who turns out to be Victor Frankenstein. A friendship grows between Walton and Frankenstein, and it is only when Frankenstein diagnoses Walton to be suffering from the very same (Promethean) disease that afflicts him that he reluctantly narrates his story.

Frankenstein describes his blissfully happy childhood in Geneva, where he grew up sheltered by his parents' love and wealth. His mother, Caroline, adopted Elizabeth, who, unfortunately, became the unwitting cause of her stepmother's death; Caroline passed away after having looked after Elizabeth when she was ill, only to fall deathly ill herself after she had nursed Elizabeth back to health. The novel drops numerous hints that Victor's obsession with finding out the secret of life is linked with his attempt to regain access to the absent body of his dead mother. Partly because of his father's dismissal of the alchemists, Frankenstein is fascinated by their work. Later, when he goes to study medicine at the University of Ingolstadt, he incorporates his readings of alchemy with his medical experiments to produce a body stitched together from various corpses. In a feverish frenzy that clearly separates him from everyone, even his beloved Elizabeth, to whom he ceases writing, he succeeds in reanimating the creature. Yet he flees from the creature out of fear and revulsion, and falls into a delirium on the edge of madness, from which Henry Clerval, his best friend, rescues him by patiently nursing him back to health.

The creature, like an overgrown abandoned child, is forced to learn how to survive on its own. It encounters the De Lacey family in the woods, and, by spying upon them teaching a beautiful Arabian, Safie, how to read, speak, and write in French, it learns how to read and converse in French, the language of its parthenogenetic father. In its loneliness, it attempts to appeal to the pity of the blind grandfather, but once its presence is discovered, the De Lacey family, too, flees in terror and revulsion. Enraged by their rejection and abandonment, the creature burns the De Lacey hut and returns to confront its creator and to demand that Victor create a mate to ease its loneliness.

In spite of his anger and revulsion, Victor acknowledges his failure as a creator-parent, and the creature eloquently manages to wrench from Frankenstein the promise that he will birth a fitting Eve for his fallen Adam. Yet as Frankenstein works over the assembled female body and glimpses the creature's self-satisfied grin (as well as fantasizing about the numerous horrors that could spring from his female creation—such as the possibility of male rape and the generation of more "devils"), he suddenly changes his mind, and violently rips apart the inert and still lifeless female body. The creature cries out, and then vengefully vows to be with him on his wedding night.

Victor thinks that the Monster plans to attack him on his wedding night, but it is Elizabeth whom the creature kills. Thereafter, the pursued becomes the pursuer, as Victor vows to kill his own creation, who eggs him on with taunts whenever Victor's exhaustion threatens to make him desire to give up the chase. It is this deadly chase that has brought both of them to the wintry North, causing their and Walton's paths to cross. Feeble with exhaustion and sickness, Victor dies. Walton momentarily leaves the body alone and returns to find the creature weeping over Victor's body. Surprised, Walton interrogates the creature, and the Monster replies that he grieves over the loss of his father. Walton turns his ship back, implying the effectiveness of Victor's narrative as a cure for his Promethean madness, as the creature disappears into the icy infinity of the North Pole.

What I aim to show is that traditional Frankenstein films in the horror genre generally attempt to excise out, or severely delimit, the novel's embedded critique of the Romantic politics of gender, as hiding a politics of masculine domination and narcissism. In place of the novel's complex characterization of the monster, these films often substitute a grotesque creation doomed to criminality and isolation; in place of the ambivalent relationships binding Victor to his mother and his bride/surrogate mother, these films obliterate the M/Other, and set up a more conventional love triangle between male figures, such as Henry Frankenstein and Victor Clerval, who seem monstrously cobbled together from fragments of Shelley's novelistic characterization of them.

Yet this severe repression backfires. At the center of these films is a re-telling of an exaggerated myth of male self-birthing—a myth whose classic analogue may be glimpsed in the story of the birth of Dionysus from the thigh of Zeus. At the heart of these transformations is a complex web of intersecting and diverging temporal and "ethical" strands. Contemporary *Frankenstein*ian films draw from an antinomic hybrid of pre-Socratic and Romantic narratives, both of which mythically configure the natural world as one of strife, in which gendered antagonisms comprise a crucial component. Pre-Socratic myths, as Nietzsche tells us, are narratives "beyond good and evil," whose "morality" derives from an unadulterated expression of the will-to-power. Romantic myths, as the novel shows us, can be a masked and murderous domination of nature, woman, the Other, done in the name of the pursuit of Scientific Truth or Artistic Creativity. Although pre-Socratic myths give evidence of a tense and creative agonism between matriarchal and patriarchal myths, Romantic myths (and contemporary renditions of these mythemes) have a predominantly patriarchal cast, in which manifestations of the "feminine" or "M/Other" are severely delimited and disciplined, often, with a great deal of narrative strain. This immense narrative strain conjures up something other than a simple victimizer (male)–victim (female) model. Rather what we occasionally glimpse are the outlines of the feminized/tortured male body, which requires, in order to sustain the borders of masculinity versus femininity, a radical repression of the powerful female body, negatively reenvisaged as either the female monster (as in the female creature in *Bride of Frankenstein*) or the feminine-as-monstrous (as Justine in *The Curse of Frankenstein*); yet this repression, even as it gains an uneasy victory, attests, in the vehemence of its negation, to its dark underside. As Deborah Wilson writes, "Victor never quite makes maternity *exclusively* male; the womb may be displaced, the maternal body reinscribed, but it will not remain subsumed."[9]

Stated differently, these Frankenstein films downplay what Janice Rushing and Thomas Frentz call the "dystopian" aspects of the Frankensteinian complex, in comparison with the novel, as is evidenced in these films' elimination of sexual ambiguity and the often tacked on happy endings. Yet the resultant strain in excising out the disturbing aspects of Shelley's novel is so great that these films often end up both veiling and unveiling their severe repression—and, as such, both reinforcing and being critical of their patriarchal foundations. Associated with this anxiety-ridden reinforcement and critique of patriarchal politics is an expression of the "flip side" of the dominant Western myth of technology as progress. To chart how this rewriting occurs, from a radical critique (in Shelley's novel) to an ambivalent affirmation-negation of a patriarchal politics of gender, alongside a veiling and unveiling of the repressed dystopic myth of technology (as evidenced in contemporary *Frankenstein* films), this book poses the following questions:

1. In what ways do these films significantly differ from the novel by Shelley, particularly in terms of their rhetorical construction of the masculine versus the

feminine, where the "masculine" realm is aligned with the divine and the human, as opposed to the "feminine" realm of the monstrous and the sub/inhuman or the machine? As a parallel question, how is "masculinity" configured as powerful, as "femininity" is associated with powerlessness, in the convergent way the "masculine" realm delineates human speech from the "feminine" realm of silence and bestial or nonhuman sounds?

2. What are some Romantic and Classical mythological roots, which may be inferred from the novel, that seem to be muted or totally eradicated in these films and when traceable, their production processes? Or, tracing the Frankensteinian complex backward to its classical roots, what major transformations have occurred to the intertwining stories of Dionysus and Baubo?

3. What evolving myths do these films generate or reflect, in terms of the Ego's mythic relationship to gender and technology? Are there significant changes/ continuities across the evolving filmic iterations, which often visually and thematically reference each other?

In very concrete ways, to engage one of these questions is to implicate the others. The main objects of this inquiry are a genealogy of the transformations of the Frankensteinian myth, and what these transformations reveal about the evolving depictions of "masculinity" and "femininity." This genealogy of the Frankensteinian Romantic myth may be traced backward, to its classic analogue, or traced forward, for example, to Whale's image-crystallizing 1931 film revision. *Frankenstein* uses the narrative of male self-birthing, or parthenogenesis, to critique the patriarchal politics of Romanticism. This critique is silenced, not without tension, by its filmic counterparts, which, in turn, appropriate and hyperbolize the parthenogenetic myth to tame the unruly ambivalences of its twin myth, the story of Baubo's *ana-suromai* (lifting her skirts to reveal her genitalia and belly) to create a more sanitized and clearly delineated demarcation separating the "masculine" from the "feminine." Yet insofar as the degree of splintering or repression required to uphold the supermasculinization of the myth of the thigh birth (and the obliteration of the myth of the exposure of the female belly and pudenda) is so great, this repression also constitutes a critical revelation of patriarchal aspirations—and the hint of a possible antidote to the nightmarish story of the hunter who becomes the hunted, or the creator whose creature turns against him. Alongside this affirmation and critique of patriarchal politics is also a revelation of the dark/repressed side of technology as gateway to disaster rather than progress.

Several clarificatory remarks concerning this theoretical framework are necessary. First, the sense in which I use the terms "masculinity" and "femininity" is not strictly confined to a heterosexual perspective; on the contrary, this approach shows precisely how, as Carol J. Clover has claimed of contemporary films, in horror "gender is less a wall than a permeable membrane."[10] However, there is also a sense in which not all male gazes upon male bodies are necessarily homosexual, and not all female gazes upon female bodies are necessarily lesbian. I am sympathetic to Harry Benshoff when he argues that "Both movie monsters and homosexuals have existed chiefly in shadowy closets, and when they do emerge from these proscribed places into the sunlit world, they cause panic and fear. . . . To create a broad analogy, monster is to 'normality' as homosexual is to heterosexual."[11]

Nevertheless, I am also aware of the risk of exchanging one hegemony for another, and reducing all gendered interactions to *necessarily* queer readings. Although that approach is compelling, and Benshoff's is a clear illustration of its illuminative potential,[12] insofar as I am doing a genealogy of the material transformations of the mythic origins of the Frankenstein narrative—myths that precede and transcend distinctions of homosexuality and heterosexuality—I aim to preserve a notion of gender that precedes and even grounds this constructed binary dichotomy. Same sex interactions comprise a complex spectrum, ranging from "homosociality" to "homoeroticism," and particularly in the realm of monsters, where not only gender, but also sex, become porous, I find it more useful to speak of the evolving deconstructions and fleeting reconstructions of "masculinity" and "femininity" in relation to power in terms of a performative continuum that resists reduction to an exclusively hetero- or homosexual perspective. In a parallel argument, Rhona Berenstein analyses Robert J. Corber's work in the following way: "[Corber] reduces the field of sexual identity to a pitched battle between homosexuality and heterosexuality. Although I sympathize with the lure of discussing homosexual desire as both central and preexistent to heterosexuality, reversing the hierarchy creates a whole new set of problems. Surely Corber is wrong when he assumes that all male gazes are homosexual in form."[13] Admittedly, there are sections, such as those dealing with the films or scripts of openly gay men, such as James Whale, where the continuum veers quite closely to an overtly queer reading. Yet in such cases, my reading of same-sex interactions are not insulated from relations with the "opposite" sex; instead "masculinity" and "femininity" remain dynamic, performative reimaginings in collaboration with and antagonism against each other.

Second, this study also builds from a large corpus of interdisciplinary scholarship on how literature is adapted, or transformed, into film.[14] Because of its focus on filmic transformation as a rhetorical act that privileges certain choices and interests, this analysis, for example, draws from some of the critical strategies of Wayne McMullen and Martha Solomon's[15] analysis of Steven Spielberg's film translation of Alice Walker's *The Color Purple*, and Brenda Cooper and David Descutner's[16] analysis of Sydney Pollack's film rendition of Isak Dinesen's *Out of Africa*. McMullen and Solomon illustrate how Spielberg alters Walker's narrative of a black woman's evolution to self-empowerment, resulting in silencing the voice of its central character and forcing the story to conform to dominant patriarchal cultural mythologies. In their words, "viewers are stimulated to see Celie as an example of the American dream. Persistence, hard work, and capitalistic acumen secure her eventual triumph. In short, for Celie the patriarchally controlled system works. . . . For viewers besieged by images of homelessness, sexual abuse, violence against women, and other critiques of the social system, Spielberg's filmic story is a tranquilizing narcotic."[17]

Similarly, Cooper and Descutner show how Pollack's film used the rhetorical strategies of "transference, redefinition, antithesis, and displacement"[18] to cover over Dinesen's complex voice and vision, and her link with Africa, in order to produce the portrait of a woman dependent on men, disinterested in personal freedom, indifferent to issues of sexism and racism, and alienated from Africa. Although this study converges with McMullen and Solomon's, and Cooper and Descutner's, conclusions regarding how film versions impose patriarchal interpretations on feminist writings, it differs in its method. McMullen and Solomon rely mainly on a frame derived from Kenneth Burke whereas Cooper and Descutner draw from Judith Mayne, a feminist film scholar, to ground their analyses. In contrast, this study is drawn from three distinct clusters of sources. These are Anne Mellor's,[19] Margaret Homans's,[20] and William Veeder's[21] converging analyses of Romantic gender politics, which I link with the Dionysian myth of parthenogenesis;[22] Winifred Milius Lubell's genealogy of the persistence and transformations of Baubo's skirt-lifting gesture (or *anasuromai*)[23] and Sarah Kofman's assertion that the myth of Baubo is the counterpart to the myth of Zeus-Dionysus;[24] and Janice Rushing and Thomas Frentz's construction of an evolving dystopian shadow myth that reveals repressed fears the culture has in its relationship toward technology.[25] I agree with Rushing and Frentz's analysis that the recurring myth of technology running wild is "Frankensteinian" and is continued in such films as *Jaws, Rocky IV, Blade Runner*, and *The Terminator*. And unlike McMullen and Solomon's and Cooper and Descutner's studies, which focus on a linear patriarchal covering over of feminist voices, this book focuses on the twofold movement of the severe repression of the "feminine," the Other, the monstrous, and the concomitant erection of a supermasculinized version of the myth of parthenogenesis. This is a twofold movement that simultaneously reveals and undercuts its patriarchal foundations. McMullen and Solomon's and Cooper and Descutner's work show how the medium of film exacts conversions that transform radical critiques into more ideologically mainstream statements. Though this study echoes that, it also takes up the issue of how these films, as volatile "shadow" myths (i.e., myths of the disowned and scandalous, but ambivalently desired as part of the Self), not only differentially repress, but also unveil, their patriarchal assumptions concerning gender and technology.

I now proceed to a more thorough analysis of the essential strands of these theoretical frames, which consist of the competing myths of Dionysus and Baubo in relation to the politics of reproduction and eroticism, and the dynamic of shadow myths as outlined by Rushing and Frentz in their analysis of science-fiction films as revelatory of anxieties concerning gender and technology.

PARTHENOGENESIS: CLASSICAL AND ROMANTIC ITERATIONS

Mellor argues that the imaginative genesis of the scene of the murder of Elizabeth Lavenza, Victor Frankenstein's bride, is traceable to a painting by Fuseli titled *Nightmare* (1781). This painting features a young woman's death/dreaming pose, with her head flung back and her hair cascading forth in an ambiguous expression of erotic desire and fear of the demonic incubus that sits upon her womb. This image is recaptured in Mary Shelley's description of Elizabeth's death-pose: "her head hanging down and her pale, distorted features half covered by her hair . . . bloodless arms and relaxed form flung by the murderer on its bridal bier."[26] Mellor strengthens her contention by stating that Mary Shelley was well aware of this painting, partly because of her mother's early passion for Fuseli.[27]

Mellor points out two striking traits of the painting, which have implications for the interpretation of Mary Shelley's novel: first, the woman's languorous pose is ambiguous, expressive of lustfulness for and fear of the incubus that leers upon her, brought to her by the stallion whose head, the only visible part of the horse, appears to tower above the bed—like a god of fertility for whom a sacrifice is being enacted; and second, that the incubus sits, not exactly upon her breasts, but farther down, closer to her womb, leading one to suspect that what is at stake is not simply a nightmarish vision of eroticism, but also its link to the propagation of life as eternally tied to the imminence of death, rendered concrete in the act of reproduction.

Thus, Mellor argues that a major theme not only sculpting this particular scene but also permeating Shelley's book is the masculine attempt to harness the female power of childbearing. Victor's nonsexual creation of the Monster provides him with a means of eliminating the female role in the genesis of progeny. His refusal to create a mate for the monster, however much he rationalizes it, is grounded upon terror in the face of the vivid possibility of an unbridled female power that is free from the social, ethical, and physical constraints that usually maintain the dominance of males over females, particularly in the spheres of eroticism and inheritance. Ultimately, Victor seems to desire his bride most passionately in death. His nonsexual treatment of Elizabeth either as a favorite pet, a dear sister, or an inspiring angel, when she was alive, surfaces in sharp contrast. As Mellor states, "Victor most ardently desires his bride when he knows she is dead; the conflation with his earlier dream, when he thought to embrace the living Elizabeth but instead held in his arms the corpse of his mother, signals Victor's most profound erotic desire, a necrophiliac and incestuous desire to possess the dead female, the lost mother."[28]

The persistence of the ghost of the dead mother as an object both lusted after and loathed readily emerges as a recurrent theme. The novel is riddled with the tragic deaths of mother figures: Elizabeth and Justine not only bear the heavy mark of Caroline's character and mannerisms, but they are also charged with having caused the deaths of their mothers. They both become replacement mother figures (Elizabeth, acting in Caroline's stead, and Justine, acting as a foster-mother for William). Subsequently they are both killed.

Homans echoes Mellor's stress on the rape and destruction of the mother as figuratively expressed in Victor's obsessive desire to "penetrate into the recesses of nature and show how she works in her hiding places."[29] The ultimate sacrilege he commits is necrophiliac in character as he thrusts into the "unhallowed damps of the grave"[30] and disturbs, "with profane fingers, the tremendous secrets of the human frame."[31] As Homans phrases it, "The mother he rapes is dead; his researches into her secrets, to usurp her powers, require that she be dead."[32] In conjunction with this ambivalent violence upon the mother, Veeder observes Victor's recurrent desire to kill Elizabeth. Victor murders Elizabeth twice: figuratively in the nightmare and actually on the night of the wedding.[33] Yet for Veeder, the deaths of all the mother figures are but a prelude to the death of Alphonse—Victor's father. The primal complex at work here is less an oedipal complex than a "negative" oedipal one, as the son murders the mother in order to kill the father, rather than the converse.[34]

Mellor's, Homans's, and Veeder's hypotheses converge, however inadvertently, with a pre-Socratic mythological parallel: the birth of Dionysus from the thigh of Zeus—a son born of a father. The Orphic version of this myth narrates how Dionysus was given to the goddess Hipta, who "assisted the child-bearing Zeus"[35] at the birth of Dionysus. This same version reveals Hipta to be Rhea, the great eastern mother goddess, who, after accepting Dionysus from his father, carried him on her head.[36] In the fifth century B.C.E., the cult of Dionysus was reintroduced in Athens, and Zeus, now bearing the name Sabazios, was glorified in a hymn as the god who sewed Dionysus into his thigh so that "when he who had been sewed in" was "ripe," he could be brought to the goddess Hipta on Tmolos.[37] However, another version of this myth from Asia Minor does render problematic the question of whether the father had indeed mutilated and emasculated himself. According to this version, after Zeus had committed incest with his mother, Rhea, he seemingly emasculated himself but actually cunningly threw a ram's testicles into the womb of the goddess.[38]

The areas of affinity between this conglomerate of myths and the Frank-

ensteinian narrative emerge: first, the male aspiration to give birth to another male, and second, the shrouding of the son's incestuous desire for
the mother. The resonance with this reinterpretation of the myth, in
Veeder's case, is even more pronounced—the desire to kill off the father
may be interpreted as the ultimate attempt at self-generation and autoeroticism. It is important to note that for Veeder, the series of deaths in
Mary Shelley's novel occur along the scale of an increasing amount of
intimacy and of primal stature, beginning with a child, a peer, the closest
male peer, the closest female peer, and, finally, the father. It is true that
the Monster does not directly murder Alphonse, yet Veeder argues that the
apoplectic fit that does kill Alphonse is caused by Victor and the progeny
he creates to effect his demonic desires. Veeder also observes the string of
deaths, alphabetically retraced, produces the sequence: W(illiam)-J(ustine)-
H(enry)-E(lizabeth)-A(lphonse). Such a sequence, (W-J-H-E-A—i.e., a
backward flow through the alphabet), indicates, to Veeder, a primal re-
gression: the unbridled ambition to return to the nothingness of generation
and to become the absolute self-generating source, which Veeder emble-
matizes using the figure of the snake swallowing its tail: "Like the snake
swallowing its tail, the male can provide both the phallus and the recep-
tacle. Siring oneself assures mortality by closing the generative cycle and
thus precluding death. Victor Fitzvictor."[39] This ambivalent myth of a father who appropriates the female power of birthing in order to generate a
son resonates with the novel's critique of male Romanticism with its thoroughgoing attempt at self-generation and autoeroticism, which eventually
breeds monsters.[40]

Nevertheless it is important to note how this myth of male self-birthing
is rewritten as it "progresses" historically. In its classical version, the myth
of the thigh birth is an ambivalent depiction of the tense and combative
interplay of masculine and feminine powers in the generation of life, as
symbolized and embodied in the act of sexual reproduction. In taking this
line of interpretation, I converge with Margaret Whitford's[41] analysis of
Luce Irigaray's mytho-politics, where Greek myths constitute a record of
how matriarchal myths gradually give way to patriarchal myths. In the
myth of the thigh birth of Dionysus, Irigaray argues, one can still detect
signs of the deadly struggle between the two forms of narratives. "In Dionysos, the fight to the death between two conceptions of the world is still
staged. He participates in both, and clearly shows he is torn apart by that
double allegiance."[42]

Rushing and Frentz also draw attention to the ubiquity of the wounding
of the male thigh as a heroic motif. Examples are "the Greek Hephaestus,
who walked with a limp; Odysseus, who received a thigh wound while
hunting a boar; the Arthurian Fisher King, whose groin wound festered
while his kingdom turned into a wasteland; the Biblical Jacob, who dislo-
cated his upper leg wrestling with God; and even Jesus, who, in some ac-

counts, walked with a limp."[43] Adopting Bly's[44] interpretation, Rushing and Frentz note that this wounding slows down the warrior, deepens his connection with the earth (a maternal figure), and enhances his capacity for feeling. Quoting Bly, this wound transforms the thigh into a "male womb," thus enabling the influx of spiritual strength.[45] It is interesting that in taking this interpretation, Rushing and Frentz also show how the archetype of the thigh wound/womb entails a complex connection between masculine and feminine elements. Like Bly, Rushing and Frentz reject Freud's interpretation of this myth as a euphemism for genital loss and fears of castration—an interpretation that already reveals the repressed fears of the overextended masculine Ego.

However, the myth of male self-birthing becomes emblematic of the absurd dream of (male) Ego-as-God. As reenvisaged by these films, the Frankensteinian complex becomes both a severe repression of the novel's critique of Romantic gender politics and an attempt to erect a supermasculinized version of the parthenogenetic myth. The extent of tension required to erect this hypermasculinized myth is reflected in its repression of its counterpart myth: the story of Baubo's impudent reassertion of female reproductive and erotic power. It is this less known mytheme to which I now turn.

ANA-SUROMAI: UNVEILING THE LOST FIGURE OF BAUBO

Baubo is a mythic figure who seems lost in obscurity. The narratives of Persephone's rape and betrayal and Demeter's monumental grief appear to have survived, yet the intertwined links concerning the roles Baubo and Dionysus play in this saga appear to have been overlaid. Part of the reason why the traces of Baubo are difficult to excavate is because the nomenclature of her name is confused. She is variously known not only as Iambe, Isis, and Bau; her numerous elusive and contrasting characterizations resist unification into a monolithic entity. As Lubell points out, Baubo is at times depicted as a nurse, servant, or priestess; at other times, she is a participant with goddesses in the *hieros gamos* (sacred marriage) ritual of ancient rites associated with fertility. One of her visages is *Bona Dea*, goddess of women, yet she is also sketched as a bawd, night demon, or the Evil Eye.[46]

The story of Baubo-Iambe is compellingly envisaged in the surviving *Hymn to Demeter*, one of thirty-three anonymous poems gathered in antiquity, which eventually became known as the Homeric Hymns. This poem describes the rape and abduction of Persephone by Hades, the god of death and the underworld; it also details the sorrow, fury, and grief of her mother Demeter and her vengeful neglect of her duties as a goddess of fertility. She mirrors her disappearance into the realm of death by vanishing into the guise of an old nurse, infertile and impotent. In this disconsolate state,

Demeter arrives at the great hall of the ruler of Eleusis. Metaneira, the queen, offers the impressive stranger a seat on a splendid couch, but the goddess remains standing, her noble head down, full of remorse. Iambe, a servant, discreetly offers the goddess a stool that she has covered with soft fleece, which Demeter accepts. Iambe then coaches the goddess out of her black mood of despair by entertaining her with lewd jokes, which causes Demeter to laugh. Lubell points out that the transformation of the sage and perspicacious Iambe into the raucous Baubo who reveals her belly and vulva to the grieving goddess, thus startling her into laughter, is a later development.[47]

Nevertheless, Kofman, in her interpretation of Nietzsche's political appropriation of the myths of Dionysus and Baubo, creates a composite picture. Briefly, Kofman's "Baubo: Theological Perversion and Fetishism" begins with an elaborate retracing of Baubo's mythological roots. Baubo makes her appearance in the mysteries of Eleusis consecrated to Demeter. Grieved by the disappearance of Persephone, Demeter, goddess of fecundity, is acting like a sterile[48] woman. For nine days and nine nights, she does not drink, eat, bathe, or adorn herself. Baubo makes her laugh by pulling up her skirts and showing her belly on which a figure had been drawn. This figure is believed to be that of Iaachos, the child of Demeter, an obscure deity at times identified with Dionysus. Drawing from several sources, Kofman arrives at an insightful interpretation:

Reinach interprets it as a magic scene whose aim is to restore to earth the fecundity that it had lost during the sorrow of Demeter.[49] Comparison with Greek legends such as those of Bellephoron, and with Irish and Japanese ones, allows us to assert that wherever a woman raises her skirts, she provokes laughter or flight, such that this gesture can be used as apotropaic means. . . . The belly of the woman plays the role of the head of the Medusa. . . . By lifting her skirts, was not Baubo suggesting that she go and frighten Hades, or that which comes to the same, recall fecundity to herself? By displaying the figure of Dionysus on her belly, she recalls the eternal return of life.[50]

Kofman strengthens her position by recalling the etymological origins and other mythological underpinnings of the name "Baubo." *Baubo* is the equivalent of *koilia*, another of the "improper" words used in Greek to designate the female sex. *Baubon*, the symbol of the male sex, is derived from *Baubo*. Through the intermediary of *Baubon*, the story of *Baubo* intersects with that of Dionysus. There are two intersections: (1) in one of the myths, Dionysus is born in Nysa, at the spot where Hades carried off Persephone (thus initiating Demeter's descent into grief); and (2) in another of the myths, when Dionysus was looking for the road to Hades, he encountered Proshymnos with whom he had "unspeakable relationships." After Proshymnos's death, Dionysus replaced him with a figwood phallus (*baubon*) to console himself. Thus, *Baubon* and *Baubo*, as personifications of the two sexes, appeared in these guises in the Eleusinian rites where Baubo is an animated *koilia*. Kofman clinches her argument: "In the Eleusinian mysteries, the female sexual organ is exalted as the symbol of fertility and a guarantee of the regeneration and eternal return of all things."[51]

Kofman's position, that "Baubo can appear as a female double of Dionysus"[52] effectively locates Baubo and Dionysus as masks for life as eternally self-generating and protean.[53] Yet if I were to carry the implications of her genealogy even further, it appears that Baubo is more than Dionysus's twin. As someone who nurses a goddess of fertility back into health, and as the woman upon whose belly the image of Iaachos-Dionysus (i.e., Dionysus as an infant) is etched, she seems more powerful than he is. Lubell echoes a similar position when she opposes the view held by Stroud and Bookidis[54] that Baubo is no more than a nasty old crone with a weakness for exhibition:

Perhaps the old nurse, who had seen so much happen during her long life, was saying to Demeter: "Remember! . . . You were raped by Zeus. You then gave birth to a girl child, who in her turn was abducted and raped by her uncle, Hades, with the connivance of Zeus; and it is Kore, this girl, who in her turn has given birth to your grandson Iaachus. . . ." I think Iambe/Baubo was saying more universally: "We are the life-givers, never forget that! . . ." In her bawdy joke was she not saying: ". . . it is our vulvas, our wombs, that are the center. We are the transformers!"[55]

Despite the differences between Lubell's and Kofman's accounts, they converge on a vigorous portrait of Baubo—a portrait whose outlines seem to shift between dutiful nurse and irrepressible trickster, a figure of fecundity and obscenity, ricocheting in between mortality, divinity, and demonism. Lubell carefully traces the gradual covering over of Baubo's benevolent symbolic participation in agricultural rituals of fecundity, where consecrated women squatted over newly plowed fields, and returned their "moon blood" or menstrual fluid to the earth with which it was intimately linked. The conclusion she arrives at is compelling: "In the fiercely misogynist climate of later patriarchal cultures, these old, old female rituals that had been closely connected with the earth and its cycles faded away or were effectively obliterated."[56]

This obliteration-demonization of the myth of Baubo, alongside the severing of the complex connections binding the myths of Dionysus and Baubo, can be further traced in the filmic transformations of the Frankenstein myth. Yet in the severity of the attempt to erase or vilify traces of Baubo (whose traces may be seen in the "feminine," "feminine-as-monstrous," and "female monster" shadows), or the amount of splintering necessary to maintain the separate spheres of the M/Other and Monster from the Ego, these films both reinforce and undercut their patriarchal underpinnings. The hypermasculinization of the parthenogenetic myth and the repression of primordial images of unbridled female power are, in keeping with Rushing and Frentz's depiction of the Frankensteinian complex, revelatory of a "dystopian" shadow myth (and its possible antidote). Finally, I now turn to characterizing, in depth, what "shadow" myths are, and why they bear conceptual weight in my analysis of *Frankenstein* films.

THE SHADOW MYTH OF TECHNOLOGY

Rushing and Frentz build their thesis of the persistence of the "Frankenstein complex"[57] from several critical insights. First, dystopian stories, such as *Frankenstein, Blade Runner,* and *Rocky IV,* regard the mechanical as monstrous and malevolent as opposed to the utopian tales that aestheticize and glorify the machine as the pinnacle of the Enlightenment dream of progress. Such dystopian stories are not only based on myth; more importantly they have attained the status of myth and archetype themselves. Such popular dystopian works expel fears that are at least partially repressed and unconscious. For example, the Frankenstein dystopic myth describes the process of the increasing mechanization of the human, and the humanization of the machine. Such a process seems to be moving inexorably toward an end in which the machine is god and the human is reduced either to slavery or obsolescence. Finally, the dystopian myth (as well as science fiction in general) is gendered in various ways, often echoing and occasionally exposing the general patriarchal bias of technology within our culture.

More recently (1995), Rushing and Frentz aim to reconstruct the tripartite story of how, with the postmodern demise of a shamanistic heritage, the myths of the Indian hunter and the frontier hunter are displaced by that of the technological hunter. In this most recent transformation of the archetypal hunter myth, the hunter's weapon evolves into a cyborg that eventually hunts down the hunter. They write, "In an increasingly technological culture devoid of spiritual influence, the ego-driven, exploitative hunter loses the soul connection with his weapon, a connection that was more prominent in our Native American ancestry. . . . The result is a threatened technological apocalypse in which humanity is replaced or destroyed by what it has made."[58]

For Rushing and Frentz, the devolution from hunter to cyborg in American myth reflects the same changes in the movement from modernism to postmodernism. Both constitute parallel records of changes in the human (e)valuation of the Ego/Self in relation to the world/Other. Both chart how the hunter becomes the hunted, and how the weapon turns against the hand that wields it. "Both describe the rise of the male to a position of supreme dominance over nature and his subsequent fragmentation as his tools, or simulations of himself, splinter his being and separate him from others, eventually acquiring the dominant status he once had."[59]

Borrowing from Jung, Rushing and Frentz lay the groundwork for an approach that attempts to speak of a " 'cultural shadow,' born in response to the limitations of the conscious perspective of an era and often appearing in the guise of archetypal symbols."[60] Although Rushing and Frentz are aware of the difficulties of attempting to speak about a "collective psyche" as opposed to an individual one, it appears that one of their aims is to resurrect the notion of "myth" as a useful concept within rhetorical criticism: "Some myths (what we are now calling 'shadow myths') are revelatory insofar as they visualize the repressed as a precursor to social change. Seen in this way, such myths are rhetorical, not in that they advance the interests of a particular social group but that they narratively advocate a view that simultaneously subverts the dominant cultural ideology and affirms a new image."[61]

In other words, Rushing and Frentz adopt Jung's term for that which is hated, feared, and disowned, yet is responded to with intense attraction and repulsion, particularly as projected on to a scapegoat. That term is *shadow*. For as long as the illusion of projection holds, we are saved from the realization that that shadow, whether personal, cultural, or archetypal, is part of us.

Rushing and Frentz differentiate between two types of shadows, or two ways through which the psyche excises out what it wishes to repress or disown. These two shadows are the "inferior" shadow and the "overdeveloped" shadow. In the first case, the ego sharply sets itself against the Other, or not-I. As postmodernism has laid bare, these "not-I" are instantiated in the realms of the feminine, body, people of color, and anything else that deviates from rational ego-consciousness.

The overdeveloped, or second, shadow results when the ego sets for itself the mission of absolute control of the Other. To accomplish this task, the ego extends itself, first to create tools, and, later, to (d)evolve into a tool itself. However, this results in a radical splintering of the psyche, where the inflated ego acts like a God, and its split off alter ego possesses the same devilish power as the inferior, or first, shadow. For Rushing and Frentz, "the primary form of the overdeveloped shadow . . . is Frankenstein's monster—the ultimate tool, the replication of our bodies and our intelligence through scientific technology."[62]

Thus, the "technological" or Frankensteinian myth unveils two primary reactions to the machine: Humans approach it as either the monstrous Other they must harness or as a part of themselves they must acknowledge. The first reaction continues the deadly projection and splintering; the second begins to recognize that the Other is a part of the Self—and points out a possible solution to the crisis presented in the myth. The process of splintering and projecting can be halted through recognizing the Other as a part of the Self. Integration with the technological, overdeveloped shadow is possible only if the hero of a narrative contacts elements in his inferior shadow (such as the feminine or the beast) through either dreams or wakeful experiences.[63]

There is a third type of shadow, which is a natural offshoot of Rushing and Frentz's framework: the "feminine-as-monstrous" or the female monster. I use the term "feminine-as-monstrous" to refer to women whose beauty, intelligence, and ambition render them dangerous. In addition, female monsters, even more so than male creatures, occupy the hybrid locus of being both powerful and vulnerable; compelling and repulsive; attractive and grotesque. Both these types of characters do not survive for very long in Frankensteinian films. They are either (justifiably) murdered, or are given no narrative alternative than to choose death. These shadows, which are a complex conjunction of the "feminized" and "technologized" types, constitute traces of the surviving Baubo myth. As such, they reveal, even if only in glimpses, the strained parameters of the parthenogenetic myth, and hint at the possibility of a different type of mythmaking.

Yet myths, and their popular emanations, films, are complex blends of archetypal and rhetorical elements that interact in a dynamic fashion: sometimes, acting in concert with each other; at other times, conflicting. Both myths and films are not "pure" outflows of a collective unconscious. Films, as partially driven by commercial interests, both reproduce and critique foundational values; they cement and subvert the existing status quo. It is precisely in this dual role that films "can show us our cultural shadow, but they can also project it onto irrelevant victims in order to preserve our guilt and preserve our innocence."[64]

Yet the ongoing saga of traditional Frankenstein films (as opposed to comedic, science fiction, and horror offshoots, for example, which I briefly comment on in my conclusion) seems, for the most part, stuck at the level of the splintering of the ego. These excise the novel's complex characterization of the Monster's, Elizabeth's, and Caroline's relationships with Victor. Unlike the novel these films systematically refashion Victor's ambivalent relationships with these feminine or monstrous Others to fit into more conventional and patriarchal molds, generating the inferior shadow of the M/Other, and the overdeveloped shadow of the Monster.

Yet, on the other hand, using Rushing and Frentz's framework, one could argue that the degree of hyperbolization required to maintain this splintering is so great that this results in a critical undercutting of the repressive movement. The tension generated by exaggerating the parthenogenetic myth, to repress its feminine and technological shadows, becomes so pronounced that these movies function both to "project the cultural shadow . . . away from us and, at the same time, insist that we see it as part of us. Neither pure revelations nor purely cynical commodities, they are a little bit of both."[65] As I shall illustrate, *Frankenstein* films are contemporary repositories of myth, and they reveal and veil, shape, as well as describe, shifting anxieties concerning power, gender, and technology.

NOTES

1. An earlier version was presented at the Speech Communication Association Conference, San Diego, California, November 23, 1996. It has subsequently been published as Caroline Joan S. Picart, "James Whale's (Mis)Reading of Mary Shelley's *Frankenstein*," *Critical Studies in Mass Communication* 15 (1998): 382–404.

2. Michael Brunas, John Brunas, and Tom Weaver, *Universal Horrors: The Studio's Classic Films, 1931–1946* (Jefferson, N.C.: McFarland, 1990), 27.

3. Joseph Lanza, "Frankenstein," *International Dictionary of Films and Film-makers—1*, ed. Nicholas Thomas, 2nd ed. (Chicago: St. James Press, 1990), 322–324.

4. The technical approaches focus on the way the shots were taken and include other formal considerations involving the way the film was created, such as acting, music, props, and makeup. The thematic approaches focus on various conceptual schemata that attempt to explain either the diegetic or intertextual elements of the film. The thematic approaches focus on various conceptual schemata that attempt to explain either the diegetic or intertextual elements of the film.

5. On Karloff's acting, see Radu Florescu, *In Search of Frankenstein* (Boston: New York Graphic Society, 1975), 192. Regarding Whale's direction, see Brunas, Brunas, and Weaver, 29; Paul Jensen, *Boris Karloff and His Films* (South Brunswick, N.J., and New York: A.S. Burnes and Company, 1974), 42; Scott Allen Nollen, *Boris Karloff* (Jefferson, N.C.: American Library Association, 1991) 47–49. For an account covering both Karloff's acting and Whale's directing, alongside Peirce's makeup innovations, Donald Glut, *The Frankenstein Legend: A Tribute to Mary Shelley and Boris Karloff* (Metuchen, N.J.: Scarecrow Press, 1973), 118.

6. For *Frankenstein*'s Romantic roots, refer to Michael Klein and Gillian Parker, *The English Novel and the Movies* (New York: Frederick Ungar Publishing Company, 1981), 54–58. For critical links binding adolescent identification with monstrous feelings of alienation and entrapment and fascination with *Frankenstein* and horror tales, see Walter Evans, "Monster Movies: A Sexual Theory," *Journal of Popular Film* 2 (1973): 354. For an account of how *Frankenstein* and other horror tales function as initiation rites, see Walter Evans, "Monster Movies and Rites of Initiation," *Journal of Popular Film* 4 (1975): 124–125. For the film *Frankenstein*'s reworking of the symbols of its European literary background, see R.H.W. Dillard, *Horror Films* (New York: Monarch Press, 1976), 14–28. For a view that characterizes Whale's *Frankenstein* as revelatory of the anxieties that haunted the 1930s and as constituting a reenvisaging of the Christian resurrection in parodic terms, see Martin Tropp, *Mary Shelley's Monster* (Boston: Houghton Mifflin Co., 1976), 88–94.

7. Women were supposed to be a later invention of Zeus, created in order to inflict pain and suffering upon men. See Edith Hamilton, *Mythology; Timeless Tales of Gods and Heroes* (New York: Mentor [Penguin], 1982), 72.

8. For work on this, refer to Anne K. Mellor, *Mary Shelley: Her Life, Her Fiction, Her Monsters* (New York: Routledge, 1989).

9. Deborah Wilson, "Technologies of Misogyny: The Transparent Maternal Body and Alternate Reproductions in *Frankenstein, Dracula*, and Some Selected Media Discourses," *Bodily Discursions: Genders, Representations, Technologies*, ed. Deborah Wilson and Christine Moneera Laennec (Albany: State University of New York Press, 1997), 109.

10. Carol J. Clover, *Men, Women and Chainsaws: Gender in the Modern Horror Film* (Princeton, N.J.: Princeton University Press, 1992), 46.

11. Harry M. Benshoff, *Monsters in the Closet: Homosexuality and the Horror Film* (Manchester and New York: Manchester University Press, 1997), 1–2.

12. Ibid. See, for example, pp. 40–58, especially pp. 50–51 on James Whale's homosexuality and a queer reading of *Bride of Frankenstein*. For an extended analysis of the Universal series, ranging from *Son of Frankenstein* till *House of Dracula*, refer to pp. 91–98. For a brief coverage of Hammer's *Frankenstein Created Woman*, see pp. 188–189.

13. Rhona J. Berenstein, *Attack of the Leading Ladies: Gender, Sexuality, and Spectatorship in Classic Horror Cinema* (New York: Columbia University Press, 1996), 46.

14. Examples of scholarship involving the translation of literature to film include Wendell Aycock and Michael Schoenecke, *Film and Literature: A Comparative Approach to Adaptation* (Lubbock: Texas Tech University Press, 1988); D. Fried, "Hollywood's Convention and Film Adaptation," *Theatre Journal* 39 (1987): 294–306; Robert Giddings, Keith Selby, and Chris Wensley, *Screening the Novel: The Theory and Practice of Literary Dramatization* (New York: St. Martin's Press, 1990); C.H. McKay, "A Novel's Journey into Film: The Case of *Great Expectations*," *Literature/Film Quarterly* 13 (1985): 127–134; Judith Mayne, *Private Novels, Public Films* (Athens: University of Georgia Press, 1988); and Neil Sinyard, *Filming Literature: The Art of Screen Adaptation* (London: Croom Helm Limited, 1986).

15. Wayne McMullen and Martha Solomon, "The Politics of Adaptation: Steven Spielberg's Appropriation of *The Color Purple*," *Text and Performance* 14 (1994): 158–174.

16. Brenda Cooper and David Descutner, " 'It had no voice to it': Sydney Pollack's Film Translation of Isak Dinesen's *Out of Africa*," *Quarterly Journal of Speech* 82 (1996): 228–250.

17. McMullen and Solomon, 171–172.

18. Cooper and Descutner, 248.

19. Anne K. Mellor, "Possessing Nature: The Female in *Frankenstein*," *Romanticism and Feminism*, ed. Anne K. Mellor (Bloomington and Indianapolis: Indiana University Press, 1988), 231.

20. Margaret Homans, *Bearing the Word* (Chicago: University of Chicago Press, 1986), 102.

21. William Veeder, *Mary Shelley and Frankenstein: The Fate of Androgyny* (Chicago: University of Chicago Press, 1986), 106, 112.

22. The myth of the thigh birth (or the parthenogenetic birth) narrates how Zeus and Dionysus form a composite figure because Zeus, the father, gives birth, through his thigh, to his son and alter ego, Dionysus.

23. Winifred Milius Lubell, *The Metamorphosis of Baubo: Myths of Woman's Sexual Energy* (Nashville: Vanderbilt University Press, 1994), 1.

24. Sarah Kofman, "Baubo: Theological Perversion and Fetishism," in *Nietzsche's New Seas*, ed. Michael Allen Gillespie and Tracy B. Strong (Chicago: University of Chicago Press, 1988), 175–202.

25. Janice H. Rushing and Thomas S. Frentz, *Projecting the Shadow: The Cyborg Hero in American Film* (Chicago: Chicago University Press, 1995); see also Rushing and Frentz, "The Frankenstein Myth in Contemporary Cinema," *Critical Studies in Mass Communication* 6 (1989): 61–80.

26. See Mary Shelley, *Frankenstein* (New York: Bantam Books, 1991), 179.

27. Mellor, "Possessing Nature," 231; see also Mellor, *Mary Shelley.*

28. Mellor, "Possessing Nature," 225.

29. Shelley, 33.

30. Ibid.

31. Ibid.

32. Homans, 102.

33. Veeder, 106, 112.

34. Ibid., 125, 144.

35. Carl Kerenyi, *Dionysos: Archetypal Image of Indestructible Life*, trans. Ralph Manheim, Bollingen Series, vol. 65 (Princeton, N.J.: Princeton University Press, 1976), 274.

36. Ibid.

37. Ibid., 275.

38. Ibid., 276.

39. Veeder, 144.

40. For a postcolonial reading of *Frankenstein*, refer to Elizabeth Bohls, "Aesthetics, Gender and Empire in Mary Shelley's *Frankenstein*," in *Women Travel Writers and the Language of Aesthetic 1716–1818* (Cambridge, England: Cambridge University Press, 1995) 230–245. For a spectrum of feminist interpretations, see Stephen Behrend and Anne Mellor, ed. *Approaches to Teaching Shelley's Frankenstein (Approaches to Teaching World Literature, 33)* (New York: Modern Language Association of America, 1990).

41. Margaret Whitford, "Reading Irigaray in the Nineties," *Engaging with Irigaray: Feminist Philosophy and European Thought*, ed. Carolyn Burke, Naomi Schor, and Margaret Whitford (New York: Columbia University Press), 383.

42. Ibid.

43. Rushing and Frentz, 172.

44. Robert Bly, *Iron John: A Book about Men* (Reading, Mass: Addison-Wesley, 1990).

45. Rushing and Frentz, 207–217.

46. Lubell, 5.

47. Ibid., 17.

48. The equation of extreme grief with sterility is Kofmann's. What she effectively seems to do is to hyperbolize Demeter's grief to the level of a type of death—a barrenness or inability to give birth, analogous to her daughter's descent into the underworld.

49. Salomon Reinach, *Cultes, mythes, religion*, vol. 4 (Paris: Leroux, 1912).

50. Kofman, 196–197.

51. Ibid., 197.

52. Ibid.

53. For an analysis of how Kofman's interpretation seems in keeping with Nietzsche's pre-Zarathustran appropriation of Greek myths, refer to Caroline J.S. Picart, *Resentment and the "Feminine" in Nietzsche's Politico-Aesthetics* (State College: Pennsylvania State University Press, 1999).

54. Lubell, 6.

55. Ibid., 11.

56. Ibid., 5.

57. Rushing and Frentz, "The Frankenstein Myth in Contemporary Cinema" 62.

58. Rushing and Frentz, *Projecting the Shadow* 5.

59. Ibid., 11.

60. Rushing and Frentz, "The Frankenstein Myth," 63.

61. Rushing and Frentz, *Projecting the Shadow*, 76–77.

62. Ibid., 40–41.

63. Ibid., 76.

64. Ibid., 47.

65. Ibid.

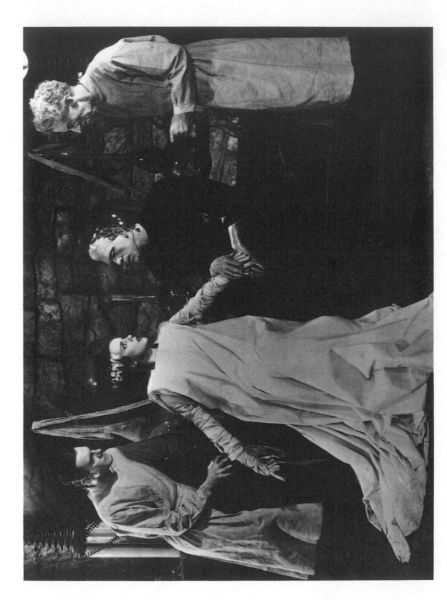

Still from *Bride of Frankenstein* appears courtesy of the Academy of Motion Picture Arts and Sciences. Universal, 1935.

CHAPTER 2

—ᴧᴧᴧ—

The Universal Series

Myths are also susceptible to "closure," or to adaptations which constrain their further development into fixed channels. In the case of the Frankenstein myth, this moment of closure arrived in 1931 in the shape of William Henry Pratt (better known as Boris Karloff), whose rectangular face and bolt-adorned neck have fixed our idea of the monster into a universally-known image from which it is hard to see further revisions breaking free.

—Chris Baldick, *In Frankenstein's Shadow*

INTRODUCTORY REMARKS

Janice Hocker Rushing's "Evolution of the 'New Frontier' in *Alien* and *Aliens*: Patriarchal Co-Optation of the Feminine Archetype,"[1] clearly converges with some aspects of the theoretical framework this book uses.

The classical myths and fairy tales that are better known today are probably revised from earlier Goddess myths to reflect a later patriarchal bias that coincided with the heroic, war-torn Iron Age. The new hero was the masculine ego, which set itself against nature and the feminine, creating the new dualism upon which the rational mind is based. Whereas nature and the Goddess were inconstant and metamorphic, forcing humans to submit to a greater law, the heroic ego attempted its own immortality.[2]

However, though Rushing sees the "Dionysian figure . . . exiled along with the Goddess,"[3] I see the mythic emergence of an apparently more triumphant and less ambiguously gendered Dionysus, who, locked in a parthenogenetic embrace with his father, Zeus, bears an outwardly Apollinian visage. In the evolution from novel to films, beginning specifically with the Universal film series, what is increasingly scapegoated is less the Dionysian, than the monstrous feminine, which results in dystopic narratives of necrophiliac and ambivalently incestuous eroticism and monstrous births.

To compare, in the original novel, Victor's initial fixation on his creature bears the obsessive temper of an unnatural and even monstrous eroticism. Shelley's novel seems to hint at the monstrosity of Frankenstein's sexuality. For a while Victor's devotion to Elizabeth is eclipsed by the feverish fit that descends upon him, driving away all save the birthing of this being. Although Universal films bring to the surface the undercurrents of female rivalry present in the original novel, they purge themselves of the necrophiliac, incestuous undertones of the novel. The "other woman" is no longer possibly the dead mother, but the proverbially faceless and safely unknown one. The relation between father and son also consequently becomes simpler, and more sanitized, devoid of the oedipal and negative-oedipal stirrings one may glimpse in the original novel. The concealment of the corpse of the mother, reflective of the excision of the novel's "inferior" shadow, is accompanied by the strengthening of the bond between father and son. For example, in James Whale's *Frankenstein* (1931), the father assures the audience of his son's recovery, and the maintenance of the patriarchal line, with his final toast to a "son of the House of Frankenstein."

Finally, as part of the critical frame, I take the view that the transformations that occurred as scripts were converted into films are as important as the transformations that occurred as M. Shelley's novel was converted into movies. Hence a genealogy of these transformations is crucial to my methodology. To illustrate: Harking back to Whale's *Frankenstein*, the final scenario, which hints at the coming marriage of Elizabeth and Victor Clerval, and the tragedy of the House of Frankenstein, was discarded. Gregory William Mank details this particular excision from the original Florey and Faragoh scripts in the following way:

Baron Frankenstein and Victor, after the chase to the windmill and the deaths of Henry and the Monster, meets the praying Elizabeth standing by the pillar, the morning sun breaking over them—while in the b.g. [background] kneeling before the shadowy altar, the broken figure of the old Baron. CAMERA MOVES BACK AT INCREASED TEMPO to the very doors of the church, which close slowly.[4]

This ending would at least have had some thematic similarity with Mary Shelley's novel, where the Monster, Victor's alter ego, has killed off everyone whom Victor loves, and weeps over Victor's body before he disappears from sight. Yet the tragedy of the house of Frankenstein, or how the hunter is destroyed by his own weapon (which is simply an extension of himself), was also taken out. Despite this scene's juxtaposition with the lighter scene of Elizabeth's impending marriage to Victor, and the implied promise of a more optimistic narrative, this more pessimistic scene had to be repressed. In other words, within the broader context of this book, this particular example shows how the dark undersides hinted at in the original script, such as the scenes depicting the sorrow of the old Baron, or the deaths of Elizabeth and Henry, were simply taken out. These traits, of straining to generate a completely triumphant version of the parthenogenetic/patriarchal myth and of attempting the total eradication of the myth of unbridled female power imaged in Baubo's skirt-lifting gesture, are characteristic of Universal films, as I demonstrate.

CREATING THE MONSTROUS: KARLOFF AS CINEMATIC ARCHETYPE

Frankenstein was released only ten months after Universal's classic horror film, *Dracula*, whose main star was Bela Lugosi. Lugosi's immense success resulted in his originally being cast as the Monster in *Frankenstein*, and Robert Florey was originally contracted to direct the film. Lugosi's test footage, revelatory of his sympathetic depiction of the Monster, was rejected in favor of a more sinister and devastating monster, and a director who could project a nightmarishly baroque view: James Whale.

Universal purchased the rights to the Peggy Webling stage adaptation of Mary Shelley's novel. The play had been performed in Great Britain, along with *Dracula*, but had never been performed in the United States. Screenwriter John Balderston sold an adaptation of the play and its rights for $20,000 plus 1 percent of the gross of the film. Apparently a number of different hands labored on different screenplays, with Robert Florey conceiving of the incidents of the criminal brain and the burning windmill. It was Garrett Fort who thought up the scene of Frankenstein being thrown off the windmill. When Florey was forced off the project, Francis Edward Faragoh took over as Fort's collaborator. Faragoh, who had written *Little Caesar*, changed Fritz from a mute persona into a character who could speak, and transformed Frankenstein's laboratory from an old windmill to an old watchtower.[5] What resulted was a plot sewn together from various odds and ends, which also unmasks many of the tensions of the parthenogenetic mytheme.

Having examined the transformations of the intertwining myths of Dionysus and Baubo from their pre-Socratic origins to their revisions in Mary Shelley's novel in Chapter 1, I now turn to the issue of the rhetorical (re)constructions of masculinity, divinity, and humanity, against those of femininity, the monstrous and the mechanical, in the Universal Series films, beginning with Whale's 1931 version. Using Janice Rushing and Thomas Frentz's framework, which converges with insights of such theorists as Luce Irigaray, Margaret Whitford, Anne Mellor, William Veeder, and Margaret

Homans, I trace how this film harnesses the inferior shadow, through the repression of the critical dimensions of the novel's depiction of the feminine, and reduces the overdeveloped shadow, which takes the form of an inhuman technological monster that turns on its creator. Whale's film also represses a third shadow—a complex amalgam of the inferior and overdeveloped shadows, which occurs through the destruction of the convergence between the feminine/mother and the monstrous/machine in the figure of the female Monster or feminine-as-monstrous in M. Shelley's novel. This third type of shadow results partly because as the repression of the feminine and the Monstrous occurs, the attempt to elevate a super-masculinized and sanitized version of the myth of male self-birthing also occurs, resulting both in an affirmation and an undercutting of the film's patriarchal depictions of gender and technology. As M/Other and Monster fuse to create an even more threatening shadow, the masculine ego as narrator goes to great lengths to maintain its myth of autonomous and perfect self-generation. In other words this third shadow is cast by the hyperbolization of the myth of Dionysian parthenogenesis and the attempted repression of the narrative of Baubo's *ana-suromai*.

To begin, one of the first things that strikes a reader familiar with Shelley's novel is that the figure of the Mother, and her ambivalent power, primordial link to both life and death, is completely effaced in Whale's film. The original novel is riddled with the deaths of mother figures. Caroline, Victor Frankenstein's mother, dies as she gives birth to William, Victor's younger brother. Justine, the surrogate mother who takes care of William, is hanged, framed as William's murderer by the creature and Elizabeth, who bears the heavy imprint of Caroline in her mannerisms and values, is killed by the Monster on the night of her wedding to Victor.

These mother figures are killed off in Whale's *Frankenstein* in a different way. They do not even appear. From the very start, Caroline does not even exist; the Baron Frankenstein, Henry Frankenstein's father, is the sole parent. Justine, because her principal function of being a mother to William has been eradicated, also does not appear. Elizabeth becomes simply Henry's devoted fiancée, who survives the wedding night.

What occurs in Whale's film is a covering over of the murder of the Mother that forms a principal motif in Shelley's novel. The ambiguous power associated with Motherhood is shorn away, leaving an effete shadow (symbolized by Caroline, Elizabeth, and Justine), which can be recognized as Other and presents no danger to the empowered masculine realm occupied by Henry Frankenstein. Thus, the tinges of necrophiliac and incestuous desire that readers such as Mellor and Homans glimpse in the novel are silenced. Another result of this silencing is the disappearance of the key motivation for Victor's creation of his Monster—the unbridled masculine aspiration to becoming the Self-generating Source. One of the peculiar features of Shelley's mother-figures is their potency as simultaneous bearers of life and embodiments of death; in denying them not only this powerful status but also their existence, Whale's film suppresses what had originally been a devastating but ambivalent critique of Romantic gender politics.

Further evidence of the splitting off of the inferior/feminine shadow from the masculine ego may be seen in the film's modification of the novel's depiction of the encounter between the Monster and a child. The death of William at the hands of the Monster he spurns as ugly in the novel is replaced by the scene of the innocent Maria's drowning when the Monster tosses her into a lake while they are playing. In the novel, William, before he is killed by the Monster, heartlessly spurns the lonely creature that had intended to kidnap the boy purely for companionship. The Monster, enraged by the child's insults and the sudden knowledge of his family name, strangles him. What occurs is a complex picture of mutual and escalating victimization, narrated from the point of view of the Monster. "The child struggled and *loaded me with epithets which carried despair to my heart; I grasped his throat to silence him, and in a moment he lay dead at my feet*" [my emphasis].[6]

In Whale's version the Monster stumbles across Maria, an innocent peasant girl, by a lake as she is picking flowers. It is Maria who initiates the contact by smilingly introducing herself, taking his hand, and asking him to play with her. It is, for a while, a touching encounter between two innocents who fling flowers into the lake and watch them float away. Then the Monster suddenly reaches over and grabs the girl as the scene is cut. The modifications within the film seem to point to the need for a completely innocent and vulnerable victim—a young girl who actively invites the Monster's attention. The changing of the sex of the victim from male to female seems completely in keeping with the film's tendency to suppress the ambiguous power associated with females in the original novel, and to reduce the female purely to the roles of powerless victim and naïve temptress (albeit, with a markedly repressed sense of eroticism).

The splitting off of the inferior/feminine shadow from the masculine realm of the ego is also seen in the film's rewriting of the encounter between the Monster and Elizabeth on the eve of the wedding. The film does replicate, at a certain level, Elizabeth's death pose from the novel. However, in the film, Elizabeth Lavenza continues to live after the encounter with the Monster on the eve of her wedding. After Henry discovers Elizabeth in this ambiguous "death pose" (albeit without the hair obscuring any part of Mae Clark's pretty face and certainly undistorted features), Elizabeth stirs, showing that there is some hope that she may live after all. This change in the original plot opens the way for the possibility of a happy ending, which does occur in the film, Hollywood style. After Henry plummets to the ground from the windmill, he is seen miraculously lying in bed, conversing with Elizabeth as the filmic curtains close with Baron Frankenstein giving a toast to a son of the House of Frankenstein. The tragedy of the House of Frankenstein is averted; Henry must live at all costs, and his immortality is signaled by his father's toast to a future son. Elizabeth lives only because it is through her that the patrilineal line continues. Like Sarah Connor in *The Terminator*, Elizabeth's primary function is that of the Madonna, who will give birth to a son through whom the salvation of the future may be ensured.[7] The conventional/patriarchal happy ending resonates with the fact that the outer narrative frames in the novel, those of Robert Walton and Margaret Saville, his sister, are removed in the film. In the novel Walton saves a yet unknown Frankenstein from an icy death as Frankenstein is pursuing the fleeing Monster. It is through Walton, retold via letters to Saville, that the story of Victor unfolds. The use of this twice-removed narrative frame in the novel is important because it allows Shelley to assume an ironic distance from the story and enables her to embed a proto-feminist critique of male Romanticism within her novel. With the removal of these concentric frames, the film loses the novel's critical voice. Because the use of these concentric frames is excised in the film, a flat and linear narrative emerges, devoid of the novel's critical stance.

Veeder also pays a good deal of attention to the presence of concentric narrative frames within the novel. To him, Mary Shelley deliberately chooses Robert Walton—a male brother-mentor-father figure—as a correspondent for Margaret Saville "because gender qualifies for judgement in *Frankenstein*."[8] What follows is an interesting, if controversial, excavation-play upon the character's names in an attempt to discern possible explanations for Shelley's use of the double-framing technique.

Together "Margaret" and "Saville" give to this native jewel the imprimatur of Mary Shelley's own initials, M.S. Moreover, since Mary affirms her Wollestonecraft heritage[9] by using the middle initial "W," rather than the expectable "G,"[10] she is all the more associated with Margaret whose maiden name of Walton gives her too the middle initial "W." Why does Mrs. Mary W. Shelley omit the "W." from Mrs. Margaret Saville's name? . . . "Walton" as "walled-town" suggests the isolation inevitable to Private Prometheans like Robert and Professor "Waldman." Only by leaving Robert's bachelor realm behind . . . can Margaret reach *Saville*, that native community which is the union of male with female and the ideal of Agape.[11]

Even if these observations may be written off as purely conjectural, it is significant that in the novel Walton relents in his Frankensteinesque obsession with penetrating the North Pole and turns back. Such a move seems very much in line with a proto-feminist critique of male Romanticism, and seems to cater more to its outermost narrator-audience: M.W.S. (Mary Wollestonecraft Shelley disguised as Margaret [Walton] Saville). That even conjecturing at this level is impossible in Whale's film version is significant, as it is indicative of the degree to which the original novel seems to have been purged of its implicit criticism of a patriarchal politics of gender. The extent to which the film modifies and replaces the original Romantic dystopic myth shows the severe fragmentation of masculine from feminine, domesticating the novel's inferior shadow.

Whale's film version also suppresses the "overdeveloped" or "technological" shadow, which is evidenced in the exaggerated sub/inhumanity of the Monstrous Machine, as opposed to the ambivalent semihumanity of the Machine turned Monstrous in the novel. The original Monster is initially as innocent as a child and eventually learns how to speak French, the language of his father-creator. In contrast, the film Monster, having been given a "criminal brain" (admittedly by accident), is implied to be inherently evil and never learns how to speak.

This rewriting again has implications, because in the novel violence and guilt are emotions the Monster grows to recognize by virtue of its tragic alienation; in Whale's film these appear to be an inevitable mode of being. It is hardly surprising, therefore, that whereas the Monster in the novel eventually learns to speak, argue, and plead in the language of his father-creator, the film Monster remains mute: growls, grunts, smiles, and gestures are his only tenuous link to the outside world. Whereas the original Monster still appears to possess a semblance of a human visage and can converse like one, and is thus empowered in some fashion other than through brute strength, the film Monster is, from the very start, an embodiment of that which is Other than human. His biological criminality and lack of speech sentence him to a life of guilt, condemnation, and social impotence. The myth of the toolmaker who himself becomes a tool in his obsession with becoming a godlike Ego becomes converted into the less problematic myth of the toolmaker whose tool turns against him because it was fashioned from inferior and criminal materials from the very start.

There is yet another shadow that Whale's film generates, which seems to be a combination of both "inferior" (feminine) and "overdeveloped" (mechanized/monstrous) shadows. In the novel, Victor, after initially acquiescing to the Monster's demands that he should create a mate for his lonely creature, destroys the female Monster he had begun to piece together. This sequence is conspicuously absent in the film.

In discussing the significance of Frankenstein's destruction of the intended bride of the Monster, it is probably best to begin with tracing Victor's fevered flow of thoughts, within Shelley's novel, that leads to this development: "I was now about to form another being of whose dispositions I was alike ignorant; she might become ten thousand times more malignant than her mate and delight, for its own sake, in murder and wretchedness. . . . She also might turn with disgust from him [the Monster] to the superior beauty of man."[12]

For Mellor, what Victor Frankenstein fears is actually a thoroughgoing form of female sexuality: one that is sexually liberated, as well as free and empowered to make sexual choices (by force if necessary). Mellor's conclusion is that the real reason why Victor rips apart the female creature he is making—an act resembling a violent rape—is due to the female Monster's potential to defy the sexist aesthetic that demands that women be vulnerable, modest, passive, and pleasing—available only to their lawful husbands.[13] Even if one were to distance oneself from the uncompromising starkness of such a contention, one cannot deny that Whale's film, by effacing this segment, smoothly elides another potential area in which the ambiguous power of the female may rear her head. In other words the visible act of rape-murdering the mother figure is replaced by invisibility. The act of rape-murdering the (M)Other is a defensive reaction to, and therefore inadvertent affirmation of, the mythic (M)Other's/Baubo's reproductive and erotic power. In effacing this segment, the film aborts this third shadow and masks the anxieties it unveils.

Alongside the fragmentation and projection of the Other as feminine and Monstrous is an attempt to shore up a supermasculinized (and sanitized) version of the parthenogenetic myth and the repression of Baubo's vulva-revealing gesture. To show how this exaggeration of the masculine occurs alongside the repression of the feminine, it is important to see how masculine relationships are rewritten in the transformation from novel to film. For example, "Victor Frankenstein" and "Henry Clerval" in the novel are converted into "Henry Frankenstein" and "Victor Clerval" in the film. That the names of "Victor" and "Henry" are interchanged in the film, as opposed to the original novel, may be explained away by an appeal to its production history. Dennis Fischer notes that Peggy Webling's play, upon which the film was based, switched the name of the Monster creator's name, Victor, with that of his best friend, Henry.[14] Despite the fact that a historical precedent for this switching occurs, the result of this renaming, particularly when viewed alongside the other filmic modifications, is that the initial intense affinity (which seems to bear hints of a homoerotic attraction) binding Victor and Henry in the original novel, is broken and their personae are changed. Instead of the fervent fraternal devotion binding the two, such that Henry may be seen as a reflection of the lighter side of Victor's psyche, the two become completely separate and competing individuals.[15]

This sundering is magnified as the friendship binding Victor and Henry, unmarred by any conflict in the novel, is replaced by a clear rivalry over Elizabeth, rendered civil only by Elizabeth's obvious choice of Henry Frankenstein over Victor Clerval. This is illustrated clearly in an early sequence of the film where Victor, calling upon Elizabeth, finds her agitated over Henry's apparent mental state, promises to help her, and speaks to her like a rejected lover. There are also indications that the film intends to grant the crown of victory to Victor, not Henry, but these get suppressed as the film is produced, for reasons to be examined later.

The friendship identifying Henry as Victor's more humanistic and optimistic side in the novel is replaced by the master–slave relationship binding Henry Frankenstein to the sinister-looking dwarf, Fritz, who functions ostensibly as simply his laboratory assistant. For Fritz, despite his mutterings, is compelled to obey Frankenstein's every command. On the other hand, it appears that a curious father–son relationship also coexists as Henry displays a curt, paternal side when he orders the dwarf to duck down from the sight of the mourning crowd as the pair scavenge for fresh body parts. It is also noteworthy that Henry does not consider Fritz's presence even worth mentioning during the scene in which Henry invites Dr. Waldman, Victor, and Elizabeth into his laboratory to witness the awakening of the Monster he had sewn together from various sources. "A great scene isn't it? One man crazy—three very sane spectators!"[16]

One could argue for a threefold explanation for Henry's strange statement that there are four, rather than five, players on the scene: first, that Henry does not regard Fritz significant enough to mention as a spectator to this momentous scene; second, that Henry does not believe Fritz is "human" enough to appreciate the miracle of a non–human being coming to life; and third, that Henry does not consider Fritz separate/disparate enough from himself to warrant recognition as a cocreator. These three possible motivations, even if taken singly, and even more so when taken together, point to a high degree of identification binding Henry and Fritz in the film, as opposed to Victor and Henry in the novel. Instead of Henry's being symbolic/reflective of Victor's lighter side, Fritz becomes the personification of Henry's darker side. Fritz is Henry's son, as much as he is Henry's tool in the creation of the Monster; he is, in some senses, already the embodiment of the hidden Monstrosity lurking behind Henry's enlightened facade. Henry's attempts to birth himself, through total absorption in masculine and technological production, via the "birthing" of a supermasculine being, result in Monstrous progeny, revealing the dystopic nature of the parthenogenetic dream. The myth of the male Ego as Self-generating Source reveals its dark underside.

In addition, the more abstract, earnest relationship linking Victor and his father, Alphonse, in the novel, is replaced by a more concrete, comic version between "Henry" and Baron Frankenstein in the film. Thus the ambivalences of male gender dynamics in the novel are considerably reduced. Indeed this vague mixture of abstraction and fervency defining Victor's relation with Alphonse, his father in the novel, enables Veeder to see less an oedipal complex than a "negative Oedipal" one.[17] Any suggestive details allowing this hypothesis to emerge in the original text disappear in the film. The Baron Frankenstein, Henry's father, is domineering but loving, and cannot understand what his son is doing, puttering around in a drafty old windmill when a pretty girl is waiting to marry him (and perhaps, more importantly, when his father and the town are expectantly awaiting the wedding celebrations). Nevertheless his eventual explanation for Henry's odd behavior strikingly renders explicit what was implicit in the original novel: "There is another woman and I am going to find her!"[18]

In the conversion from script to film, two endings of *Frankenstein* were filmed, and of the two, the absurdly unrealistic one was retained. In the first ending, Henry Frankenstein was supposed to die when he was thrown from the windmill; in the second, which was retained, he lived.[19] The explanation seems to lie in a disastrous preview that alarmed Universal executives because of a large number of walkouts. Throughout the film, Victor seemed to be being set up, in traditional Hollywood fashion, to take Henry's place with Elizabeth after Henry's death, and Henry even gave a speech to that effect before he went off in pursuit of the Monster in the mountains. Instead, in the revised version, a voice was dubbed in, ridiculously saying, "He's alive," just before the burgomaster called out his name, got no response, and said, "Take him to the village." Finally the scene with Baron Frankenstein drinking a toast outside his son's sickroom to a "son to the House of Frankenstein"[20] was simply tacked on.

It is at this point that the tension necessary to uphold an exaggerated or triumphant version of the parthenogenetic myth, alongside the blunting of the critical edges of the novel's inferior and overdeveloped shadows, undercuts the film's patriarchal foundations. The lengths the film goes to in order to sustain these movements uncover its dark underside and reveal the myth of male self-birthing, devoid of any feminine participation, to be a lie. The destructive consequences of a patriarchal politics of gender and of the dark side of technology are visible, in spite of their heavily painted facade of a conventional "happy ending." The strain of upholding the parthenogenetic myth, and of repressing the Other, strains the film's credibility as a narrative; artifice emerges as artifice.

A second part of the film reveals the ironic undercutting of Whale's patriarchal reenvisaging of Shelley's novel. The scene with the Monster flinging the girl into the village pond also proved a source of some controversy. Apparently this was one of the few times that Karloff (and the rest of the crew) vehemently disagreed with Whale concerning how it should be shot. Mank quotes Karloff's thoughts on the matter: "Well, that was the only time I didn't like Jimmy Whale's direction. . . . My conception of the scene was that he would look up at the little girl in bewilderment, and in his mind she would become a flower. Without moving he would pick her up gently and put her in the water exactly as he had done to the flowers— and, to his horror, she would sink."[21]

Controversy plagued this particular scene. "I won't forgive Junior Laemmle or James Whale for permitting the Monster to drown a little girl before my very eyes," screamed *Motion Picture Herald*.[22] Although Whale and Laemmle agreed with the censors to cut the scene where the Monster killed the little girl to see if she would float, Karloff objected vehemently. He believed this was the sole scene whereby he could display the Monster's single spark of humanity by wringing his hands and emitting cries of agony. This scene did play in England, but the British board of censors excised the scenes where the Monster threatened bride-to-be Elizabeth (Mae Clarke) and killed Dr. Waldman (Edward Van Sloan).[23] Later MCA released new videocassette and disc versions, which included the long-lost footage of Frankenstein's Monster tossing the little girl into the pond after he ran out of flowers to throw. However, initially, with this controversial scene cut, there emerged the unwanted suggestion that the Monster had molested the child in the scene of her father carrying her drowned body through the midst of the village celebration.[24]

The degree of scandal associated with the inadvertent suggestion of the Monster's possible sexual assault of Maria can be better understood against the backdrop of another transformation of the narrative, from script to film. From Mank we learn of one more excised section of the Florey and Faragoh scripts.

There is a wild episode with two peasants, Johann and Gretel, preparing to make love as the Monster plays Peeping Tom at the cottage window. Johann teasingly plays with Gretel's chemise, and then the chemise is flung into the camera, draping itself rakishly over the foot of the bed. The excited Monster breaks in "eyes gleaming bestially," throws Johann into a corner and attacks Gretel. The episode ended with a "flash close shot" of the peasants' children trembling with fright, wide-eyed, listening—too terrified to utter a sound.[25]

Mank thinks that the reason why the Monster's violent attack of Johann and his implied rape of Gretel was taken out was because "it was very strong stuff and certainly destined to kill any sympathy the audience might have felt for the Monster."[26] Although this may have been a consideration, it seems clear that for the most part, Whale's film makes it very difficult for the audience to be sympathetic to the Monster, especially in comparison with Shelley's novel. The splintering off of the technological shadow is more complete in Whale's film than it is in the original narrative because the film's Monster is more dehumanized than the one in the novel. Another effect of this act of censorship is ridding the Monster of its sexuality. The Monster is acceptable as a playmate, but not as a rapist, because then it becomes too masculine, too much like its creator, who wishes to disown it. Ridding the Monster of its sexuality renders it Other, and yet domesticates or harnesses its Otherness within safe limits. By refusing the Monster an expression of magnified bestial desires characteristic of the dark side of the parthenogenetic myth (with its undercurrents of matricide and rape), the dissociation of the technological shadow reaches its highest expression. The narrative of the father giving birth to his son can only be compelling if it exacts the rape and murder of the ruptured female body, both seductive and maternal.

Yet again the ironic undercutting is evident here. In the attempt to repress any account that might allow the fissure dividing Machine/Monster from humanity to heal by granting the Monster its sexuality—an account that could give back to the technological shadow some of its ambiguous power—the unwanted suggestion of its repressed (supermasculine) sexuality emerges when the apparent rape of Maria surfaces. The Monster, even as it is, from the start, designated as Other by virtue of its biological criminality and inability to speak and argue as a human being does, reveals itself to be simply a masked extension of the (masculine) Ego.

The convoluted genealogy of the film reveals an anxiety concerning the depiction of the Monster. Whale and Karloff both seemed to want to depict the Monster as a being whose humanity coexisted with his in/subhumanity in a complex fashion. However, whereas Whale appeared to wish to exploit the fascination with the grotesquely monstrous, which one can glimpse in the Monster's pseudohuman visage, Karloff envisaged the Monster more as a pathetic and lonely creature, capable of the same emotions, curiosities, and motivations as any human being. The audience, in its overwhelming desire for a "happy ending," shunned even these attempts to wrestle with this complex blend of subhumanity and humanity in the Monster, resulting in a repression so great that it inverted itself into an admission of the myth of Otherness as a lie.

In addition, the deviations from the script, in terms of Elizabeth's appearance after the Monster's attack, and the effacement of Marilyn's mother, achieve the same effect of allowing critical distance from the triumphant patriarchal myth of parthenogenesis. In the original Fort and Faragoh script, the relevant scene is detailed as follows: "J-18 INT. ELIZABETH'S BEDROOM: As seen from the doorframe—Elizabeth is lying across her bed, apparently dead. Her wedding gown is in tatters; the lace and silk hang in shreds, but on her head is still the wreath of orange blossoms. We see the broken window, through which the Monster has escaped."[27]

In the film, Elizabeth's clothes are anything but in tatters and shreds. Sprawled elegantly over the edge of the bed, with her hair cascading over the edge, she seems the very picture of the inviolate virgin bride. The change is important, for it again illustrates the film's suppression and streamlining of potential Romantic gender conflicts, as well as the attempt to tame recurrences of Baubo's *ana-suromai*. The replacement of Maria's mother with a sole father may be seen as simply coincidental, not really demanding an explanation. Yet alongside the other changes, it seems to be more than it initially appears to be. It seems to be an extension of the general effacement, domestication, and diminishing of the role and power of mother-figures present in the novel, which are strikingly absent in the film. This further splits off the effete feminine shadow from the masculine, godlike Ego. Yet the extreme measures taken in order to ensure this effacement undercut these repressive movements, because the resultant story does not appear credible and is filled with gaps that cry out for explanations.

There was another transformation, from script to film, that shows the dark underside of this film. This time, the changes revolved around some aspects of the film that seemed to have an antireligious bent. Originally, when Dr. Frankenstein (Colin Clive) had his "It's alive!" scene, he then continued, "Now I know what it's like to be God!"[28] Another version of this emendation narrates how at first, after Henry Frankenstein has shouted "It's alive!" several times, Victor was supposed to respond, "Henry, in the name of God!" However, this was considered too blasphemous and upsetting to the clergy as Hollywood tightened its moral code in the thirties and so was replaced by an obvious jumpcut with the sound being covered over by a peal of thunder just as the scene faded out and Henry collapsed.[29] This pessimistic, anti-Christian outlook appears endemic to Fort and Faragoh's script and Whale's interpretation of it, and was not simply a careless slip within the dialogue among characters. As proof of this, it is important to note that in both the original Fort and Faragoh script and the resultant film, a Gothic, parodically anti-Christian setting forms the backdrop against which Frankenstein and Fritz make their entrance.

Fade in:
A-1   EXTERIOR . . . LONG SHOT HILLSIDE
DUSK
Sunset. The torn, bloody banner of the sky. Purple and black shadows that creep stealthily in the wake of the sun, which are now gone. The hill springs out of the landscape—stark, parched. Its weary slope carries the eye toward a bleak summit. This is the cemetery. There are crosses here, rude, primitive, tilted at crazy angles, like so many symbols of the inevitable decay.[30]

Whale emphasizes the visual impact of the three crosses askew. It seems no accident that when Fritz and Frankenstein enter the graveyard, they enter from behind a statue of Death. As the pair haul up a casket in front of the statue of Christ crucified, a third crosslike structure, built from Frankenstein's draping of his clothes around a stake he has pulled from a grave and relocated, is in between the statue of the crucified Christ and the figure of Death—reinscribing a Calvaryesque scene. Frankenstein's trance-like utterance as he cradles the casket continues this impression: "He is just resting . . . waiting for a new life to come."[31] Martin Tropp again succinctly captures the ironic and anti-Christian reworking of the mythology of the Resurrection: "This scene is a perverse Resurrection, and the Monster destined to parody Christ."[32] This motif fits nicely with Rushing and Frentz's notion that repressed spirituality (which is part of the myth of progress) reemerges as demonic. This is seen most clearly in the "technological" man,

who acknowledges no spiritual guidance, and thus unleashes "demonic su-
pernaturalism" in his inventions, as in the case of Frankenstein.[33]

The dystopic nature of the Frankensteinian myth again emerges, this
time, given further concreteness by an anti-Christian dimension. In Whale's
films, beginning with *Frankenstein*, the myth of the Resurrection is ironically aligned with the myth of technology-as-progress, revealing its dark
underside. Frankenstein, who aspires to be God, and to re-create the human
race in his image, is punished as his parthenogenetic son turns against him.
The son born from the father's labors turns out not to be a Christ through
whom redemption becomes possible but a demon who wreaks havoc and
destruction.

The shadow myth entails a refractory dimension: Shadows deny as well
as magnify that which is hated, repressed, treated as Other—and yet are
responded to with intense attraction and repulsion. This refractoriness, particularly with respect to the patriarchal relation to technology as simply an
extension of the Ego-as-God, is glimpsed in the film's indulgence in the
magical fascination of gadgetry. The laboratory in the ruined watchtower,
the most memorable set in all the Frankenstein films, evokes the spellbind-
ing attraction and fear that science embodies for the layperson; its centrality
also underlines the mythic shift from female bodily reproduction to male
technological production. Though there is evidence of fluctuation and tension, this general mythic shift holds through its various filmic iterations.
The laboratory's central structure is a gleaming gadget that raises the Monster through a skylight in the midst of a raging electrical storm in order to
infuse the Monster with "the great ray which first brought life into the
world."[34] The rising crescendo of special effects that usher in the awakening
of the Monster is unforgettable. It is a "controlled catastrophe combining
our fascination for electronic wizardry with the horror of its product."[35]
These laboratory scenes serve to glorify as well as caricaturize modern technology—conjuring in electrical splendor the birthing of the Monster. This
parthenogenetic birth illuminates the relationship between the Monster
whom Henry creates and the monster who functions as Henry's assistant
and double—Fritz; both function as servant-sons and extensions of Henry-
as-Ego.

Tropp follows a similar line of argumentation and hints at a historically
grounded explanation for the film's rewriting of the Frankensteinian myth.

In many ways, the 1931 *Frankenstein* plays upon the particular collection of fears
that haunted the thirties. The scientist and hunchback personify the forces of mad
authority and sadistic servitude that brought disaster to the world and perhaps,
were plotting new horrors for the future. Their "science" is both technological and
political; the Monster is weapon and victim, a mechanical engine of destruction
and a collection of misused human beings. Its rage and rejection threaten all of
society. At the same time, the film plays upon the seduction of gadgetry (our affin-

ities with the scientist) and our identification with the isolation and sexual force of the Monster.[36]

What Tropp does not point out is that the excessive degree of splitting necessary to maintain the Otherness of the inferior and overdeveloped shadows in Whale's rendition hints at a possible resolution. The symbolism of the hunchbacked dwarf in relation to his master-father-employer may be envisaged as a way of showing how the Monstrous Other is simply part of the Self. The same may be said especially of the Monster. This is most evident in the scene in which the Monster, in the course of the chase, confronts Henry Frankenstein at the very spot in which the gibbet of the hanging murderer once stood, and whom Frankenstein had ordered Fritz to cut down for the purpose of scavenging usable body parts. Whale has the camera pan back and forth effectively uniting them. A similar visual-thematic effect is accomplished by the shot-reverse shots Whale has of the Monster and his maker within the windmill, as they face one another, separated by a revolving structure, which extends from the floor, whose numerous slats resemble windows through which the two look at each other.

In Fritz's case the dynamic is slightly more complex. Although Frankenstein effectively regards Fritz as an extension of himself (as evinced in Frankenstein's omission of Fritz's presence in the laboratory scene involving the awakening of the Monster), there is a sense in which Fritz resists such a thorough assimilation. Whale, with his characteristic black humor, endeavors to give him a personality of his own, seen in Fritz's abruptly comical attempts to drive away Dr. Waldman, Victor, and Elizabeth on the fateful night that Henry attempts to bring his experiments to their climax: Fritz's leaning down to pull a loose sock as he stumbles up and down a long flight of steps, muttering irritably to himself; Fritz's hilarious dropping of the "normal" brain when he accidentally bumps into a hanging skeleton and a gong that reverberates in Dr. Waldman's classroom, and his consequent, naïve stealing of the "criminal" brain instead. It is as if the figure of the evil double, embodied in the Monster, is prefigured in Fritz such that the hunchback becomes a hideously laughable and traditionally American stock character—the sidekick. As Tropp phrases it, "Like Hawkeye and Chingachgook, Huck Finn and Jim or at a later date Matt Dillon and Chester, Frankenstein and Fritz face the future together, partners on a scientific frontier."[37] The Romantic Doppelgänger or evil twin/alter ego, via Whale's rewriting of the Frankensteinian myth, becomes the laughable sidekick. This transformation still maintains an illusion of projection, as Fritz may be seen purely as Henry's subservient helper or tool; on the other hand, however, the closeness and complexity of identification binding this first monstrous son (this son-tool-servant who acts as midwife to the birthing of the second monstrous son) to Henry unveils Fritz's identity to be primordially tied up with Henry, the monstrous father. Henry, in some ways, simply births himself through his tyrannical molding of Fritz's acts; in so doing, he attempts, unsuccessfully, to excise through projection the monstrosity that lurks in himself.

(UN)VEILING THE BRIDE

Barely two years after the release of the overwhelmingly popular *Frankenstein*, Universal Pictures had already begun plans on a sequel. This second film was publicized as one designed to "surpass the original in greatness,"[38] and to cast Bela Lugosi, the actor who had turned down the original role of the Monster, as a mad doctor. Lugosi eventually withdrew, and the project remained stagnant until 1935, when Whale began casting. After much debate the film was labeled *Bride of Frankenstein*. There apparently seemed to be a gravitation toward *The Return of Frankenstein* as well as *Frankenstein Lives Again!* because of the fear of confusion: more precisely, the bride was the Monster's bride, and not Frankenstein's. Though billing interests seem to have dictated the choice of the title, the use of *The Bride of Frankenstein* is intriguing as it reveals a further complication of the evolving Frankensteinian myth. The title seems to spotlight, rather than efface, the shadow of the not-I or the "feminine Other"; on the other hand, it hyperbolizes the necrophiliac glimpses in the novel and renders them overt, closely intertwining feminine beauty with monstrosity and death in a simplistic, rather than complex, manner. Baubo's life-giving gesture is transformed into an attractive-repulsive symbol of death. It is no accident that the bride first appears as a mummy and then later in a white wedding gown that resembles a shroud. In so doing the film combines the inferior and overdeveloped shadows, heightening the fascination with the feminine-as-monstrous, and overtly justifying why this hyperbolically monstrous shadow should be ruthlessly expelled. Similarly, it is interesting that the telltale sign of monstrosity—the "?"—is transferred from the male monster to the female one. In the credits, Karloff takes top credits as the Monster; Elsa Lanchester's name is in the middle, identified as the actress who plays Mary Shelley, whereas the female Monster, who is at the bottom of the list, is cryptically identified as "?" in spite of the fact that press reviews and releases had identified Lanchester as playing both the parts of Mary Shelley and the female Monster.[39] Lanchester herself wrote of the deliberate conjunction of femininity with monstrosity, characteristic of Whale's film, in a letter to Life magazine issue for April 5, 1968. She said Whale's casting of the same actress for both parts was "because he wanted to tell that Mary Shelley indeed had something in common with the dreadful creature of her imagination." Although it is true that Mary Shelley did seem to identify with the Monster, in its loneliness and alienation from a detached father and a nonexistent mother, the film splits monstrosity into two. The male

Monster takes on appealing human characteristics and displays a consciousness of self; in contrast the female Monster becomes the embodiment of the fearful and fascinating, who, when she begins to assert her will to choose a mate, is ruthlessly destroyed.

Similarly, Paul Jensen points out how the prologue of the film serves an additional purpose: to imply that within the dainty and delicate Mary seethed "a nasty spirit, a real evil" and that the two were "the same person."[40] Thus, Whale meticulously insisted that the dress Lanchester wore as Mary Shelley be of "the finest possible white net, with iridescent, sequined butterflies and moons and stars on it," even if such details would not be obvious onscreen; he also deliberately modified the script's description of the female Monster's hair from being "curled close" and hanging "straight and dark on either side" to the famous hairstyle stiffly standing away from her head.[41] This hairdo, which seems to have been inspired partially by Nefertiti's bust, once again ambivalently aligns the female monster with beauty, death, and the exotic/Oriental. Interestingly enough, Jensen also constructs a compelling argument for an artistically camouflaged misogyny that runs through Whale's work, which he traces biographically to Whale's breakup with set and costume designer Doris Zinkeisen.[42] Finally, Donald Glut stitches together the details of Jack Peirce's (the makeup artist) and, reputedly, Whale's vision of female monstrosity to reveal this paradoxical conjunction of the beautiful and grotesque via the evocation of the exotic and mysterious.

Pierce's own readings on the subject of Egyptology entered into his creating the Bride's make-up. Remembering statues of Queen Nefertiti, Pierce gave the Bride a similar appearance by making her thick mass of hair, streaked with lightning-like silver, stand out from her head. This matched the gauze on her arms for effect. The eyebrows shot up like those of a movie vampire. The Bride's neck showed stitched scars where the head had been attached. The "Bride of Frankenstein" stood seven feet tall in the disguise. She was a veritable monster, a suitable mate for Henry Frankenstein's first attempt at creating a human being. Yet despite her terrible appearance, there was something *weirdly attractive* about the Bride that made her even more bizarre [italics mine].[43]

It is true that in the novel, unbridled female sexuality, as Mellor has shown, is associated with violence and death. This motif recurs, for example, in Victor's dream, after he has given his creature life, of Elizabeth's transmogrification into his mother's corpse, as well as in the train of Victor's thoughts as he rationalizes the rape-murder of the female creature that he, for a while, attempts to fashion. However, in Whale's second rendition of the Frankensteinian narrative, he takes away the technique of concentric frames Mary Shelley uses in order to throw suspicion upon Victor's motives in obsessively creating the male Monster and just as compulsively destroying the female Monster. Mary Shelley embeds Victor's account in Walton's letters to his sister, and in so doing, reveals Victor and Walton to suffer from the same mad ambition—the desire to rape, penetrate, and master nature. It is striking that Sir William Crookes, a physicist who addressed the annual meeting of the British Association in 1898, used the same tropes of sexual intercourse, birth, claims to paternity, and aspiration to Creatorship so pervasive even, according to various feminist critics, in contemporary scientific practice: "Steadily, unflinchingly, we strive to pierce the inmost heart of nature, from what she is to reconstruct what she has been, and to prophesy what she yet shall be. Veil after veil we have lifted, and her face grows more beautiful, august and wonderful, with every barrier that is withdrawn."[44]

Whale instead replaces Shelley's subtle undercutting of Victor's (and Walton's) perspectives through the use of slippery and concentric narratives with a more stable story: the tale of how Mary Shelley conceived the plot of *Frankenstein*. The film begins with the usual Gothic atmospheric effects: torrential rains, blinding flashes of lightning, and the crash of thunder. In a castle are Lord Byron (Gavin Gordon), Percy Shelley (Douglas Walton), and Mary Shelley (Elsa Lanchester). Byron, styled as a prolix dandy, proclaims himself the virtual cause of the storm—the target of those divine bolts from heaven, as England's greatest sinner. He then shifts and conjectures that perhaps they are an accolade to Percy, "England's greatest poet." When Percy interjects, "What of *my* Mary?" [italics mine], Byron calls her an "angel" as the soft and feminine background music subtly swells. Mary is described by Byron as an "astonishing creature"—one whose "bland and lovely brow" surprisingly conceived of the story of a Monster created from the cadavers of rifled graves. Mary protests that her purpose in writing the tale was to draw a moral lesson: "the punishment that befell a mortal man who desired to emulate God." She accidentally pricks her finger over her needlework, ostensibly distracted by Byron's vivid recall of the morbid aspects of her novel. Nevertheless, with but a little bit of prodding, particularly from Byron, she proceeds to resurrect the tale of the Monster. The phallic pricking of her finger, which draws blood, inverts the fairy-tale correlate of the birth of Snow White ("her lips blood red, her skin like snow, her name, Snow White"), spawning a nameless Monster with black lips and greenish skin.

It is interesting that an iteration of this version of the events has been immortalized in both film and literature. Emily Sunstein, by no means alone in framing the tale of the tale in a similar way, recounts the genesis of the novel from a storytelling competition at the Villa Diodati, Switzerland. The contest evolved partially from the boredom and restlessness of being trapped indoors by the storm raging outside, but was also inspired by their reading aloud from a German book of ghost stories translated into French, *Fantasmagoriana*.[45] Although Sunstein reveals that there were two other people who were present, Claire Clairmont (Mary's half-sister) and Sir John Polidori (a physician who idolized Byron), she nevertheless depicts Mary as a poor soul who is unable to keep up with the poetic and imaginative talents of Byron and her husband. " 'Have you thought of a story?' they asked each day, to which she had to reply 'with a mortifying negative.' " Sunstein's source is Mary Shelley's preface to the 1831 edition, the source of contemporary versions of the novel.[46] Yet John Polidori's diary reveals a very different story: It appears that it was Mary who proposed the competition[47] and who boldly volunteered the story of the "pale student of the unhallowed arts kneeling beside the thing he had put together."[48] Mary, even in Sunstein's accounts, was not a naïve girl who was more interested in sewing than in intellectual discovery and growth; on the contrary, Godwin, her father, described her as "singularly bold, somewhat imperious, and active of mind. Her desire of knowledge is great, and her perseverance in everything she undertakes almost invincible."[49] It is interesting that even Mary Shelley's account is not one that can be taken at face value; her "factual" rendition of events is itself fictionalized, which does not render it either frivolous or false, but powerfully revelatory of the gendered expectations concerning the authorship of shocking and horrifying tales during the Victorian era. Indeed, Stephen Behrendt reinterprets Shelley's use of the deferential, self-deprecating introduction or preface, a standard literary fixture, as a strategic rhetorical gesture of ownership.

In her own 1831 Introduction to *Frankenstein*, Shelley pointedly reminds us that her story originated with a set of conversations between Percy Bysshe Shelley and Byron to which she was essentially a silent auditor. Yet *hers* is the story that was completed *and* published *and* that became sufficiently popular to demand republication. Making her claim of authorship explicit, Mary Shelley in the process claims possession not only of the novel's language but also of the material—the apparently unremittingly *male* material—of its subject matter.[50]

It is also noteworthy that Whale's Mary Shelley justifies her authorship of the Monster's story through an insistence on the moral lesson it intends to teach. However, as Steven Forrey shows us, Mary Shelley's 1831 version of the novel is very different from the original 1818 version. The earlier version's moral ambiguity is replaced by a heavy, moralizing stress, partially in keeping with the commercial viability of the overtly didactic *Presumption; Or The Fate of Frankenstein*, which was performed thirty-seven times during its first season in 1823.[51] It is revealing that it is this sanitized version that Whale chooses to comprise the outermost frame of his film—rendering it, despite the greater complexity with which it characterizes the Monster, ultimately a rather simplistic cautionary tale.

The film's tale within a tale (i.e., Mary recounting her novel) begins with a series of flashbacks:[52] of Henry Frankenstein (Colin Clive) and Fritz

(Dwight Frye) scavenging for parts in graveyards; of the laboratory "birth-ing" scene; of the inadvertent murder of Maria, the child who dared to invite the Monster to play with her; of Henry being flung from the top of the mill by the Monster. The action resumes to reveal the smoky ruins of the mill, which Whale films as a series of burning crosses, toppling to the ground, thus continuing his motif of the parodic Resurrection from his first film. In a continuing ironic rewriting of the account of the Resurrection, two women conjecture on whether the Monster is finally dead. The bur-gomaster (E.E. Clive) dismisses the Monster as simply a "strange man," and refuses to acknowledge his monstrosity, in again an ironic rewriting of the nonbeliever's dismissal of Christ's messiahship. Hans (Reginald Bar-low), the father of Maria, insists on attempting to see the Monster's black-ened bones, in spite of his wife's (Mary Gordon) entreaties not to enter the ruins. In line with the film's effacement of the feminine-as-Other, although Maria's mother finally appears in this version, as opposed to the first film, she remains nameless and ineffectual. Hans falls through the fire-weakened roof and is attacked by the Monster. In characteristic Whale-ean black humor, Hans's wife hears his screams and, thinking it is her husband who is reemerging, takes the outstretched hand of the Monster, and helps him out. The Monster strangles her as an owl blinks dispassionately, a fellow predator unmoved by the screams of the victim.[53] Minnie (Una O'Connor), one of the women earlier gossiping about whether the Monster is alive, is a witness to the Resurrection of the Monster and runs off, screeching. Min-nie functions as the ironic counterpart of the women who had found Christ's tomb empty, and had run off proclaiming that Christ is again alive. Yet it is not an angel she has seen, but a devil; and because she is disbelieved by everyone, she, like Pontius Pilate, washes her hands clean of responsi-bility. As Alberto Manguel points out, Minnie functions as a comic Cas-sandra, and shifts the *Bride* from the realm of tragedy to grotesque comedy. "The old couple had uttered terrible, dramatic screams; Minnie's are too shrill to be terrifying—an artifice, an exaggeration."[54]

Yet Minnie's part is far from one of simple mimicry. It is she who locates the plot line of the movie in relation to the plot of the novel; she reveals that Henry had intended to marry Elizabeth (Valerie Hobson) on this very day, an affair that seems to have ended tragically, with his apparent death. Yet it is also Minnie who utters the latest iteration of the all-too-famous line: "He's alive!" as Henry's hand stirs, to Elizabeth's relief. The move-ment of Henry's hand is shot, interestingly enough, in the same way the Monster's hand was shot during his awakening in the first film, forming an equivalence relation. If Whale hints at a kinship binding Henry and the Monster, he also gives Minnie the role of proclaimer of life (a distinction that is solely Henry's in the first film). In addition, Whale undercuts Min-nie's status as life-proclaimer by coupling that role with comedic relief. Tinges of a decadent version of Baubo's *ana-suromai*, with its life-affirming proximity to eroticism and the cycle of life and death, emerge. This is a Baubo whose display of female power is tied up with barrenness and comic relief. The type of laughter she evokes is no longer the life-affirming type but is linked with ridicule. Finally, Minnie becomes, in some ways, the female equivalent of Fritz in the initial *Frankenstein* film because it is she who witnesses the reemergence of the Monster from the smoky ruins of the mill, and, like Fritz, she later actively torments (with words, rather than a whip) the creature when he is captured. This renders her an accomplice to Frankenstein's crimes, in a manner analogous to Fritz's assistance to Frankenstein and his hyperbolization of Frankenstein's actions in the earlier film.

The lovers' wedding night seems to be destined to be disrupted, as a "Dr. Pretorius" (Ernest Thesiger) is theatrically announced by Minnie, the maid.[55] The kinship between Minnie and Fritz is clearest during the scenes prior to the meeting between Henry and the sinister doctor. Minnie's mannerisms and antics are reminiscent of Fritz's: Like him, she shuffles along with rapid, clumsy movements, and mutters constantly to herself. Yet, unlike Fritz, who has the nerve to turn away unwanted guests, Minnie is unable to withstand Pretorius's imperious demand to be let in, despite the lateness of the hour. Interestingly, after Pretorius (whose name Tropp genealogizes as Latin for "causing to be known" and "of the ruling class"— indicating his lust for absolute power)[56] has been ushered in, Henry opts to send away Elizabeth rather than their unexpected guest. When Pretorius suggests that they collaborate on the creation of life, Henry initially resists, but then eventually gives in to his curiousity, and consents to Pretorius's invitation to see the results spawned by the doctor's experiments in the creation of life "in God's own image." This effectively rewrites, not only the Resurrection motif, but also the biblical story of creation and the Edenic fall. This time, it is not a serpent who tempts a woman, but an effeminate man who tempts a doubting creator.

Pretorius and Henry sneak off to a hidden laboratory, where Pretorius toasts their partnership with the words: "To a new world of gods and monsters." Although Henry does not drink to the toast, it is significant that even he makes no attempt to include or even inform Elizabeth of their whereabouts or intentions. It seems imperative that her role as a passive, nonsexual creature be maintained in order for the narrative to gain momentum. In the hidden laboratory, Pretorius carries out a casket-shaped container that houses his bottled specimens. They are fully developed homunculi: a miniature queen, king, archbishop, a devil who bears Pretorius's features, a ballerina, and a mermaid. Whale gives the scene another touch of dark humor when he depicts the king (resembling Henry VIII) to be a slob who is slave to the dictates of his bodily desires; when he is not busy devouring a chicken leg, he is attempting to get into the bottle of the protesting queen, and is easily picked up and deposited into his own bottle by the watchful Pretorius. It is Pretorius who ensures that his creatures do not reproduce on their own, and that the domain of reproduction remains fully in the realm of male production, devoid of female participation. Interestingly enough, the analogy he uses to defend his work from Henry's charge that his work is "black magic" rather than "science" locates himself as a divine gardener who "grew [his] materials from seeds as nature does." The botanical model is instructive, as plants, particularly in a well-kept garden, are rigorously pruned and pollinated in keeping with the gardener's desires—a process of generation that requires the cool detachment of a creator rather than the passionate involvement of lovers.[57] Similarly it is also Pretorius who proposes to Frankenstein that they create a woman with the words: "Male and female he created them. . . . 'Be fruitful and multiply . . . ' Alone, you have a man; now together, we will create his mate." Pretorius's words are a double entendre—it is clear that there is an erotic dimension to their proposed partnership, which aims to displace woman from the site of (M)Other to daughter-slave. In Shelley's novel the monster himself demands the creation of a mate to relieve his loneliness; in Whale's version Pretorius's Mephistophelean dream of power is the starting point. The new world of gods and monsters is to be spawned through masculine self-birthing.

Pretorius was principally constructed by Whale, and was designed to eclipse even Henry's character. Ernest Thesiger undoubtedly stole the show with his performance as Pretorius, settling down to a feast on top of a grave, toasting a skull atop a pile of bones, before settling down to his graveyard endeavors. Pretorius's character, combined with the prologue, "intertwines a coy fascination with death, an ambivalent attitude toward religion, a suspicion of women, and a disdain of human nature in general."[58] In Pretorius, an ambiguously gendered role combined with the power of a scientist and the cunning of a criminal produces a demonic figure against whom Henry appears angelic. Yet both mirror and need each other in order to continue with their parthenogenetic ambitions.

In a scene that seems to mime and reverse the earlier scene with Maria, the Monster rescues a shepherdess (Anne Darling) from drowning, but she screams when she regains consciousness. The town mobilizes itself against the Monster, who throws rocks at them before he is finally subdued by the angry and desperate mob. Manguel eloquently captures how the film Monster's characterization fluctuates across hunter and hunted, undead and child. "In a beautiful close-up, lit from the left, the Monster's face becomes young, frightened, almost angelic: . . . The face of evil possibilities has become a face of possible goodness."[59] In addition, Jensen details how Whale achieves the cinematic parallel between the capture of the Monster and the torture and Crucifixion of Christ, and shows how Whale forcefully conveys the script's description of the Monster "raised against the sky, a terrible but pathetic sight—friendless, persecuted and almost crucified."[60]

Strangely enough, it is Minnie again who is given the significant role of Judas, gloating over the capture of the Monster, who is bound, Christlike, on a pole, elevated as if he were crucified, before he is dropped into a wagon of hay amidst jeers and cheers. Minnie, at the head of the mob, peers into the prison, where the Monster is shackled, ironically, in a throne-like structure. It is also Minnie who calls him a "nightmare in the day," linking her comical utterances with the vision that leads to Mary Shelley's generation of the tale of Frankenstein and his monster. Like Christ, whose power as a Messiah is denied by the mob that crucifies him, the Monster's power is scoffed at when he is bound in chains. Yet the Monster escapes, and the bodies of three more victims, one of them a young virgin on the way home from her first communion rites, are found. Interestingly it is again Minnie who discovers two of the three victims, and it may be no accident that the dead couple are called "Neumann"—literally translated, "new man"; their violent murders possibly underscore, once again, the parodic resurrection of this "new man" who has turned monstrous.

As the Creature lumbers on, nursing an arm that has been shot, he hears violin music. What follows is a touching scene as the blind man (O.P. Heggie), who, in the novel, is prevented from befriending the Monster by his protective son, Felix, welcomes and feeds the Creature. As the Creature is unable to communicate using words, the blind man—here a hermit living alone—assumes that his unexpected guest, too, suffers from an affliction, and vows to look after him, reasoning that the Monster's companionship will bring him comfort in turn. Manguel points out how the double entendre of sickness, dark eroticism, and isolation probably had some resonance with Whale's personal predicament as an openly gay man. "There is something tacitly but strongly erotic here; the meeting of two men, both outcast, both unwanted, who find they can share house under a common bond."[61] A mirror-imaging set of male homoerotic relationships emerges: the Monster–blind man dyad, which produces nurturance and companionship, and the Henry–Pretorius partnership, which spawns alienation and the master–slave relation.

Nevertheless it is significant that Whale's film excises out three characters in the novel: Agatha and Safie, the two women who are part of the De Lacey family in Mary Shelley's novel, and Felix, the son of the blind man. In the novel the Monster learns how to speak through voyeuristically participating (though at a much faster pace) in the lessons Safie, the exotic Arabian, receives from her French-speaking protectors. The film replaces that with an exclusively paternal relationship between the blind man and the monster; even Felix has to be eliminated because in the novel he possesses the feminine characteristics of gentleness and sensitivity. The De Lacey family, as Mellor has shown, functions in the novel as an alternative type of society to the tyrannically gendered world in which Victor belongs, where the public realm of action is masculine and the private realm of domesticity is feminine. In such a society, the realm of adventure is not limited to the male (Safie undergoes many trials as she goes in search of Felix), and males are capable of vulnerability and passivity (Felix is sad and inconsolable until Safie arrives). In contrast Whale's film returns to a world in which ideal companionship is an exclusively male province, and paternalism replaces a communion of equals. It is both ironic and fitting that the music the blind hermit plays is the *Ave Maria*—a hymn dedicated to the image of the eternal mother, but precisely as inviolate virgin and bride—a mother shorn of the novel's emphasis on motherhood as the meeting point between eroticism and the dark passions, and of life and death.

As the Monster recovers, the blind man tries to teach his unorthodox student some words: "bread," "drink," "good," "smoke," and "friend." Yet whereas the blind man sees fire as "good," the Monster calls it "bad." Again, the complex characterization of the Monster in the novel is replaced by a simplistic one in Whale's film. The Monster whose sexuality remains ambiguous in the novel is capable of not only eloquent sentences, but also of paradoxical insight—he is able to discern that fire, which brings joy through warmth, can also bring pain and destruction. In contrast, the Monster in the film is unambiguously male, is capable of uttering only words clumsily strung together, and simplistically views the world in terms of "good" versus "bad." What occurs is a caricature vulnerable to both domestication and ridicule, as the *New York Times* film review points out: "[The Monster] learns to speak, to smoke cigars and drink wine. 'Good,' he says gluttonously, and points to the things he wants. 'Bad!' he growls and shakes his square and metal-clipped head at fire. One will be amused at his softening, but it will be respectful amusement; one would not dare to laugh: he might snarl."[62]

The context of the humanization of the Monster—his depiction as a persecuted victim, a comic child of simple pleasures, and his noble and justifiable rage at rejection—is important to note. No reference is ever made back to his "criminal" brain, and his behavior is easy to sympathize with. Yet the context of this normalization crystallizes most clearly within the context of an exclusively male relationship, though one must add, a relationship "feminized" through its kinship binding two malformed outcasts.

Hunters accidentally pass by and recognize the Monster; they forcefully take away the blind man and try to kill the Monster by burning down the blind man's hut, despite the hermit's protests. The Monster escapes and pathetically cries out for his friend, but only succeeds in scaring away a small group of children, most of whom are schoolgirls—an all-too-poignant reminder that female companionship is an inadequate replacement for the original father-son relationship.

At a graveyard the Monster wreaks havoc, toppling even a papal statue.[63] Again, harking back to the theme of a perverse Resurrection, instead of being raised up after a period of suffering, he lowers himself into a tomb underneath an overhanging crucifix. A mob follows in hot pursuit of him. Underground in a mausoleum, the Monster stumbles across the body of a dead woman, whom he pathetically addresses as "friend," upon whom he smiles and at whom he waves. It is significant that it is only with a dead woman that such "communion" is possible; the sterile and necrophiliac tendencies the novel associates with Victor are grafted on to the Monster, further emphasizing his Otherness. Though there is an increased humanization of the technological shadow, there are boundaries to maintain. The creature remains associated with death and sickness, as if by destiny. As Glenn Erickson points out: "The Monster first embraces a skull while contemplating his future love, and at one point, enters a mausoleum to be where he feels most at home, with the dead."[64]

Dr. Pretorius arrives to scavenge graves, and the Monster (and the audience) are privy to the doctor's necrophiliac tastes. Pretorius orders two men to dig up the grave of a nineteen-year-old girl. The Monster is lured out by the smell of cigar smoke and food, which he associates with friendship. Somehow the Monster senses that Pretorius is planning to create a being like himself, and is overjoyed to find that the doctor is planning to create a "woman, friend, like me." It is noteworthy that the film never explains how the Monster comes to learn of the differences between men and women; instead, in the same way he is conceived in Henry's image, he conceives of "woman" in *his* own likeness—a slip that again emphasizes the collapsing of the inferior and overdeveloped shadows in Whale's second *Frankenstein* film. The female monster emerges as conceived in the liminal realms of the "not-I" (the feminized shadow) and the monstrous (the technological shadow). She is constructed as a double-lack—lacking masculinity, and, as a monster, lacking humanity.

Pretorius questions the Monster to find out if he knows of his origins. The Monster replies that Frankenstein was his creator, and that he, the Monster, loves the dead and hates the living. It is interesting that the referent "he" is ambiguous in the novel, as Victor seems to be the one drawn to death in his desire to penetrate the secrets of life—an act not without the symbolic desire to possess and obliterate the dead (m)other. In Whale's film, however, that ambiguity is lost, and is replaced by the Rousseauesque narrative of how an artificial man becomes monstrous by virtue of his maltreatment by others. Once again the covering over of the murder of the mother occurs, this time, with barely a trace, as Whale's narrative completely expunges the novel's refractory references to Victor's ambiguous lust for his dead mother. In place of the novel's subtle irony, Whale establishes a sardonic, dark humor, as Pretorius applauds the Monster's love for the dead with the words: "You are wise for your generation." The necrophiliac and megalomaniac tendencies in the original novel's Victor are hyperbolized to form a fusion of infernal forces that unite to conceive the plan of creating a monstrous woman. As Jensen writes, "The figure of Death meets a living corpse in the house of the dead, the God-like Devil and the Devilish Christ come face to face, and the two social outcasts join forces."[65]

Pretorius comes to fetch Henry, who cowers behind the protective Elizabeth (now his wife), who in turn declares the doctor's visit "most unwelcome." Although this revision seems to provide Elizabeth with greater power than the novel does (where she is alternately treated either as a favorite pet, an angel, or an untouchable virgin), it is important to note that Elizabeth, in both the film and the novel, functions effectively as a surrogate and unerotic/Good mother figure, rather than a lover. Her function is more to ensure that Pretorius does not "disturb" Henry, much as a devoted mother would protect a vulnerable child from a bully; it is strangely a supremely maternal role sanitized of the castrating and arousing potential of the Baubo's *ana-suromai*.

To convince Henry to continue with their "supreme collaboration," Pretorius orders "another assistant," the Monster, in. What occurs is a mirror-image of the first *Frankenstein* film. In a manner paralleling the first encounter between Monster and maker, the Monster motions with his hands and orders his creator to sit, before he is sent away by Pretorius. Frankenstein still resists, and the Monster, following Pretorius's cues (and an inevitable theme of the Frankensteinian myth—the perpetual deferment of the consummation of the wedding night), abducts Elizabeth to coerce Henry's cooperation in completing his end of the bargain. This reenvisaging of the novel is again interesting as it reveals the gendered dynamics at work. Instead of acting autonomously as in the novel, the Monster in Whale's film is no more than a muscle-clad pawn in Pretorius's mad scheme of absolute power. Similarly the complex Milton-inspired appeals to responsibility in the confrontation between Creator and creature in the novel are replaced by a simple story of blackmail, with Elizabeth being the quintessential helpless female Henry is compelled to rescue at all costs. Minnie, as usual, performs the function of divine and ridiculous herald: she possesses the gift of premonition, as evidenced by the fact that prior to the kidnapping, she feels nervous about leaving Elizabeth alone; yet the power of that position is shorn away by having her cut a ridiculous figure, screaming hysterically as she announces Elizabeth's abduction.

It is obvious that the scene of the second birthing forms the dramatic climax of the tale. Accented by the driving beat of Franz Waxman's eerily romantic score, the business of bringing the female Monster to life becomes a montage of tilted camera angles, tight close-ups of the faces of Henry and Pretorius, and sparks issuing forth from various electrical devices. The parthenogenetic myth reveals itself again in full glory. This time two men birth a woman (a not-man) (not) made in their images. The female corpse is borne upon an apparatus that exposes her to the lightning bolts, which inseminate her with the spark of life.[66]

This scene is rife with intertextual filmic references: again, a violent storm rises, again, an inert figure, dressed like a mummy, is shown. As Pretorius speaks fondly of the artificial brain he has cultivated like a plant, he murmurs Frankenstein's earlier line, steeped in a parodic revision of the Resurrection, as Henry scavenged for parts at the cemetery in the first film: "It is waiting for a life to come." The substitution of "it" in this film for "he" (in the 1931 *Frankenstein* film) is crucial; it is clear that Pretorius thinks the creature is like a plant he has germinated. Kites are dispatched to function as conveyors of lightning bolts to the apparatus, as the female body is carried upward, heralded by the fury of the storm, in a parodic and modern reenvisaging of the Ascension. The experiment proves successful: When the bands are removed, the fingers move, a sound emerges from the hitherto inert figure and its eyes open. Frankenstein again utters the line he has immortalized (on film): "She's alive! Alive!" This implies that he has slipped back into his former persona, and that Elizabeth's safety was far from the primary consideration once the experiment had gotten underway. The female Monster extends her arms outward, much like the first Monster; yet she is depicted as weaker, as she falls asleep, seemingly sapped from her efforts at movement.

Pretorius theatrically announces her "the bride of Frankenstein" to the ghostly peal of wedding bells, and she clumsily jerks toward Henry for a while, as both Henry and Pretorius support her—a choreographed act that reveals the men's attempt to orchestrate her every move. Manguel captures the ambivalences of the film's unveiling of the female Monster, which couples beauty with the macabre and new life with death. "Standing between Pretorius and Henry, the female creature is clothed in all her splendour, half-Nefertiti, half ghost with her long white bridal gown, or death robe, or swaddling clothes . . . her face carrying . . . Lanchester's pouty look . . . her hair unforgettably coiffed streaked with white lightning, she stands halfway between a zombie and a future punk, outlandishly sexy."[67] The references to Nefertiti are far from accidental. They emphasize Nefertiti's famed beauty and exoticism. The dominance of her upturned hair, made to resemble the dead queen's famous headpiece, draws attention to the bride's animal sexuality. With scars prominently showing under an otherwise unmarred face and lightning streaks in her stiffly standing hair, the conjunction of the images of Helen and Medusa—the beautiful and the terrifying—is uneasily held together.

The ambiguously baptized "bride" then frees herself from both the men's grasp when the Monster appears and the two man-made creatures stare at each other. The Monster attempts to woo his bride, but she repulses him twice in favor of the scientist. The scene is both grotesque and humorous, particularly when the Monster caresses his bride's hand as the two unnatural father figures anxiously look on, only to elicit a shriek from his beloved. The Monster, heartbroken, declares, "She hate me—like others," and starts to break things in the laboratory. He reaches for a lever and is sharply warned against doing so by both Henry and Pretorius when Elizabeth knocks sharply at the door, pleading that Henry leave with her. The Monster orders Elizabeth and Henry to leave, but mandates that Pretorius and his monstrous bride should stay. "We belong dead," he says, as a tear rolls down his face. The bride utters an enigmatic sound (an exaggerated swan's hiss—a creature that again combines beauty with nastiness), and her face contorts into something in between a grimace and a smile. Henry and Elizabeth escape as the tower is blown up (which, shot from below as if to emphasize the tower's height, recalls the destruction of the Tower of Babel). The ending is significant because the female Monster is set apart from all the other characters. The final sound she utters—in between laughter and horror—is an indecipherable mark. She is a cipher that resists understanding, unlike even the male Monster, whose motivations we understand only too well.

Despite the sympathy with which the male Monster's portrait is sketched, it is important that the film arrives at the same conclusion that the novel does: that the female Monster should be radically eliminated. In the novel her body is violated even before she has had the chance to become a sentient being. Similarly, when the female Monster in the film begins to exercise her right of choice as an erotic being, the only resolution to the problem is that of killing her because in her, the monstrous and the desirable lie in close proximity. As William Everson points out, "No . . . explanation is . . . vouchsafed for why the Monster survives the ensuing holocaust (in the sequel), but his mate does not."[68]

The changes from novel to film hide another source of slippage—the reinscriptions that occur as a script is translated into visual form. In the case of *The Bride of Frankenstein*, a *Variety* film review[69] notes that seventeen minutes from the original footage was clipped off in the final version.

Perhaps the most striking excisions surround Karl, played by Dwight Frye, who had acted as Fritz in the first *Frankenstein* film. In the original script, Karl is given more footage and depth of characterization: He is a homicidal maniac who scavenges dead bodies for dissection by doctors and medical students. Pretorius, in a scene deleted from the final version, attempts to impress Henry by telling him the story of how Karl had once brought him the body of a woman known to suffer from catalepsy. Noting that the "corpse" was still warm, he proceeded to dissect; when he had cut away many of her parts, the woman suddenly gained consciousness, and screamed. He killed her. Pretorius ostensibly tells Henry that story to illustrate that Karl fears him; yet his ultimate goal is to make Henry afraid of him. By illustrating the power he has over Karl, a dangerous, unstable maniac, he draws a parallel between Karl, the Monster he now controls, with the two Monsters over which he will eventually gain control, as the film progresses: the male Monster and Henry Frankenstein.

Karl is a character steeped in the tradition of the doppelgänger. Through him, the vile, inhuman aspects of Pretorius's and Henry's madness are mirrored. Thus, when the Monster goes on a rampage after his "Crucifixion" and brief incarceration, Karl is shown simultaneously creeping through windows of homes and wantonly attacking his own victims, exploiting the confusion generated by the Monster's attack. Glut conjectures that these scenes were excised from the film, "probably for the sake of better pacing."[70] Jensen gives a slightly different account. He narrates a long sequence in which an unbelieving burgomaster conducts an inquiry into various deaths and dismisses all reports of the Monster as "all nonsense and poppycock." After he has the courtroom cleared, the Monster appears, grabs the sceptic through a window and drags him out, cuffs him on both ears, then drops him, and turns to the fleeing villagers.[71]

Jensen conjectures that the reason this section was excised was because the courtroom scene resembled Inspector Bird's inquiry in Whale's *The Invisible Man* too closely, and the Monster's semicomic punishment of the burgomaster might have significantly diminished the impact of the Monster's rampage. In addition, the Hays Office, responsible for making certain the film stayed within the restraints of the code, had wanted the number of killings reduced, and had specifically pinpointed this sequence as an expendable one.[72]

Although either or both explanations may be true, it is also important to see the impact of the excision of these scenes upon the resultant cinematic narrative. In the original script, Karl, more than the male Monster, rivals the female Monster in potential evil. He appears to have no qualms about murdering or looting. As such he seems a character more deserving of the title "monster" than the creature disfigured by Henry's mad attempt at creating a superior race, and by the ravages of fire and (in)human torture. Like the female Monster, he is a mystery because there is ostensibly no explanation for his necrophiliac and murderous propensities. If the original script had been kept, then he would have deflected some of the limelight away from the monstrous "bride," whose fascinating and inexplicable monstrosity seems central to Whale's second filmic narrative.

There is another set of revisions that deserves attention. Whereas the original (male) Monster's notoriety is explained via the criminal brain Henry inadvertently transplants into his creature because of Fritz's bungling, the female Monster's brain is cultivated using Pretorius's method of growing flesh from seeds. The female Monster's mind is supposed to be a blank slate, and is designed to follow its creator's (Pretorius's) commands. Interestingly it turns out that the part that becomes crucial to manufacturing a female Monster becomes, in this version, not the brain, but the heart, carrying on the cliché that men think and women feel. It is the heart that becomes the crucial organ to harvest in this sequence, and it is this heart that is the only plausible explanation for this female Monster's assertion of autonomy, despite the precautionary machinations of Pretorius.

Henry, now completely wrapped up in the task of creating another being, demands a "fresh" heart—one young and healthy. In the earlier conception of the story, Karl creeps into the cave where Elizabeth is held captive, kills her, and returns with her heart. That was supposed to be the explanation of why the female Monster, who, in this version, has the heart of Elizabeth, chooses Henry over the Monster. However, this was deemed too grotesque for the film, and the "happier" version of Karl's choice of an unknown woman whom he ambushes in a dark alley was substituted.

This suppression is significant, not only because of its commercially driven search for a more conventional "happy ending," but also because it does emphasize the supreme lengths the film goes to in order to harness the monstrous. In splitting apart the kinship the novel establishes between Elizabeth and the Monster as rivals for Frankenstein's affections, and as common victims sacrificed upon the altar of his mad dream, the film substitutes the sanitized narrative of the virtuous woman as completely separate from the monstrous woman. The virtuous woman deserves to live, whereas the monstrous woman deserves to be obliterated. The unknown woman, who fits neither category easily, is quickly dispatched, and her heart, the only trace of her that remains, becomes reappropriated into the realm of the "monstrous," implying that even potentially virtuous women have to be severely harnessed, lest they transmogrify. The virtuous woman's motivations are completely transparent; the monstrous woman remains an impenetrable cipher. Nevertheless it is important that both figures of the feminine—the virtuous woman and the monstrous woman—never gain self-consciousness. Elizabeth seems incapable of defining her identity away from her maternal role in relation to Henry; the female Monster, unlike the male Monster, is never able to look upon her own visage, and completely gain, however painful, a genuine sense of selfhood.

Other deletions from the film seem to have been exacted by the then powerful Catholic League of Decency, through the militant censorship of the Catholic journalist, Joseph Breen. The implicit intertwining of blasphemy, humor, and eroticism found in Baubo's *ana-suromai* that converges with Shelley's novel, which is hyperbolized in the *Bride*'s campy irony, became targetted. All overt references comparing Frankenstein's ability to create with God's were struck down, as was a scene in which the Monster witnesses a couple exchanging love vows together with the word "mate" because of the potential implication concerning the Creature's latent sexual physicality. Manguel details how Whale scrupulously sought to appease Breen's every objection, which, nevertheless, still resulted in the final screen version containing the very elements Breen had originally objected to: God, immortality, entrails, and mermaids.[73] Still, the battle with censors was complicated, entailing various concessions: a haunting design by Charles

Halls, depicting the Monster tugging at the loincloth of the crucified Christ, while a large figure of death looms in the foreground, was sacrificed. In addition, much of the prologue, in which the three characters boast of their infidelity, immorality, and adultery, particularly Mary, was excised; so was a shot that exposed and accentuated Lanchester's breasts in that iridescent dress with a seven-foot-long train. Mary is made to look like an "angel" in an extremely circumscribed fashion, again hinting at the suppression of Baubo's mythic heritage, with its moral ambiguities and unruly sexuality.

Manguel recounts a genealogical footnote that is important to under-standing Whale's use of the prologue. When *Frankenstein* opened in 1931, the Quebec censor board, one of the most influential in North America, vehemently protested against its Faustian theme. T.B. Fithian of Universal appeased them by suggesting that perhaps *Frankenstein* could be intro-duced through a foreword or preface "that would indicate the picture was a dream."[74] The board relented, and eventually, *Frankenstein*, with its tragic and realistic tone, was shown as it had been conceived by Whale. Whale appears to have anticipated similar objections to *Bride of Frank-enstein* and strategically appropriated Fithian's suggestion. The overall im-pact of the use of this style of narrative framing, however, undercuts Mary Shelley's own use of multiple frames in her novel. In the novel the use of multiple frames serves to problematize and underline authorial power, which is cast as the ability to (re)create reality. In contrast, in the film narrating becomes simply "making up a story"—an innocuous activity that must not be taken too seriously, and thus should be allowed certain liberties because it is explicitly set up as fictionalizing. The radical envisaging of Mary as both bearer and victim of the tale is rendered acceptable by making it simply an entertaining nightmare.

A final set of revisions deserves mention. There seems to have been a great deal of consternation concerning how to end the film. As Glut points out, the final shooting script, which was still titled *The Return of Frank-enstein*, indicated that Henry suspected that it was Elizabeth's heart that throbbed in the female Monster's breast.[75] In yet another version, Elizabeth does appear in the final scenes, but perishes in the explosion. Even more absurdly, an earlier scene, which depicted the destruction of the laboratory, shows not only the Monster, his bride, Pretorius, but also Henry, dying in the cataclysm. Because this scene was shot prior to that depicting Henry and Elizabeth's escape, and the costly scene had already been filmed, wreck-ing the set, the shot was retained, in the hope that the inconsistency would be lost in the spectacle of grand disintegration. The resultant narrative, like the earlier *Frankenstein* film, strains credibility, and the escape of Henry and Elizabeth leads one critic to conjecture that "Universal may have an-other follow-up in mind."[76] Even more importantly the film again reifies the parthenogenetic myth and its counterpart: that the dream of male (auto)genesis somehow survives its monstrous progeny, and that the feminine (inferior) shadow is allowed to survive only when it is expunged of its darker shades, and is kept divorced from its monstrous (overdeveloped) double. As Manguel points out, given the bride's characterization as a femme fatale, death is the only way to maintain the boundaries of the patriarchal narrative.

In this world of men, the Bride is damned if she does and damned if she doesn't. Were she to consent to the coupling, she'd be a complacent whore; unwilling to submit to what she is told is her duty, she becomes a reluctant whore, and an instrument of male perdition.[77]

BEARING A SON IN THE NAME OF THE FATHER

Although Whale was still at Universal in 1939, Rowland V. Lee was receiving the more lucrative assignments, such as *Son of Frankenstein, Tower of London*, and *The Sun Never Sets*. Lee combined a sober and realistic portrayal of the characters with a surreal Germanic atmosphere, creating a nightmarish world of rain, thunder, and gloomy darkness. Everson enthuses over *Son of Frankenstein's* visual elegance, leading him to crown it "the second best film in the series" (with *Bride of Frankenstein* ranked as first) in spite of its unusual length of ten reels.

The little town is as unreal as Douglas Fairbanks' Baghdad, but is as convincing, since Lee never shows it to us in juxtaposition to things that *are* real. Everything— from the rain to the door knocker and the distorted stairway—is magnified to giant, dreamlike proportions.[78]

Son of Frankenstein unabashedly makes the parthenogenetic myth its fulcrum. The defining relationship here is between Wolf Frankenstein (Basil Rathbone) and his dead father, Henry (Colin Clive). This is visually established early in the film. When Wolf walks into his father's study, and stands underneath his father's portrait, Benson, the butler (Edgar Norton), immediately points out how similar he is to his father. Wolf wistfully remarks that he wishes he had even a small portion of his father's genius. As Benson looks on, Wolf reads his father's letter to him, which justifies the deceased Henry's work as a result of an "irresistible desire to penetrate the truth." Wolf then toasts his dead father as Ygor, unseen by the characters furtively looks on.

Wolf speaks of his father in heroic and even divine terms. To calm his apprehensive wife, Elizabeth (Josephine Hutchinson), during a thunderstorm, he remarks: "Nothing in nature is terrifying when one understands it. My father drew the very lightning from heaven and forced it to his own will to bring life to a being created with his own hands. Why should we fear anything?" Somehow, Wolf's reverence for his father is tied up with

the successful usurpation of the powers of nature for the task of autonomous male birthing. His father is more than a modern Prometheus; he is
virtually a Zeus who infuses life into his unnatural son with bolts of lightning. The contrast between Wolf and his wife is visually emphasized during
the thunderstorm sequence. While the light cast on the wall behind his wife
shimmers turbulently, reflecting the flashes of lightning and peals of thunder, Wolf seems bathed in a steady halo of light. Wolf is constructed as
the very epitome of masculine bravery and strength and his wife as the
quintessential example of feminine timorousness and weakness.

The film repeatedly drives home the point that Wolf's relationships with
other people are secondary to his adoration of his father. As he struggles
with whether to kill the sick and sleeping Monster (Boris Karloff), Wolf
decides in favor of restoring the Monster to health on the grounds that it
"would vindicate his father and his name would be enshrined among the
immortals." When the agitated Benson warns of the danger of continuing
experiments on the Monster, and reminds Wolf of Elizabeth and Peter, his
son (Donnie Dunagan), Wolf, clearly in an afterthought, distractedly agrees
that both should be sent away in the morning (rather than immediately,
which would have been the logical choice had he truly considered their
safety the most important priority). Finally, when Elizabeth confesses to
having lost confidence in her husband, due to his nervous and distracted
manner, Wolf replies, "I've been working too hard . . . There's a terrific
experiment . . . one I wanted to surprise you with; one that would establish
me and my [looks at father's picture] work." Wolf's refusal to divulge the
true nature of his motivation is tied up with the secret rivalry between
Elizabeth and his father, Henry. Henry is not simply his father and his role
model, but is also the object of his desire. The movie effectively replaces
the novel's hidden fascination with the unseen body of the dead mother
with an obsessive gravitation toward the visible and living spirit of the
father, whose ghostlike presence haunts the castle, and appears to impregnate Wolf with the desire to rebirth his father's satanic progeny as a re-
habilitated Adam.

Indeed the most crucial relationships in the film are among men. Ygor's
(Bela Lugosi) relationship to the Monster is particularly complex, as his
role varies from lover, father-brother, and master. Although Ygor constantly addresses the Monster as simply his "friend," the tie that binds these
two monstrous beings is much greater than that. As Wolf himself muses
out loud to Benson, the butler: "Amazing the control he [Ygor] exercises
over that thing. It's hypnosis or something more elemental perhaps. . . . He
loves Ygor and obeys him."

It is to Ygor that this film grants the original Monster's eloquence. However, even though the rhetorical control of the novel's Monster is flawless,
Ygor, both like and unlike Whale's second film Monster, speaks, not in
monosyllabic replies, but definitely broken sentences that violate the logic

of grammar. It is also Ygor who manifests the original Monster's criminal cunning; he manipulates both Wolf and the Monster for his own designs. The Monster, devoid of both the power of speech and the ability to reason for himself, degenerates into both a vulnerable child and a mindless killing machine. As *The Encyclopedia of Horror Movies* states, "[*Son of Frankenstein*] reduces [the Monster] to a superhuman destructive force foreshadowing all those indestructible creatures that were fathered by mad doctors in the forties."[79]

Indeed, the scene of the Monster's self-recognition in the laboratory mirror is particularly revealing. Here, as Wolf fearfully enters his father's laboratory, armed with a knife, the Monster surprises him from behind, and lays a heavy hand on his shoulder. Petrified, Wolf can only watch as the Monster examines him, caresses his face, and reaches for his neck. Yet the Monster releases him, startled by his own image in a mirror; visibly frightened and perturbed, he turns to Frankenstein, as if seeking an explanation, and grabs the scientist to place him in front of the mirror to emphasize the visual contrasts in their appearances. As the Monster waves his hand at his own visage, and Frankenstein rubs his wrist, Ygor emerges and comforts his friend. In the course of the ensuing dialogue between Ygor and Wolf, the Monster, in fascination and horror, gravitates back to the mirror; Ygor protectively turns over the mirror.

The erotic entanglements binding the three men are difficult to miss. The Monster feminizes Wolf momentarily by immobilizing him, rendering him the object of male erotic desire and destruction/domination. In a reversed rendition of the myth of Narcissus, however, the Monster, (un)like Blake's Eve, is riveted, erotically medused, by his own image; it is thus to Ygor that the role of Blake's Adam, who forcefully claims Eve from her fascination with her own visage, falls. Brooks clearly draws out the mythic parallels the film, consciously or not, hyperbolizes.

Narcissism is here a temptation to which Eve, immediately enamoured of her own image, would succumb "with vain desire," were it not for the intervention of a divine voice that commands her to set aside this moment of primary narcissism in favor of sexual difference. . . . As the Miltonic scenario unfolds, Eve's first perception of Adam is not itself sufficient to move her beyond primary narcissism. . . . She would return to the "answering looks" of the lake were it not that Adam at this point seizes her hand, and she yields to what is for Milton, in his thoroughly misogynist scenario, the explicit hegemony of the male.[80]

Yet Ygor functions not to awaken the Monster to (subordinated) sexual difference, but to render him an empowered extension of himself. Wolf does not view the Monster any differently, as he aims to make Ygor obey him, so that he may gain control over the Monster. Love, in both men's worlds, is closely tied up with the power to dominate, and an intense, unremitting rivalry over the affections and obedience of the Monster weaves itself into the plot. The rivalry climaxes in another scene in the laboratory, where Wolf calls Ygor a fool for having used the Monster for his murderous and vengeful purposes, warns that if Inspector Krogh finds the Monster, "he won't be any good to either of us," and demands that Ygor leave. Ygor, like a possessive lover, counters, "He's mine! He don't belong to you! You go away, not me!"

The rivalry ends with Wolf shooting Ygor, as the latter swings at him with a hammer. When the Monster discovers his friend's corpse, he cries out in despair. Later, he tenderly lifts Ygor's body to a bed, then roars in anger, wreaks havoc on the laboratory, and then, seeing one of Peter's fairy-tale books, heads for the nursery, a devilish plan forming in his mind. It is as if Ygor's spirit infuses him, and he is now capable of the criminal reasoning his lover-master-friend had done for him when he was alive.

Wolf's relationship to the Monster, too, is complex, as it varies from brother to spurned lover-master. Ygor enlists Wolf's aid in restoring the Monster's strength by implying that the Monster, too, is a son of Frankenstein, sired with lightning. Even more interestingly, Wolf's near violation and death at the hands of the Monster—an encounter that is not devoid of erotic tinges, and may be seen as a masculinized version of Fuseli's *Nightmare*—intensifies Wolf's obsession with gaining control over the Creature. "Never in my life have I known cold fear until that moment that I felt his hand on my shoulder. I was like a child's doll in those huge hands. He could have crushed me as I would have crushed an eggshell."

Wolf's substitute for the Monster is Benson, in whom he confides and entrusts the secret of his experiments on the Monster. In response to Ygor's objections to including Benson in their activities, Wolf threatens not to do anything to help the Monster, claiming that Benson's services are invaluable as a note-taker. Significantly, it is not with Elizabeth, but with Benson, that Wolf shares his ambivalent elation over the unexpected success of his efforts at resuscitating the Monster. "Benson, it's alive! . . . yes, alive! Alive!" The repetition of his father's lines to Benson harks back to Henry's collaboration with Fritz in birthing the Monster for the first time. Yet when Benson is killed by the Monster, Wolf treats him as an expendable pawn, and he does everything he can to allay the suspicions of both Elizabeth and Inspector Krogh concerning the sudden disappearance of the faithful butler.

Inspector Krogh (Lionel Atwill), too, is another complex character. On one hand, he appears to be simply the keeper of order, and he appears a sympathetic character when he offers Wolf protection from his father's poisonous name, and from the paranoid fears of the villagers. Yet his stiff doggedness at coercing the truth out of Wolf is motivated by selfish rather than altruistic motives. Krogh claims with nostalgia that were it not for his arm having been ripped out of his shoulder by the Monster on the rampage when Krogh was still a boy, he could have become a great hero, instead of being the commander of merely seven gendarmes. Revenge (and a lust for power), then, seem to be his principal motives—characteristics that link him with Ygor, who, like the Monster, and Krogh himself with his artificial arm, is an unnatural creature who has cheated death. In some senses they are all sons of Frankenstein—hovering between the realms of life and death, sickened with compulsions for revenge and power. Even Wolf's desire to reinstate his father may be seen as a vengeful attempt to prove everyone wrong about his father. In a distinct sense, the sins of the sons may be traced to the crime of the father. Resentment and the desire for revenge against life's fleeting potency and its proneness to physical degeneration motivated Henry Frankenstein's attempts to pierce through the secrets of nature, and his legacy lives on through his progeny.

Peter, Wolf's son, is also a son of the house of Frankenstein. His fearlessness, love of lightning, and ease in the castle mark him as a genuine heir. The Monster chooses him over his father Wolf, and befriends him by giving him the murdered Benson's watch. In return, the boy gives him one of his fairy-tale books. Peter thus becomes the revised version of both Maria, the innocent girl whom Whale's first Monster inadvertently drowns, and William, the name-calling brat in the novel who enrages the Monster and becomes his first notable victim. Peter seems the rock upon whom the House of Frankenstein may be built, for he survives disaster at the Monster's hands through his trust. Yet lest Peter be construed as purely a salvific character, it is important to note the types of games he plays in his imagination. They are games involving the hunting of prey: elephants, tigers, rhinoceros, and alligators, and wild boar/bores like Aunt Fanny. Amusing as the pun and his games are, they are not completely free from the world of domination and misogyny his father and grandfather inhabit.

Correspondingly, the roles of women in this movie are severely simplified and truncated. Elizabeth's complex characterization in Whale's second film is replaced by the depiction of a fearful and cowering woman who, unlike her husband and son, is never comfortable in the castle with beds whose heads are drawn together ("If the house is filled with dread, place beds at head to head" is the way a female servant explains the unusual placement of the beds). Similarly her relationship with her husband is strangely devoid of eroticism, and he seems to treat her more as a sister rather than as a lover. When she breaks down and admits to being unable to match his bravery, he calms her with the words, "That's a good girl," much like the way a father would soothe a child. Amelia, the nurse, is given the role of surrogate mother; yet she, too, like the mother figures in the original novel, does not have long to live. The Monster murders her when he comes with the intent of kidnapping and murdering Peter in retaliation for Wolf's murder of his friend, Ygor. The rest of the women given a brief appearance in this movie function merely as heralds of doom, screaming and ineffectual Cassandras who alert others to dead bodies. Unlike Whale's films, which reveal a complex and refractory (un)veiling of the feminine and Monstrous shadows, *Son of Frankenstein* is an unabashed hyperbolization of the parthenogenetic myth and thoroughgoing repression of the gesture of *anasuromai*.

RESURRECTING THE (UN)DEAD

It was not until 1942 that Universal attempted to resurrect the specter of the Frankensteinian Monster. Although the names of Sir Cedric Hardwicke (Ludwig Frankenstein), Ralph Bellamy (Erik Ernst), Lionel Atwill (Dr. Bohmer), Bela Lugosi (Ygor), Evelyn Ankers (Elsa Frankenstein), and Janet Ann Gallow (Cloestine Hussman) appear first in the credits, it is undoubtedly Lon Chaney (who dropped "Jr." from his name then) who is the star attraction, singly introduced as "The Monster."

Jack Pierce again crafted the makeup for the Monster; nevertheless, given that Chaney was stockier than Karloff had been, and did not have Karloff's gaunt looks, the new Monster assumed a very different appearance, in spite of the persistence of the now-familiar electrodes and scars. The Monster's characterization, too, changed significantly, now being a homicidal maniac who kills wantonly, though very faint glimpses of humanity may be seen in his interactions with the little girl, Cloestine.

There is little logical continuity moving from *Son of Frankenstein* to *Ghost of Frankenstein*. At the end of *Son of Frankenstein*, the town cheers and applauds the departing Wolf Frankenstein; at the beginning of *Ghost of Frankenstein*, the town of Frankenstein is again disgruntled over the continuing curse. The whole countryside reputedly shuns the village, and even the prevalent hunger is blamed on the apparently deceased Monster. Everson points to other glaring narrative inconsistencies: "At least two of the town council, killed off in *Son*, are still in office here. The Monster learned to talk in *Bride*, and he was mute again in *Son*; here he talks again with Lugosi's brain in his skull. . . . The dialogue has some curious anachronisms: 'There'll be a new Mayor after the Fall election!' is a threat that seems far too American to apply to middle-Europe."[81]

The inconsistencies are not as egregious as one would think if one were to return to the original script by W. Scott Darling titled, *There Is Always Tomorrow*, which foretells the narrative's relatively rosy ending. The script begins with an extended sequence detailing the decadence and squalor of the ruined Frankenstein castle, after which the town is named. It also reveals the saddened Ygor playing a death dirge in honor of his friend, the Monster, buried in the hardened sulfur. Thus, it lends some credence to the villagers' hostile demands that the castle be destroyed. Not only do the ruins set the atmosphere of the town; Ygor's presence and music have a factual as well as a mythical/symbolic basis. The villagers are not simply superstitious children in search of a bogeyman upon whom to pin the blame, but are actually tapping into the secrets of the castle. Almost as if in impatience, the film immediately shows them at the town meeting, irately and irrationally demanding that the castle be destroyed. The film does not seem to want to bear the weight of explaining the revulsion, terror, and desperation that prompt the town. The castle represents the abode of the monstrous: that seems adequate justification for its violent eradication.

In his attempts to flee from a mob, Ygor accidentally comes across his newly resurrected friend, who has been preserved in the sulfur pit. The Monster, rendered pale by the sulfur that covers him, indeed looks like a ghost that has returned from the dead. The hunchback rescues the Monster, and declares the sulfur pit to have been "good" for his friend. This is, in some ways, an intertextual reference back to the earlier Whale-directed film, *Bride*, where the concept of what is "good" and "bad" is interpreted by the Monster in terms of pleasure. However, "goodness," as uttered by Ygor, refers less to pleasure, than to power, for he lays great store on the apparent indestructibility of the Monster. In addition, the relationship between Ygor and the Monster is rendered with greater vividness and complexity in the script. The script details how the Monster is like a newly wakened child, and does not seem to recognize Ygor. Ygor, on the other hand, is visibly moved; tears come into his eyes, and he is eager to touch his friend, though that affection is not untinged with selfish motive. "Ygor pats the immobile Monster as if it were a little child. His voice is cooing as over a newborn babe, and yet it contains a certain note of triumph as he continues. . . . He strokes him again, looks at him affectionately, almost lovingly."[82]

A thunderstorm brews, and the Monster actively pursues lightning bolts in spite of Ygor's objections. At a climactic moment, the Monster pushes Ygor aside and actively embraces a bolt of lightning that appears to infuse him with new life. The elated Ygor enthuses, "The lightning is good for you. Your father was Frankstein [*sic*] but your mother was lightning; she has come down to you again." The feminization of lightning is an interesting turn, yet again reveals a hyperbolization of the parthenogenetic myth. For it is still the spirit of the absent Father who can completely restore the health of this monstrous son; this is why the pair go in search of Ludwig, the second son of Frankenstein, who is heir to the secrets of the Frankensteins. Lightning, though nourishing and restorative, is simply a palliative; in order to grant the Monster his full strength, lightning still has to be harnessed via the mechanical coercion of Frankenstein's (the father's) machines. It is equally interesting that unlike *Son of Frankenstein*, there is now a marked separation between the two Monstrous beings. Whereas the Monster functioned basically as a beloved slave to Ygor in *Son*, in *Ghost*, he retains his own will, and repeatedly refuses to do as Ygor begs him. The Monster in *Ghost* is himself similar to a force of nature—a lightning bolt that unexpectedly strikes—relentless, unpredictable, immovable. The monstrous shadow concentrates its infernal strength and grows increasingly dehumanized.

The ambivalences binding Ygor and the Monster are even more clearly delineated in the script. The Monster is less impassive and Ygor, less sinister, in the script. After the lightning bolt has struck him, he loses his ghostlike veneer and becomes more animated, flexing his fingers and delighting in his newly recovered faculties. In contrast, the film maintains his ghostly veneer, and his blank face only shows the merest flicker of exultation in regained power. In the script, the Monster cries out inarticulate entreaties as he tries to chase the lightning bolts that scatter very close to him but elude his grasp. A sudden doubt assails Ygor, and he clings to his friend desperately and eloquently with the entreaty: "You must save your strength . . . you cannot waste the vital fluid that nature has poured into you by accident."[83] Ygor displays the same paternal-tyrannical urges as Henry Frankenstein; unlike Henry, however, his monstrosity is both physical and spiritual, rendering him more capable of genuinely feeling compassion for his monstrous friend-weapon. Unlike the final film, which simply shows the Monster impassively following Ygor, the Monster in the script is both active and expressive: he snarls with rage and hatred when he hears the name, "Frankenstein"; he stares with doubt when Ygor comes up with his plan; he growls like an animal when he grows convinced of the justness of the plan of hunting down the other Dr. Frankenstein. All these are excised or radically muted in the film, rendering the Monster indeed a ghostly specter of his scriptic self.

At a chateau, Ludwig Frankenstein, a doctor tending to the "diseases of the mind," is in the process of completing a successful brain transplant. Dr. Bohmer, one of his assistants, is envious and embittered, as he used to be Frankenstein's teacher-"master"; however, through a "slight miscalculation" and the failure of one of his crucial experiments, he finds himself overshadowed by his former pupil. The rivalry between both men is evident as William Everson humorously points out: "Dear old Sir Cedric Hardwicke, rather tactlessly reminding Atwill of the incident [that led to him being drummed out of the medical profession], winds up with a lame and condescending 'But you blazed the trail!' while Atwill glares daggers at him."[84] This is generally consistent with the script, except that the script grants Kettering, Frankenstein's other assistant, a more thorough characterization. It is clear that Kettering worships Frankenstein with the same intensity that Bohmer hates him. This characterization is essential to why Ludwig later thinks Kettering's brain would be best to use to replace the Monster's criminal brain. Again the parthenogenetic myth reifies itself. By aspiring to transplant Kettering's brain into the Monster, Ludwig, like his father, Henry, aims to reclaim his lost son-devotee, Kettering, and harness the Monster.

In the film the Monster and Ygor enter Vasaria where they inquire for

Ludwig Frankenstein's residence from a goosegirl who keeps throwing fearful and curious glances at the Monster. While Ygor is talking to the goosegirl, the Monster wanders off to find Cloestine, whose balloon has been deliberately kicked to hang from a rooftop by one of the neighborhood bullies. The young girl turns to the Monster in wonder as the older boys flee, and he towers over her. Like Maria in Whale's *Frankenstein*, Cloestine shows no sign of fear and takes the initiative: "Hello, are you a giant?" she asks as she takes his hand and examines the scars on it. The camera shoots with a high angle from below, presumably from the point of view of Cloestine, emphasizing the Leviathanesque appearance of the Monster—a filmic device that continues the demonization of the technologized shadow in the figure of the Monster as hulking, speechless, and alien.

Again it is interesting to note how the film elects to make a virtually a-sexual girl the object of desire for the Monster. Unlike the goosegirl who exudes sexuality and is ignored by the Monster (yet is noticed by Ygor), Cloestine's appearances are always heralded by idyllic music, and she is depicted as devoid of sexuality. Unlike Whale's Maria who exudes the ambiguous allure of both virgin and whore, Cloestine is virginal through and through, pointing yet again to the repression of the feminine shadow and traces of the myth of Baubo's genitalia- and belly-revealing gesture. Unlike Maria, whose gestures of friendship have a faintly voluptuous quality to them, Chloestine remains safely harnessed within the realm of chastity and childhood; thus she survives her kidnapping by and friendship with the Monster.

The script differs a fair bit. Here, the Monster becomes the object of fascinated horror as a crowd of children cluster around him. Some shriek; others make catcalls; still others run on ahead of him and make faces at him. To them, he is no more than a freak that has escaped from a sideshow. The Monster plods on implacably until he comes across Cloestine, who has a "wide-eyed seriousness about her,"[85] which distinguishes her from the rest. The Monster stops and looks at Cloestine; the rowdy crowd of children also look at her, apparently jealous of the attention he is paying her. One of the older boys then spitefully kicks her ball away as she gives a cry of dismay. The result of these omissions weakens the Monster's enigmatic allure. In the script he is an object of attraction, fascination, fear, awe, and repulsion. In the film he is simply the bearer of fear. Interestingly the script flattens not only the Monster's character but also Cloestine's. Cloestine in the script laughs with childish glee when the Monster has brought her to the top of the building; she smiles and touches his cheek with ingenuous charm; she confidently gives him her hand to hold and instructs him firmly that she must not be allowed to slip. In the film she expresses delight only at the return of her ball, and she possesses only a shadow of her poise in the script when she requests the Monster to return her to her father.

In terms of father-daughter ties, interestingly, the script also renders overt the strong relationship that binds Elsa to her father, Ludwig Frankenstein. When Erik, Elsa's fiance, for instance, expresses concern for her safety because of the type of clientele to which her father caters, Elsa replies proudly, "I am never in any danger. My father knows what he is doing. . . . He has just been offered the especially endowed research chair at the University of Plowdorf . . . and his election to the Society of the the Royal Academy is assured!"[86] Erik then humbly replies that it is because of her father's brilliance that he has come to ask for help in diagnosing the psychiatric condition of their mysterious prisoner. Ludwig's position, as both ideal father and scientific authority, seems unassailable at this point.

As Ludwig is working in his study, Martha, the maid, announces an unknown visitor from the village of Frankenstein. In the script she is given a more fully developed role, as she struggles to conceal her revulsion when she first sees Ygor; in the film she does not react at all to Ygor's appearance. She simply becomes the dutiful nurse who fades into the background, and shows no reaction to any of the events unfolding. As if based on a premonition, Ludwig agrees to see the visitor, but instructs Martha not to reveal anything concerning this strange caller to Elsa. Ygor chuckles and greets Ludwig with a sinister smile as he says, "How does it feel to see a man you thought your brother killed, doctor?" As Ludwig is rendered temporarily speechless, Ygor demands that as the earlier Frankenstein had done, Ludwig should restore the Monster to new life by harnessing the power of lightning.

It is significant that again the power of speech is given, not to the Monster, but to Ygor, whose diction and rhetoric are flawless in selected instances, such as this. In other circumstances his speech is cracked and deformed, like his body. The allusions to Christ are made not in relation to the suffering of the Monster as parallel to a suffering Son of Man, as in Whale's *Bride*, but in relation to the godlike power of Ludwig as a scientist who can subvert natural laws to suit unnatural ends. Yet Frankenstein's power, particularly under the tyrannical grip of Ygor's threat to reveal Ludwig's true identity, is associated not with harrowing hell, but with a descent into the demonic. Ludwig weakly gives in to Ygor's demands, yet imperiously orders him out of his home.

On the way out, Ygor encounters Elsa on the steps. The two exchange glances, and Ygor smiles in a sinister manner. Elsa's reaction is one that hangs poised between the realms of horror and fascination as she runs to her father and tells him of the strange man and his "cruel smile." Ludwig, who had begun to pore over his father (Henry's) and his brother's (Wolf's) notes, puts these aside, and reassures his daughter with the words, "You know what my patients are like," implying that in the realm of the sick, among whom he dares to tread as a savior, such behavior is typical. In contrast the script details the doctor's response as less composed. He projects his own nervousness and embarrassment to her and gives her a slight put-down by laughing tensely and saying, "Getting rather nervy, aren't you, dear?"[87] When Elsa's mood is not dispelled and she asks when he will return, he kisses her, and uses a tone that verges in between what one would use to soothe a worried child or anxious wife: "Just as soon as I can, dear. Now I have to go to the hearing in the village."[88] There is never any mention of Elsa coming along. In keeping with the domestication of the power of the feminine archetype, the spheres of domesticity and public involvement remain tightly circumscribed.

At court, a crowd jostles about, bristling with excitement over the trial of the chained stranger. The judge and Erik hold a sidebar, where the judge expresses confusion over why the trial has to be held immediately; Erik replies that because the prisoner is both dangerous and insane, it would be best to remand his case to a higher court, and transfer him immediately. Erik then proceeds to interrogate the Monster, who, like Christ, does not reply. However, whereas Christ's silences are eloquently posed, the Monster's silence only serves to underline his subhuman nature. The judge then suggests that some attempt to establish contact with the Monster through Cloestine be done; as her father objects, the young girl walks fearlessly up to the Monster, as the same idyllic musical motif wells up again. At the point of a breakthrough, Ludwig Frankenstein causes a stir by arriving, and the child is whisked to safety.

The Monster appears to recognize Frankenstein and smiles, but Ludwig denies recognition of him. Enraged, the Monster breaks free of his chains and goes on the rampage as the crowd flees. As the Monster is on the verge of strangling Frankenstein with his broken chains, he hears Ygor's horn. He heeds his monstrous pied piper's call, leaving the scientist unharmed. Ygor and the Monster make their getaway on a horse-driven carriage. The script makes the rivalry between Ygor and Ludwig over the control of the Monster surface clearly. "Using intense concentration which makes him look almost *diabolically determined*" [italics mine], Frankenstein tries to quell the Monster by sheer strength of personality. The music of Ygor's pipes continues to come over from the outdoors. The Monster suddenly becomes conscious of it and stops.[89]

The encounter is a significant one because it is Ludwig's refusal to acknowledge his kinship to the Monster that awakens the Monster's murderous rage. The salvific power of Cloestine's innocence is radically undercut by Ludwig's veneer of virtue and respectability. Even more significantly it is less Cloestine's gaze that animates the Monster's springing into action, but Ludwig's averted gaze. It is the brother-father tie that ultimately counts most. Ludwig is also a son of (Henry) Frankenstein; because he is also a doctor, he possesses the same godlike power his father did—and as such, functions as the surrogate of Henry Frankenstein in this film. It is his approval, rather than Cloestine's, that is of considerable significance.

The Monster forces entry into Frankenstein's house; he attacks the young assistant, Dr. Kettering, and kills him. The script again harks back to its filmic/novelistic predecessor: Ludwig's instructions to his daughter are the same that Henry/Victor shouts to Elizabeth: "Go to your room. . . . Lock yourself in" (63). Elsa, however, uncertainly decides to follow her father rather than obey his orders. Ygor attempts to pull away the reluctant Monster in the attempt to shield him from his crime, but the Monster resists and this time drags Elsa away; Ludwig releases soporific gas into the hallway where the Monster, Elsa, and Ygor are. As Ludwig calls Bohmer, he lifts the unconscious Elsa gently; Bohmer comes running to help, and stares, fascinated, at the body of the Monster. In the script Bohmer's fascinated gaze upon the Monster does not occur; quite simply, Frankenstein keeps his envious assistant-rival in the dark until he needs his help. Either way, in both film and script, male rivalry over and fascination with the Monster constitute a crucial narrative force.

When Elsa wakes up, she anxiously inquires after the Monster; her father reassures her that the Monster has been subdued. What is striking about this particular scene is that father and daughter do not seem to speak to each other the way a father and daughter would. Instead it is as if they speak as lovers, with Elsa remarking, "Last night, I felt as though something had come from the past to threaten our happiness." A rather erotic shot, revealing her breasts heaving underneath her nightgown, is quickly shown, and then replaced with a more conservative shot. It is interesting that Elsa's relationship with Eric is overtly romantic, yet completely devoid of any erotic tinges. What occurs here is an interesting reversal: Instead of the ambivalent lust and loathing for the hidden mother by the son is the suppressed passion of the present father for his daughter-as-virginal-mother. For Elsa functions as more than his daughter; she, like the novel's Elizabeth, is a creature sequestered and protected. Yet she also possesses strong maternal instincts, and essentially mothers both Ludwig and Cloestine, when the girl is brought as a captive to the chateau. Elsa begs her father to find a way to "keep the past from threatening their happiness," and her father concurs. A shadow of Baubo, combining the feminine powers of eroticism and motherhood, fleetingly reveals itself, only to be harnessed within the patriarchal narrative.

The script gives Elsa an even stronger character. It is Elsa, and not Ludwig, who conceives of destroying the Monster through dissection. And it is Elsa's determined conviction that the Monster be destroyed that finally moves the reluctant Ludwig to destroy his father's handiwork. "Father, you cannot evade this issue. . . . It is a part of the Frankenstein destiny, the Monster must be destroyed . . . bit by bit . . . piece by piece. . . . Just as your father created it—!"[90]

As soon as his daughter disappears from his study, Ludwig turns to the old notebooks and finds himself swept into the feverish excitement of his father's and brother's experiments. With visible effort he retrains himself; he is about to throw these documents away but then changes his mind and locks them up in a cabinet. He begins to pace up and down like a caged animal. The script details what the film smooths over: the struggle for power between father-daughter-lover and Ludwig's divided loyalties to Elsa and his paternal-fraternal heritage.

What occurs next is the fulcrum of the entire film. As Ludwig looks over his father's diary again, the ghost of Henry Frankenstein manifests itself in the instruments in the laboratory. The ghost of the Father chides his son with the words: "Would you destroy that which your father dedicated his life to creating?" Ludwig attempts to argue against the ghost, who keeps shifting his location from one instrument to the next, as he argues for preserving his work of discovering the "secret of life artificially created." His son protests that the Monster has brought death, not new life, to all it has touched. The ghost shifts ground by claiming that it is because he inadvertently gave the Monster a criminal brain that the Monster is pathological, but suggests that the creature could easily be redeemed by giving him a new brain. It is interesting that Hardwicke, who plays Ludwig Frankenstein, also plays the part of the ghost of Henry Frankenstein. The movie seems to suggest that ultimately, despite (and perhaps because of) the vehemence of Ludwig's arguments against preserving the Monster, he is ultimately more interested in continuing rather than terminating his father's experiments (which is obvious in the script, but is not readily apparent in the film). Even more significantly perhaps it is not so much against the spirit of his dead father that Ludwig (apparently) argues, but against a part of himself that attests to his dark kinship to his father. Interestingly enough the parthenogenetic myth, with the identities of father and son blurring into each other, reifies itself again in this scene.

Erik arrives with witnesses who claim they have not seen the missing Kettering leave via the morning train, which constitutes Frankenstein's attempt to cover up the Monster's crime. Ludwig has no choice but to give in to Erik's imperious demands that the premises be searched. He does, however, threaten Erik with no longer being welcomed as a guest in his home. In the script Erik steals a look at Elsa at this threat, but she remains firmly on her father's side. In contrast, in the film, they don't exchange looks, and it is clear that this a matter for the men to decide. In keeping with the progressive repression of the feminine shadow, Elsa does not have a position of authority from which to mediate conflict. Erik and the police examine the large table upon which the Monster formerly had been strapped, and then notice the opening to the underground dungeon. Requiring that Ludwig lead them, the men descend into the dungeon, uncover a loose stone, and find themselves in a deserted secret room. Ludwig defensively remarks that due to the nature of his work, he keeps this room ready for use all the time for the more violently insane.

It is significant that this scene is rife with yonic imagery, the converse of phallic imagery, with its dark and winding secret passages that harbor the Monster. The police unsuccessfully attempt to penetrate these passages, which resist their advances. As Arnold Mindell points out, vaults, caves, holes in the earth, and crevices[91] are associated with power of the earth goddess, instantiated in the gesture of the *ana-suromai*. Interestingly, as James Hillman notes, "Rottenness, putrefaction, decay are part of the underworld."[92] However, in *Son of Frankenstein*, these dark subterranean passages are interestingly swept clear of the discarded, excremental, and elemental traits of the underworld because they serve as a secret/inferior version of the laboratory. Although these passages provide the Monster, Ygor, and Frankenstein with a safe harbor, the amount of protection they can offer is limited. The film implies that despite this temporary solace, it is the male womb, the Father's scientific laboratory, which provides the key to health and rebirth.

The Monster abducts Cloestine, and accidentally sets the house on fire. The script details essentially the same events, though the characterization of the Monster's relationships is much more complex. A sob of joy escapes his throat when he sees Cloestine smiling at him, and he reverently touches her head. Cloestine is alternately delighted and worried, declaring that he must hide because the others are hunting him down. Interestingly the Monster does not leave on his own initiative; Ygor's pipe summons him, and he obeys, bringing Cloestine. In contrast, in keeping with the progressive alienation of the technological shadow, the film renders the Monster stoic and impassive as he takes the little girl from her bed; she, too, appears a more wooden character, and simply goes along silently, apparently unafraid.

Similarly, in this version, the ambiguous power of the dead (M)Other that so characterizes the original novel is severely harnessed. Not only is Elsa motherless, she herself is a virgin-mother, whose sexuality seems to be tightly tied to her father. Cloestine, the other major female character, and the object of desire for the Monster, is essentially an asexual creature that is incapable of the ambiguous power of life and death associated with motherhood. Similarly the hyperbolization of the monstrous shadow occurs concurrently; Chaney's Monster is a homicidal maniac—a killing machine that resists control, even by the cunning Ygor.

The script details a confrontation between Elsa and her father, which the film deletes. Frankenstein assumes the mask of the calm professional and apologizes for his treatment of her. Yet he simultaneously implies that she deserved this because she had been "a little hysterical," and he had been "forced to doubt" her loyalty. When Elsa refuses to reply, he adds sharply, "You intend to be discreet, don't you, my dear?" The script details his fluctuations graphically: "There is a little threat in his voice and a little betrayal that he is far from rational on his face now."[93] Elsa argues with her father over the merits of his decision to transplant Kettering's brain into the body of the Monster, but the doctor remains egomaniacally convinced of the justice of his decision. "I have removed the evil . . . and replaced it with goodness . . . with intelligence. Do you think they can criticize Frankenstein when I offer mankind the priceless gift of immortality?"[94] The use of "Frankenstein" is ambiguous because it refers to both his father and himself, who unabashedly share the same dream of parthenogenesis. Frankenstein's daughter is no longer as important to him because he can replace her with a son purely of his own creation; in her father's eyes, Elsa has become as invisible as her dead mother, who is never once mentioned in the film. Elsa sadly declares revolt, and announces her intention of leaving and going to Erik, taking Cloestine with her. Her father still has a hold over her; he firmly reiterates the need for discretion, and orders her not to leave until the experiment is over. Surprisingly, Elsa obeys.

In contrast, in the film, Erik storms Ludwig's office and again demands to know what has happened to Dr. Kettering. Ludwig decides that it is time for a showdown, and again characteristically, both men leave Elsa behind to descend into the secret room where the Monster is recovering. Ludwig shows Erik the Monster, and when the young man asks why he had been concealing the Monster, he replies like his brother, Wolf, as a true son of Frankenstein: "It was necessary for a while . . . Kettering lives again . . . I have made amends for the great tragedy my father and my brother unintentionally brought to this community and restored the good name of Frankenstein."

However, it is not Kettering's but Ygor's voice that emanates from within the body of the Monster. He boastfully remarks, "I am Ygor! I have the strength of a hundred men; I cannot die; I cannot be destroyed. I will live forever!" The script draws out this sequence even longer. Initially the Monster's voice is not immediately recognizable as Ygor's. When Frankenstein asks the Monster to identify him, it answers correctly, and the doctor looks triumphantly over to Elsa and Erik, who acknowledge the apparent miracle with nods of amazement. However, when Frankenstein asks the Monster about its own identity, it simply smiles and remains silent. Frankenstein mistakenly reveals the creature's identity to be Dr. Kettering's, but the Monster laughs the cynical snarling laugh associated with Ygor. The fused Monster indulges in an extended speech gloating over his rebirth into immortality and unlimited strength. The parthenogenetic myth of self-birthing and its hubristic desire for masculine immortality again rears its head.

Ludwig fearfully declares that he has "created a hundred times the horror my father created" and accusingly lunges for the traitor, Bohmer. The Monster stops Ludwig from attacking Bohmer, and refrains from killing Frankenstein with the words: "I should kill you, Frankenstein, but after all, your father gave me life and you gave me a brain." The importance of the paternal line of inheritance, and its transmission of (malignant) life and power is starkest at this point. In contrast, in the film, though the Monster does intervene to protect Bohmer in the script, he does not utter the line that stresses his contempt of and indebtedness to Ludwig and his father, Henry.

Meanwhile the villagers storm Frankenstein's abode in search of the missing Cloestine. Suddenly the Monster loses his sight and cries out for Bohmer. Frankenstein, slumped against the operating table, informs Bohmer that his dream of power is over: because the blood types of the Monster and Ygor do not match (as opposed to Kettering), the sensory nerves of the Monster's eyes cannot be fed, resulting in blindness. In the film the loss of his sight causes the monstrous Ygor to become even more vigorous in his movements. The father's mistake manifests itself in the loss of his son's sight, which in effect castrates him, and brings him closer to the realm of instinctive body—a realm that is associated with the feminine. The Monster's hulking body, thrashing about, reveals the ever-lurking possibility of a male body tortured and vulnerable, which the Ego attempts to suppress. But this is a revelation the Frankensteinian myth cannot sustain.

In the script a moment of epiphany occurs as both men realize their grand ambitions—Ludwig, of birthing a "great good," and Bohmer, of spawning a tyrannical ruler—have both been "slight miscalculations."[95] This consciously ironic twist is deleted in the film, and action is substituted for reflection. The Monster-Ygor demands that his sight be returned, and remarks, "What good is a brain without eyes to see?" When Bohmer remains silent, he angrily flings Frankenstein's assistant against one of the laboratory machines, killing him. The monstrous Ygor then goes into another rampage, causing a fire that eventually consumes him (and, by implication, Ludwig Frankenstein) and explodes the castle. However, whereas the camera lingers over the physical disintegration of the Monster, voyeuristically emphasizing how his pale face begins to melt and peel, there is no evidence of physical suffering on the part of Ludwig. It is the Monster's spectacular destruction that the camera highlights, almost with a trace of vindictiveness, bringing the demonization of the monstrous shadow to a new pitch. As Glut remarks, "The Frankenstein Monster had a new image. No longer did he motion pathetically for an explanation of his humanity; nor did his face show the torment of a creature existing in a world of aliens. He walked stiffly with one purpose—to kill."[96]

The movie closes with a typical Hollywood ending, with Erik and Elsa embracing and walking away from the ruins into the dawning of a new day. In the script, Elsa attempts to look back, but Erik prevents her from gazing upon the scientific Sodom and Gomorrah from which they have fled. In the film Elsa's loyalty to Erik is complete, and she feels no need to look back upon the ruins where her father perishes. She has passed from dutiful daughter to domesticated wife-to-be. This time the repression of the monstrous and feminine shadows is so great that none of the ambivalent tensions of Whale's films manifest themselves.

IN THE WOLF MAN'S SHADOW

By the 1940s declining box office receipts made Universal think that the Frankenstein Monster, though it had been infused with even greater physical strength by the two sons of Frankenstein, would be too weak to sustain its former box office draw. A different type of horror film would have to be spawned—one that pitted two monsters against each other. Lon Chaney, although he had played the Frankensteinian Monster in *The Ghost of Frankenstein*, and actually preferred playing the Monster to the Wolf Man, seemed the natural choice to play the Wolf Man's part because his portrayal of this creature in *The Wolf Man* had made it the second most popular monster. Controversy raged over who should play the Monster.

Because the Frankensteinian Monster in the last film had been shown as blind and speaking with the voice of Ygor (played by Lugosi), Lugosi seemed like the natural choice. That would save the studio the trouble of dubbing Lugosi's voice if the part were played by someone else. Lugosi's strategic blunder of turning down the part of the Monster in 1931 because it did not speak haunted him, and he enthusiastically signed up for the part, partially because his career and health had both radically declined, but also, Lugosi rationalized, because in Kurt Siodmak's original script, the Monster could speak. However, Lillian Lugosi, Bela's former wife who died in 1981, admitted that Lugosi's motives were less than pure. "Isn't it crazy? After turning down the original, Bela winds up doing it anyhow—THE MONSTER MEETS THE WOLF MAN, or something? He finally did it because of MONEY. He didn't do it any other way."[97]

Interestingly enough top billing was not given to either of the two Monster actors, but to Ilona Massey, a blonde Hungarian soprano, who played the part of Elsa von Frankenstein (formerly played by Evelyn Ankers in *Ghost of Frankenstein*). Ilona had been hailed as "The Singing Garbo" by MGM, and was formerly the pampered protegee of Louis B. Mayer.[98] Second billing went to Patrick Knowles, who functioned as an all-purpose leading man in many of Universal's films. Knowles was judged as well cast in the role of Dr. Frank Mannering ("Dr. Harley" in Siodmak's original script), with his appeal lying in "sound[ing] sincere when he cries, 'I can't destroy Frankenstein's creation! I've got to see it at its full power,' and handsome enough to give Ilona someone to cling to in the final reel."[99] Third billing went to Lionel Atwill, who had played the one-armed Inspector Krogh in *Son of Frankenstein* and the vengeful Dr. Bohmer in *Ghost of Frankenstein*. Universal appeased Chaney with the special "and" billing in the credits.

Roy William Neil's *Frankenstein Meets the Wolfman* features the Frankenstein Monster only in the second half of the film; consequently my analysis is concentrated principally upon what is relevant to the mythic unfolding of the Frankensteinian narrative. The movie immediately makes clear that the star monster in this movie is not Frankenstein's Monster, but the Wolf Man. Ironically it is Lon Chaney's performances that both reduce the Monster into a mechanical prop and mindless killing machine, and animate the character of Larry Talbot as a Byronic hero seeking death as a permanent release from lycanthropy.

Fleeing from angry villagers, the Wolf Man falls into underground catacombs, attempts to jump out unsuccessfully, and then collapses in a faint. Larry Talbot, the human alter ego of the Wolf Man, awakens to find himself human again. He finds himself trapped inside another virtual womb, with one end sealed by nature in the form of glacial ice, and the other, a humanly built stone foundation. Nevertheless, Talbot chances upon the dormant figure of the Frankensteinian Monster frozen in a block of ice, and releases him.

What ensues in the original script is a conversation between both fugitives regarding their fates. It appears that the Monster is both blind (in keeping with the ending of *Ghost of Frankenstein*) and extremely weak. He speaks, though with difficulty, in the original script of how he ended up being buried alive in a block of ice.[100] Hatred of "futile little mortals" and the experience of having been buried alive bind the two Monsters in an unsteady alliance. However, whereas the Monster lusts after regaining the strength of a hundred men and living forever, the Wolf Man desires peace through death. Interestingly enough the original script traces a certain ambivalence in the characterization of both the Monster and the Wolf Man, which is absent in the film version. In the script the Monster's motives for regaining his health are ambiguous: part of it is a power trip, but there seems to be some mistaken or self-aggrandizing paternalism mixed in with the Monster's desire to rule the world. Similarly Talbot reveals traces of morbid self-absorption that are brushed over in the final film version.[101] The film excises all these out, and instead substitutes the image of an extremely proactive Talbot, and a mute, effete, and power-hungry Monster— very much in keeping with the increasing demonization of the technologized shadow toward which the Universal series' treatment of the Frankensteinian myth gravitates. The subordination of the Frankensteinian Monster to the Wolf Man is easily evident in *Frankenstein Meets the Wolf Man*; not only does he lose his powers of speech and reasoning to the Wolf Man, but he is also transformed into a flat caricature, with whom identification and sympathy is impossible.

Mank details Siodmak's remarks on why, behind the scenes, the Monster's dialogue was cut out: "Do you know why they took the Monster's dialogue away? Because Bela Lugosi couldn't talk! They had left the dialogue I wrote for the Monster in the picture when they shot it, but with

Lugosi it sounded so Hungarian funny that they had to take it out! Seriously!"[102]

Regardless of the reason/s cited, the effect achieved is that of rendering the monstrous shadow even more alien. With the Monster's mouth flapping open mutely in some places, and his seemingly inexplicable groping, Lugosi's Monster loses the human spark one glimpses particularly in Karloff's rendition of it. He becomes nothing more than a power-crazed automaton, a concentrated repository of the demonized technological shadow.

The two creatures are disappointed when they find that Frankenstein's diary is missing. Their pathos and confusion, so vividly sketched in the original script, is edited out. However, they do find Elsa von Frankenstein's picture, and Talbot determines that it is to her that they must turn for help. Setting out alone, Talbot unsuccessfully tries to convince Elsa to reveal the whereabouts of her father's diary; the Monster causes a commotion when he arrives looking for his missing friend. In the original script, the Monster recognizes Talbot and smiles faintly at him; in the movie, however, the Monster simply roars at him when he approaches, but Talbot grabs him, and urges him on to a wagon, and both make their escape, impeding their pursuants by dropping barrels in their wake. Again, in the original script, the barrels simply accidentally fall off the wagon; in the movie, the Monster actively and maliciously initiates the process of their descent. The overall effect is again that of demonizing the Monster, and rendering him devoid of human emotion, causing the split between Ego and monstrous shadow to grow even more insurmountable. At the same time, though, it renders the creature both physically weak and emotionally needy, two all-too-human traits which, nevertheless, ironically further alienate the monstrous shadow.

What follows next in the original script is a conversation between Talbot and the Monster, explaining why the Monster had made such a dramatic entrance at the village. The Monster who speaks in this script is one who is vulnerable, not only emotionally but also physically, and is mortally afraid of being abandoned. When Talbot hears Frank Mannering's voice calling him, the Monster cries, "Don't leave me—don't go! I'm weak. . . . They'll catch me and bury me alive!"[103] All this is removed, and the only transition made is that of Maleva (the old gypsy woman who functions as a surrogate mother to Talbot, acted by Maria Ouspenskaya) spotting the smoke ensuing from the fire Talbot had made, and Talbot suddenly appearing before the small party composed of the doctor, the baroness, and the old gypsy woman. Elsa volunteers to show Talbot where her father's diary is, and Talbot looks at her searchingly before turning to Maleva, who reassures him. As Talbot leads the three visitors into the old Frankensteinian castle, Elsa seems riveted by horror and cannot seem to move into the castle, but Frank Mannering boldly moves to the Monster. Talbot introduces the doctor to the Monster, who, in the original script, inquires if

Mannering has arrived to restore his original strength. Talbot replies in the affirmative, lying in accordance with his plan, yet his fascination with the Monster is evident.

But as he gazes at the giant, it is clear that Dr. Harley [Mannering in the film] is fascinated by this phenomenon—his scientific curiosity is unleashed. He takes the monster's arm, pushing up the sleeve of the burned, torn clothes, and stares at it wonderingly—this arm put together from parts of human bodies—the stitches of the surgeon's needle still plainly visible. Then Harley looks at the monster's face, gently moving the ugly head and touching the steel bar, which runs straight through the giant's throat.[104]

Elsa watches apprehensively and calls out, a perplexed, pleading expression on her face. The doctor suddenly realizes he has shown too much interest in the creature and feigns surprise. The rivalry between Monster and woman again occurs, though this time expunged of the dark incestuous and murderous desires for the dead mother in the original novel.

As preparations for the experiment are in full swing, ostensibly to grant the two creatures their greatest desires, Elsa again pays a visit to the laboratory. This time she addresses the doctor by his first name, "Frank." The use of the first name not only establishes the romantic liaison between the two, but also points out his potential similarity with her father and grandfather. She reminds him of the obsession and horrible deaths that befell these men, and urges him to keep his promise of destroying the Monster. Yet as a daughter of Frankenstein, her ultimate motive appears to be, like Wolf Frankenstein, clearing the name of the Father. "It's in your hands to clear the name of Frankenstein—to undo the crimes my father and grandfather committed! We must clear the name of Frankenstein."[105]

When Mannering is left alone in the laboratory to destroy the creature, however, he falters, and as a mad gleam enters his eyes, he declares, "I can't do it; I can't destroy Frankenstein's creation. I've got to see it in its full power." Elsa stares at the Monster as he regains consciousness and struggles against his straps. Horrified, Elsa shakes Frank, who appears to be under a spell; undaunted, she then pulls a switch that causes an explosion and seems to shake Frank Mannering back into consciousness.

What transpires next in the script is very different from what occurs on film.[106] The revisions are significant because they dramatically reshape the narrative. Repeatedly, it is the Monster who is demonized, and the Wolf Man who is rendered the heroic figure. The Wolf Man saves the doctor and the baroness for no apparent reason than residual humanity utterly lacking in the Monster. The Monster in the script is motivated only by the survival instinct; in the movie he appears to have sexual designs on Elsa.

As the two superhuman creatures battle against each other, Frank and Elsa embrace and escape. In the meantime, Vazek (Rex Evans), whose daughter was killed by the Wolf Man, is shown climbing the dam and planting dynamite. As the dam explodes, water cascades down and engulfs the castle, drowning the two monsters. This is the last shot of the film. In the original script, Maleva rescues the lovers, and then unobtrusively slips away as the villagers watch the spectacle of the debacle of the Frankenstein castle. Again the power of the (M)Other is covered over in favor of a conventional romantic ending, with the gallant doctor rescuing the helpless baroness. By now, though, it is clear that the vigor of the filmic Monster is waning; the Ego has overextended itself, resulting in the alienation of the monstrous shadow. The Monster has now become a caricature—flat, devoid of humanity, the unthinking slave of aspiring tyrants. As Leslie Halliwell writes, "Henceforth, in the rest of its appearances for Universal [the Monster] would remain in its dormant state until the final reel, when, electrically impelled, it would stagger forth to be disposed of—momentarily—by the angry mob."[107]

EFFACING AND HOUSING THE MONSTROUS

With the physical and intellectual deterioration of the Monster, alongside the need to appeal to a younger audience, Universal adopted a new strategy. Instead of having just two monsters, they decided to crowd in as many as five monsters in one film. This resulted in two sequels, *House of Frankenstein* (1944) and *House of Dracula* (1945), both of which were directed by Erle C. Kenton.

House of Frankenstein resurrected both the Wolf Man (Lon Chaney) and the Frankensteinian Monster (Glenn Strange), and added Count Dracula (John Carradine), Daniel the hunchback (J. Carrol Naish)—a character derived from Victor Hugo's Quasimodo of Notre Dame, and a mad scientist, Dr. Gustav Niemann (Boris Karloff). Karloff declined the part of the Monster, but accepted top billing as the mad scientist. Apparently this caused some confusion that worked in favor of the film's publicity; according to Glut,[108] many viewers entered the theater, expecting to see Karloff in his famous Monster makeup. Apparently some even surmised that Karloff played both the parts of the scientist and the Monster. The confusion is instructive because the resultant trend not only reduces the Monster to a mindless and mechanical prop, but also begins overtly to demonize the scientist. Part of Karloff's draw was his association with the Monster, with its fearful and terrifying body. Moving Karloff from the site of the Monster to that of the scientist imbues the scientist with these characteristics. This is a trend that is implicit, in both the novel and many of the Universal films, but becomes explicit particularly in the Hammer films.

Erle C. Kenton's *House of Frankenstein* opens with the usual stormy evening, but the setting this time is Neustadt Prison for the criminally insane, where a guard brings food to two prisoners: Dr. Gustav Niemann

(Boris Karloff), the brother of a former assistant to the original Dr. Frankenstein, and Daniel (J. Carrol Naish), a homicidal hunchback. Like Wolf Frankenstein, Niemann is immediately established as an adoring and devoted son, determined to claim and hallow Frankenstein's mantle. Niemann grabs the guard by his throat and demands, of all things, that he return his chalk to him. When the guard acquiesces, the doctor releases him. Coughing, the guard threatens Niemann with solitary confinement, and calls him a "would-be Frankenstein." Niemann treats the guard's derogatory remarks as the supreme compliment, and speaks reverentially of Frankenstein: "Don't profane his name with your dirty lips. He was a genius in whose footsteps I will follow when I get out of here." Similarly the dynamic between Niemann and Daniel is reminiscent of the relationship between Whale's Henry Frankenstein and Fritz. Like Henry Frankenstein, Niemann is paternal toward his deformed pupil, slave, and devoted follower. Not only Niemann, but also Daniel, reveals himself to be a son of Frankenstein in his obsession with rebirthing himself through the acquisition of a new body.

Interestingly, though, the final version is quite different from the original script. The earlier version reveals some hesitation, the faintest hint of self-doubt in Niemann, as he claims not to know "all" of Frankenstein's secrets, but only "some." He also hesitates slightly when Daniel asks if he has the power to grant him a healthy body as he admits that he needs Frankenstein's records to "guide" him in order to "go further." Then, almost in compensation for these moments of weakness, he comes up with even more outlandish claims than in the final film version. "With [the Frankenstein records], . . . I could give you not only a perfect body, but a new mind—a brain built from parts of a dozen others, and perfect brains!"[109]

The changes from the initial version to released film are significant because they not only condense what would have been long soliloquies into more pithy remarks, but also because Karloff's character becomes more menacing through the removal of these obviously all-too-human fluctuations from insecurity to overconfidence. Niemann, the resurrection of Henry Frankenstein's spirit, no longer possesses the hysterical instabilities of his progenitor. He has, in every sense, bested the father.

A violent storm breaks out; as thunder peals and lightning flashes, the roof and a section of the prison wall caves in. After ducking to avoid getting hit by the falling debris, both Niemann and Daniel escape through an underground passage. Outside the prison the escaped convicts come across Professor Lampini's (George Zucco) wagon that is stuck in a mudhole. Both men help free the wagon, and Lampini offers them the hospitality of his wagon. As Daniel sits back quietly, Niemann and Lampini verbally spar. It becomes clear that Lampini displays the same pride as Niemann does and that both men fancy themselves explorers of dangerous and arcane realms of knowledge. For a significant period, they take turns revealing their knowledge concerning the possibility of resurrecting as well as destroying a vampire. Power over a supernatural creature is power over life and death, and both men glory in this idea.

When Lampini resists making a detour to Riegelberg, where Hussman, one of Niemann's enemies has become mayor, Niemann gives Daniel the signal to kill off Lampini. In the final version, after Daniel is shown discarding of Lampini's corpse like a ragdoll, Niemann coolly instructs him to dispose of the driver as well and Daniel moves off wordlessly. The way the scene is shot makes it clear that Daniel is not only a potential parthenogenetic son, but also one of the film's monsters. He looms close, reaching for the camera with his powerful, gigantic looking hands as Professor Lampini's horrified face is shown.

The scene changes to reveal Burgomaster Hussman checkmating his police chief (Lionel Atwill). The police chief, with an ambivalent mixture of frustration and admiration, accepts defeat as Rita (Anne Gwynne), the burgomaster's granddaughter-in-law arrives. Rita is sprightly and irrepressible, and she teases the policeman for tempting fate by playing chess with her unbeatable grandfather-in-law. Rita's vigor and charm dominate the scene; she leans down to kiss the burgomaster, calling him "old darling." She is the first of the two "feminine-as-monstrous" figures we meet in this Frankensteinian film.

Rita declares confidently that Carl and she have decided "to take in the midnight show of the Horror Exhibit at the crossroad." Carl, her husband (Peter Coe), impishly interjects that it is actually Rita who has decided. She imperiously ignores him and orders her husband to bring old Hussmann's hat and coat. When the burgomaster objects, she simply dresses him; the inspector is also bundled up in spite of his objections because of the vigor of Rita's request-commands. There is a teasing banter between husband and wife that reveals a battle of wills.

It is evident that Rita is used to getting the last word in because it is her will that moves the men toward the show of horrors. In the original script, the police inspector manages to elude the grasp of Rita's will, and playfully calls out "Checkmate" to Hussman as he bids them good night. Nevertheless, Rita, laughing, promises to take good care of her grandfather, implying that she will take the place of the police chief, who normally functions as his bodyguard. The Rita in the script is even more outspoken than that in the final film version because she uses stronger language in her teasingly combative banter with her husband, daring to call him a "beast" and openly throwing him dangerous looks with great frequency—all of which are excised in the released version. In the script the portrait of a female character secure in her sexual potency, like the figure of Baubo, emerges; this is watered down in the film, and even in attenuated form, cannot last for long.

However, at the show, Rita is transformed into a little girl and "silly goose" who delights in shivers of fear. A short but exceedingly strange episode occurs, which differs greatly in the transformation from original to released version.

The original script describes the scene as follows: "Our group enters . . . pausing at the first exhibit—a medieval rack, on which a wax figure with an agonized expression is being drawn and quartered by another dummy who has his hands on the crank of a large wheel which, when turned, stretches the rope tied to the sufferer's wrists and ankles."[110] Tony turns to his wife and musingly tells her to remind him to purchase one of these gadgets. When his wife says, "For me, my sweet?" he deadpans grimly: "To stretch my salary check."[111] Again evidence of the power skirmishes between husband and wife emerge.

In the released version, however, the prisoner is not male but female, and there is no obvious tormentor as she is locked in a stockade, with her neck, hands, and feet secured cruelly. Carl looks at this female wax figure and muses loudly that he would like to know where to get one of these contraptions. When Rita takes the bait and asks what he could possibly use it for, he replies, "Just the thing to keep your wife under control." The misogynous disciplining of the feminine shadow is rendered overt. No longer is violence resentfully directed at a paycheck—an allusion to the power of the purse strings, which Rita obviously holds—but at the woman herself, who challenges male authority. The other men enjoy the joke, and Rita forces herself to join in the laughter. Although the brief scene is intended to be a lighthearted moment, it is interesting that combined with the earlier scene, Rita's character, as determined and willful, is clear. The joke turns on what type of husband would need a rack in the first place: only a beleaguered one. The men's collective laughter is an attempt to tame Rita, and her attempt to join in their laughter reveals her awkward awareness of the power dynamics of the joke. Rita is not the only figure simultaneously powerful and vulnerable; another is soon to be introduced.

Niemann takes out the stake thrust into Dracula's skeleton, not really thinking at first that anything unnatural would happen. Dracula (John Carradine) regains both form and consciousness, and attempts to hypnotize Niemann. In the script Niemann weakens and almost succumbs, but is saved by the crucifix attached to the dead Lampini's watch, which he raises before the cowering vampire. In contrast, in the film, the doctor, though he feels the force of the vampire's hypnotic gaze, successfully resists. He then manfully gives the vampire a choice as he holds the stake over the creature's heart: "If you move, I'll send your soul back to the limbo of eternal waiting. Do as I ask and I will serve you."

The interaction between the doctor and the vampire is fascinating because Niemann speaks both the languages of violence and devotion. He both blackmails and woos the vampire into submission, and in so doing, feminizes him. His voice is simultaneously caressing and threatening, allowing no room for either defiance or rejection. When the vampire agrees, it is an unconditional oath of slavery: "For that, I will do whatever you wish." The shadows of the monstrous and the feminine momentarily converge in the figure of the enslaved vampire, who is slated, like the female monster, to be killed off.

In the released film version, the police chief only now parts company with the Hussmans. For the first time, Rita's identity is revealed. She is addressed respectfully as "Mrs. Hussman"; in contrast, old Hussman affectionately calls the chief of police "Arnz." Naming is crucial to the gender dynamics at work, and it is significant that in the original script, Rita is the direct genetic link to Hussman, rather than Carl (Tony in the original script), as it appears in the final movie version. Rita's last name in the script is "Holt," and she is Hussman's American-born granddaughter. The attempt at disciplining her renders her simply an accidental, rather than central, character to the unfolding of the plot. The issue is one of ownership, and Rita will be the pawn used in the patriarchal struggle between old Hussman, Baron Latos, and Carl/Tony.

Old Hussman, Carl, and Rita move through the mist, and the resultant dialogue further illuminates the nature of their relationships to each other. Rita's fantasizing about the supernatural irritates old Hussman, while it gives Carl latitude for treating her as his "pet"—a pubescent girl whose hyperactive imagination can be indulged. In the script version, the interaction varies slightly, though it again hints at the misogyny at the heart of this subplot. Hussman pays scant heed to Rita, totally wrapped up in his musings over Niemann's identity, while Tony takes every opportunity to reduce his wife into a screaming and frantic fool by hiding himself and then gloating over her concern and earlier proclamation that being frightened is "fun." In the continuity and dialogue, no one in particular takes heed of the noise of a carriage coming toward them, but in the film, it is Rita, who is still the active one, who alerts the men.

With a flourish, Dracula offers them the hospitality of his carriage. Rita is the first to enter the coach, and the vampire fixes his hypnotic gaze on her. She falls silent and stares off, as if in a trance. In the original script, Dracula's influence on the young woman causes her to become even more animated, with her eyes sparkling. Interestingly enough, in the film version, both Carl and old Hussman do not notice Rita's subsequent reticence and passiveness even though it is so much out of character. Carl introduces himself by his full name, his wife as "Mrs. Hussman," and explains that they are here enjoying their honeymoon. After the vampire offers his congratulations, Carl introduces his grandfather (which in the original script is Rita's grandfather), and Dracula introduces himself as "Baron Latos from Transylvania." Dracula then takes advantage of the information concerning the newlyweds and invites them to join him for a bottle of celebratory wine. It is significant that the vampire specifically addresses the question to "Mrs. Hussman," but it is Carl who enthusiastically accepts, with the hesitant proviso that old Hussman does not object, an addition that is not in the original script. Neither the older nor the younger Hussman consult Rita on the matter; they almost seem happily oblivious to her sudden silence and lack of initiative. It is as if they wish to extend the period in which they remain in the company of this stranger who has finally managed to place the irrepressible young woman in an invisible stockade.

The burgomaster insists on playing host, and the four end up drinking wine at the Hussman home. In the original script, Rita waxes poetic, comparing the wine they drink to blood, which she describes as "beautiful"; in the film she is simply silent. Dracula continues his courtship/enslavement of Rita both visually and verbally: "I drink to your love. A union to last throughout eternity. A love free from all material needs." Blind to the double entendre, Carl replies with smug wit: "I'll drink to that lack of material needs myself, Baron. But not until I raid the wine cellar, I won't. Excuse me, darling. Be right back, Baron."

Because old Hussman has fallen asleep, Dracula is unencumbered in pursuing his victim-beloved. He impales her with his gaze, and Rita glimpses shadows of his world in his ring, signaling her vulnerability to temptation. In the original script, Rita is now completely aroused and enslaved, offering no resistance. In the film Rita still hesitantly recoils, defining herself in terms of her relationship to her husband. Dracula gently takes her hands in his and slips his ring upon her finger. Initially the ring is too big, but it glows as it tightens and Dracula describes it as "the bond that links us together," as a bridegroom might to his newly wedded wife. Rita's words now reveal her lack of will: "I see your world more clearly now. I am no longer afraid." Rita's transformation from willful wife to monstrous slave is instructive as it reveals the proximity between the feminine-as-monstrous and the female monster. Her full domestication as feminized shadow is possible within the Frankensteinian myth only after the rite of passage of becoming a female monster as Dracula's potential bride.

As Hussman is killed by the vampire bat, Carl and Rita are in their bedroom. Carl is still initially blissfully aware of Rita's trancelike mood until she effectively utters a strange and eloquent soliloquy: "It's a wonderful night! The darkness beckons to me. . . . The world I see is far away—yet very near—a strange, beautiful world, in which one may be dead, yet alive!" Finally awakened from his own trancelike oblivion, Carl seizes her and spies Dracula's ring upon her finger. He desperately tries to get it off her finger, but she begins to fall and he catches her.

The original script differs slightly. Tony initially thinks she is drunk when she confesses to feeling as though she were in a dream. He mocks her gently with the words: "Look not upon the wine when it is red!"[112] Rita quotes Dracula eerily: "To live throughout eternity, without material needs," and when he advises her to lie down, she complains of being "hurt" by "her" ring. Her husband discovers the Dracula crest with alarm; his wife replies to his questions dreamily, and then suddenly sobs: "Get it off, Tony! Get it off!"[113] Tony, the stronger one, soothes her by telling her not to get excited, and assures her they will try to get it off with soap and water. Although the changes from script to film are minimal, it is evident that in the script, any vestiges of will left in Rita inhere in her relationship to her husband; it is he who grants her integrity of identity despite her outward show of independence. In the film even this possibility of resistance is removed—once again, deepening the domestication of the feminine shadow.

Dracula, fleeing with Rita, directs his coach in pursuit of Lampini's wagon, where his coffin is, but Daniel throws out the vampire's coffin. The vampire loses control of the horses and the carriage crashes; the vampire attempts to open the coffin as the sun hits him in the face. Carl and three policemen dismount and come running; they see Dracula gradually reverting back into a skeleton. In the script a stake is violently driven through his heart by accompanying villagers—a phallic gesture which blatantly underlines the feminized nature of the monster. Reunited with his bride, Carl holds Rita in his arms and smiles at her. He then looks off, and she follows his gaze to observe that Dracula's ring again glows, slowly becomes large and falls from her finger. The vampire has been effectively disposed of, yet his spell remains. It is clear that Rita has become domesticated and disciplined, no longer a threat to her husband's authority. Rita has effectively cycled through the realms of feminine-as-monstrous and female Monster to emerge, transformed, into a properly harnessed feminine shadow.

Unimpeded, Niemann and Daniel drive on to the town of Frankenstein, where they encounter a camp of gypsies. In the center of a circle, the pretty and young Ilonka (Elena Verdugo), the second feminine-as-monstrous figure, dances. She ends her dance by provocatively flinging herself to the ground, and the crowd, delighted, showers her with coins. Fejos, one of the gypsies, demands that Ilonka turn over all of the money to him. When she resists, Fejos lashes the screaming Ilonka with a whip, and Daniel leaps from the carriage and begins to strangle Fejos. Niemann intervenes, and the two make their getaway, keeping the unconscious Ilonka with them.

When she awakens, Ilonka instantly transforms from uncertain child to teasing coquette. She asks if Daniel (whom she does not yet see fully) likes her (which is not in the original script), and he awkwardly blurts out that he finds her pretty. She is now in full control, and provocatively asks whether Daniel is afraid of her. When he registers surprise, she triumphantly flings out the courtship gauntlet: "If you weren't, you would come up here where I could see you better." Daniel, as though in a trance, smilingly climbs up to the driver's seat; his smile freezes when he notices the look of shock and distaste on her face. In the script Daniel fills in Ilonka's incomplete sentence: "Oh! You're . . . An ugly hunchback." In both film and script, Daniel's voice trembles with hurt and vulnerability as he asks,

"But you will talk to me sometime, won't you?" Ilonka looks sympathetic as she holds his hands and replies, "Of course I will. You've been kind to me and I like you." Daniel's worshipful silence and joy is short-lived, however, as Niemann imperiously calls to him. Ilonka's doom is long foretold in this sequence. Unlike Rita, her blatant sensual energy and flirtatiousness is untamed, and she distracts Daniel from his awe-filled worship of Niemann. Baubo's untamed and scandalous *ana-suromai* sits well with Ilonka. Unlike Rita, who can be domesticated because her sensuality is kept in tow (save for that dangerous close brush with Dracula), Ilonka exudes an untamed eroticism that marks her as the perfect scapegoat.

Niemann and Daniel stumble across a glacial cave, where they find the bodies of both the Wolfman (Lon Chaney) and the Frankensteinian Monster (Glenn Strange) frozen. It is the Wolfman's figure that first thaws out, and he reverts back to Larry Talbot. To Daniel's dismay, Niemann orders Talbot to do the driving while he keeps his hunchbacked assistant with him, applying hot compresses to the Monster, whose flesh seems to have been damaged by exposure to ice. As they drive off, Ilonka, who has been asleep, awakens. In the film Ilonka again unabashedly displays her unconventional boldness. Initially thinking it is Daniel who is driving, she teasingly tickles his leg. When Larry rubs his leg, she laughs, touches his hand, and remarks that he must be suffering from bites. When she finally realizes it is not Daniel, her demeanor grows more cautious, but she still remains forward. She introduces herself, gently coerces his name from him, and offers to speak with him in keeping with her promise to keep Daniel company. She voluntarily sits beside him; he remains silent and uncommunicative. In the script she simply sits beside him without preamble, and when Larry verbally repulses her, she leaves him alone, but not without flirtatiously addressing him by his first name. She then falls asleep, smiling happily to herself as she gazes upon Larry desirously. Her fate is twice-sealed. Not only has she appropriated the masculine gaze, but she also has rendered the disguised monster, Larry Talbot, into an object of desire—a move that can only backfire, resulting in her destruction. The patriarchal structure of the Frankensteinian narrative cannot survive either the radical masculinization of the feminine, or the feminization of the masculine/monstrous, and she is fated ruthlessly to be destroyed.

In the original script, Ilonka's status as a monstrous feminine figure is very clear: She exposes her legs as she emerges from the lake—an image that resonates with visions of Venus rising from the sea. Instead, in the film, she has been gathering flowers, and she presents them to him as a gift—a much-domesticated representation of the same theme. Larry murmurs "pretty" diffidently, which finally causes Ilonka to erupt impetuously: "What's the matter with you? We've been together three days and you haven't smiled once." In the original script, she says, "You've hardly looked at me"—a much bolder statement.

In the original script, Larry finally breaks down and confides his secret to her by drawing the pentagram, the mark of the beast, upon the ground. She is initially shocked and draws away, to the delight of the spying Daniel. Yet she recovers from her shock and edges closer, saying hesitantly that she is not afraid as she rests her hand on his arm. Larry looks ahead, as if trying to pierce through the mists of an uncertain future. In contrast, in the film, the revelation of Talbot's secret identity occurs much later, when Daniel jealously volunteers the information to the shocked girl who accuses him of jealousy and runs off, screaming "I hate you!" The change is slight, but it is clear that the Ilonka in the script, though she often clings to Larry's arm, is a stronger and more composed woman than the woman in the film. The script persona is able gently to wrest Larry's secret from his own lips, as well as to give him hope and solace; the film version is unable to accomplish any of these. Again this modification is in keeping with the progressive domestication of the feminine as monstrous to the realm of the feminine shadow.

In both the film and script, Daniel asks his master that he be given Talbot's body. In the script Niemann frankly tells Daniel of his plans: Talbot's body, because of its youth and vigor, would be given to the Monster, to create the perfect man. When Niemann leaves Daniel to clean up after him, Daniel snarls as he whips the inert figure of the Monster viciously: "So he's going to give you the Wolf Man's body!"[114] He then spits at the Monster's face.

The film version differs significantly. Niemann remains vague concerning the nature of his plans, and thus manages to keep Daniel dangling hopefully, further enslaving him. What transpires next are a series of short clips in which the scientist and his assistant kidnap Strauss and Ullman, and Niemann maliciously exults in informing his victims of his intended plans for them. Niemann does not mention anything concerning Talbot's body until Daniel, when they are again working side by side in the laboratory, raises the issue again. Niemann finally informs him, and when Daniel reminds him of his promise, replies haughtily: "Do you think I'd wreck the work of a lifetime because you're in love with a gypsy girl?" Daniel reminds Niemann that he has killed four men for him and implicitly demands payment for debts owed, but Niemann refuses to be blackmailed and hisses: "Do as I say or I'll never help you." The cinematic Niemann is a more formidable creature than the version in the script. More subtle, cunning, and manipulative, he exercises tyrannical control on all those around him, and embodies the full strength of the parthenogenetic myth, while ironically revealing its dark underside. The appropriation of the female power of birthing unto male figures leads not to a utopia of healed souls within perfect bodies but estranged and alienated creatures, among whom the worst is the scientist himself.

In the script the Monster is shown slowly coming to life. From the moment he opens his eyes, he is hostile. He glares at Niemann, and when he sees Daniel, he seems to remember the flogging he received at the hunchback's hands. He strains against the straps to break free. Daniel makes a final plea to be given Talbot's body but is roughly turned down by Niemann. All these are cut out in the film, rendering some aspects of the complex rivalry between the two Monsters invisible. In contrast, in the film, the Monster seems to acknowledge Niemann's preference for him, and smiles trustingly at the scientist when he first opens his eyes; when he spies Daniel, he struggles to break free, but Niemann soothes him with a few words and he lies back willingly. This is the only time in the film that Niemann is intimately tender with anyone, again reifying the monstrous eroticism between parthenogenetic father and son.

Larry, the neglected Monster-son, is left to his own devices. This time, as Larry stares at his image in the mirror, and Ilonka breathlessly aims her gun (with a silver bullet), the film does show the transformation from man to werewolf. The transmogrification completes itself; the Wolf Man forcibly opens the doors that lead to the terrace. In the film, as if to stress his bestial nature even more, the creature crashes through the door. In the script Ilonka is allowed an epiphany as she aims the gun, with pity and understanding, at the snarling creature. Instead, in the film, she immediately becomes hysterical and starts screaming as soon as she spots the Wolf Man, who attacks her. Again in contrast, in the script, there is a slight pause as Ilonka lowers the gun; the werewolf also hesitates, but then grabs Ilonka and drags her out of sight beyond the trees. The script features Ilonka's sobbing and then the sound of a pistol shot; the film reveals the Wolf Man grabbing her by the throat and then as the young woman is pulled off-screen, a gunshot sounds. In the script violence done to both woman and werewolf are implied rather than shown; in the film the vicious attack upon the woman is shown, but the damage she wreaks upon the werewolf is not directly visible. Repeatedly, Ilonka is divested of autonomy and reflective deliberation. Whereas the Wolf Man is allowed a tragic heroism, Ilonka's death seems both deserved, and the only means through which she may be authorized to occupy the space of the Good Woman.

In keeping with its trend of simplifying relationships, the film version substitutes a thoroughgoing devotion between monstrous father and son for a complex rivalry between two pseudohuman sons, and a fluctuation across the realms of power and helplessness on the part of the scientist in the script. Once again the parthenogenetic myth looms large, emphasizing the fusion of father and son, rather than their monstrous fragmentation.

To illustrate: When Daniel blames Niemann for Ilonka's death and attacks him, the Monster finally breaks his straps and strides across the room. Wordlessly, the Monster picks up the speechless Daniel and hurls him through a window, who screams as he plummets to his death. Protectively and gently, the Monster returns to the scientist's inert form. He lifts him up the way a lover does, and when Niemann opens his eyes, he finds himself gazing into the face of the Monster—rendering overt the homoeroticism of the parthenogenetic tie. Once again the Monster flees from torch-bearing villagers, carrying Niemann with him. The villagers set fire to the dry brush, sending the Monster rushing into the bog, into which Niemann and his Monstrous son sink.

The script version is slightly different. Here the ambivalences of Niemann's relationship to Daniel are still evident. Although Daniel actively attacks Niemann, the scientist tries to defend Daniel from the Monster when the creature breaks free; this parthenogenetic father at least tries to preserve both his monstrous sons. The Monster is also hostile to Niemann, and his criminal brain is again cited as the main reason for his lack of gratitude for all that the scientist has done for him. As the Monster grabs Niemann with a snarl, the villagers arrive, and Niemann actually cries out to them for help before he passes out. The sequence of events that follows is the same as in the film, except that in this version, it is the Monster's, rather than Niemann's head, disappearing underneath the quicksand, that constitutes the final spectacle of the film.

Closing the Universal saga, *House of Dracula* received several favorable reviews despite its obvious attempt to capitalize on whatever remained of the box office-generating power of the Frankensteinian myth. The *Hollywood Reporter* predicted: "Box office expectancies should match, possibly even better, the hit grosses of . . . *House of Frankenstein*;"[115] *Variety* also extended its kudos, claiming that the film "upholds traditions of the company's past offerings in this field."[116] Naturally there were also dissenting voices, such as the *New York Daily News*, which decried the film as perhaps "an attempt to write a few debits in Universal's income tax blank . . . a cold-blooded experiment to determine audience saturation point."[117] Despite its possession of a more coherent script than its predecessor, *House of Dracula*, with its cost-cutting budget, is often seen as a swan song, "the last serious chapter of the once-great Frankenstein series [that] croaked an ugly and pervading death rattle."[118] Nevertheless the film does have its unforgettable highlights, such as Dracula's (John Carradine) attempted seduction of Miliza Morelle (Martha O'Driscoll).

Like some of the earlier Universal offerings, beginning with *Frankenstein Meets the Wolfman*, the Frankenstein Monster is but one of a coterie of freaks in this movie; however, the parthenogenetic myth is now coupled with not only the Christian myths of Resurrection and Transubstantiation, but also the Faustian myth. At Dr. Edelmann's home, Dracula unveils his identity to the incredulous doctor; the vampire claims to be seeking a cure for his "condition" and requests Edelmann's help. The conversation between Edelmann and the vampire hinges upon an analogy between the belief in partaking of Christ's blood through the transubstantiation of wine, and the myth of attaining physical, rather than spiritual, immortality by drinking people's blood. Interestingly, though Dracula could compel the doctor to do his bidding, he seems bent on wooing Edelmann. This is a pattern that recurs throughout the film. Later on, for example, the vampire repeatedly defers to Dr. Edelmann's interruptions of his attempted pursuit of Miliza; in addition, Dracula dares to hypnotize Nina only when Edelmann has fallen unconscious during the transfusion. The physician's volition seems essential to the vampire as he tempts Edelmann with the prospect of a new scientific breakthrough. Yet what is at stake is again a Faustian bargain: in exchange for an increase in scientific power, Dracula will demand the scientist's very soul.

In Edelmann's laboratory the doctor alerts one of his beautiful nurses, Nina, to Baron Latos's visit in the evening. Edelmann looks at a sample of Dracula's blood and requests Nina to make an "antitoxin" for it. Until now the camera has focused on Nina's face. Yet when she gets up from her desk, it suddenly steps back from her, revealing that she is a hunchback. Edelmann's relationship to Nina is complex. It seems to be a lighter version of Henry Frankenstein's relationship with Fritz. Edelmann speaks the language of father, superior, and potential lover; Nina's devotion to Edelmann also runs the gamut of daughterly affection, worshipful awe, and the stirrings of erotic love. Nina combines the two shadows, the monstrous and the feminine-as-monstrous (because she has beauty, intelligence, and the conviction to use them—though without the manipulativeness characteristic of, for example, Justine in Hammer's *Curse of Frankenstein*). This renders her a potentially disruptive agent in the unfolding of the patriarchal narrative, and, like Ilonka, she is fated to be ruthlessly destroyed.

Evening rolls in, and Baron Latos reports for his appointment. He comes across Miliza Morelle, the other equally beautiful nurse whose body and face are unmarred by any physical defect. It appears the two have met earlier, and the baron remarks amorously, "You left Schvonheim just as we were becoming acquainted." The young woman replies that she could not possibly pass up the opportunity of becoming Dr. Edelmann's assistant. The conversation hints at the (latent) rivalry between the baron and the doctor; Miliza is being given the choice of following two apparent saviors who both pursue the promise of eternal life. Yet Miliza's character does not seem as vibrant as Nina's. Unlike Nina, who possesses initiative and even dares to oppose Dr. Edelmann (like the earlier Rita), Miliza, for the most part, is passive and can only beseech Dr. Edelmann for help in moments of crisis (like the transformed Rita). Whereas Miliza remains safely within the realm of the feminine shadow, Nina ricochets in between the realms of the feminine-as-monstrous (like Ilonka) and the female monster (like the unnamed Bride).

The doctor arrives at a diagnosis: Dracula's blood has a peculiar parasite he has never before seen. He hypothesizes that if a pure culture of that parasite were introduced into the vampire's blood, these parasites would attack their parent cells and eventually destroy themselves as well, thus getting rid of the baron's "problem" (as the doctor phrases it delicately). Hints of the power struggle between the two men again emerge as Edelmann sternly tells the vampire that his treatments will occur on a strictly regulated schedule, whose dates and times will be determined/dictated by the doctor. It seems clear that the procedure has more than a literal dimension. It is through the power of "good" science, symbolized in Edelmann's eminent blood, that the vampire's monstrosity is meant to be purged. The exchange of blood between both men is not devoid of erotic tinges, and, once again, Edelmann also emerges as a Christlike figure who sacrifices his body and blood to save others. Yet this film, more so than the other Universal offerings, unveils the dark side of the myth of technology as progressive and salvific. Ultimately Edelmann not only fails to cure the vampire, but also proves incapable of saving himself when his blood becomes contaminated with the vampire's own.

Edelmann and Miliza respond to a police call for help at the headquarters. Just as Edelmann attempts soothingly to convince Talbot that lycanthropy is simply a "belief that exists only in your mind," a shaft of moonlight falls upon Talbot. In front of the terrified and fascinated doctor, inspector, and nurse, he transmogrifies into the Wolf Man. The beast, now seething with murderous urges, savagely attacks the bars of the cell, and even attempts to claw at the men, who step back. Miliza appears rigid with fear, though her look communicates compassion as well. With his strength finally spent, the Wolf Man grovels on the floor and loses consciousness. The gendered dynamics of the gaze are again significant to behold. Although Miliza also shares the fascination and horror with which the men view Larry's transformation, she is capable of something they are not: compassionate identification. Although she is physically further away from Talbot than the doctor and the inspector, who view Talbot's transformation as keepers of the law (natural and political), she is spiritually and emotionally closer to him than they are. Part of the attraction seems to be that Talbot is a curious combination of the monstrously powerful and tormentedly vulnerable—a figure both unnaturally masculinized and feminized. Like Ilonka she gazes with desire upon Talbot; unlike Ilonka her gaze remains safely within the realm of the domesticated shadow.

When Larry finds out that the corrective surgery to cure his condition is not immediately possible because of the need to germinate a certain spore crucial to enabling the surgery, Larry jumps off a cliff into the sea. Edelmann conjectures that because there are many caves at the bottom of the cliff, it is still possible that Talbot's body would wash up unharmed in one of these, and he could still be saved. Inside the cave the Wolf Man attacks Edelmann; just as Edelmann is on the verge of passing out from the pressure of the Wolf Man's grip on his throat, the moon sinks from view, and the Wolf Man again transforms back into Larry. The conversation between

Larry and Edelmann thematically matches that of the prodigal son being welcomed back by his forgiving and benevolent father.

Larry: I might have killed you. Why did you follow me here?

Edelmann: To bring you back, my boy. . . . You wanted to die but instead you will live because God in his divine workings has led you to the very thing which makes help possible. Look about you—the temperature and humidity down here are ideal for growing the spore-producing plant. Before the next full moon we should have more than enough to help you.

The film repeatedly stresses that Edelmann basks in his role as life-giver and savior. However, when he encounters Dr. Niemann's skeleton on top of the unconscious Monster's body, he displays Niemann's fanatical awe over Frankenstein's creation. The film once again shows that underneath the most benevolent patriarchal mask may seethe murderous and power-hungry urges. Scientific prowess is not necessarily indicative of progress. Unlike claims of vampirism and lycanthropy, the myth of the Frankenstein Monster is one he readily accepts because it is framed by the language of (masculine) science. Both Talbot and Edelmann are startled to find that the Monster is still alive when its fingers twitch feebly. Kenton resists the temptation of alluding back to Whale's signature close-up shot of the creature's moving fingers; instead he uses the camera to frame the three figures, keeping the focus on the triadic relationship binding Edelmann to the Monster and the Wolf Man. Edelmann crouches down and tests the Monster's motor reflexes while Talbot disappears. The rivalry between the two monstrous sons begins anew, and it is clear that this is going to be one of the central conflicts of the narrative. Nina and Talbot watch, horrified, as Edelmann attempts to reanimate the creature. It is noteworthy that the essence of the Frankensteinian Monster no longer lies in the creature's brain (as in the earlier films, beginning with Whale's *Frankenstein*), which no longer seems capable of any thinking, but in his heart—not as an organ of emotion, but of death-defying force and power. Even the "feminized" and human aspect of the creature, its heart, becomes transmuted into masculine and mechanical terms.

Nina grabs Edelmann's arm to stop him from pulling a lever, but he resists. Talbot steps in, and reasons that "this thing" destroyed Frankenstein and has brought death to everyone who has tried to follow in his footsteps. Edelmann plays the part of the enlightened and compassionate savior again, reasoning that the Monster cannot be held responsible for what it is. Talbot's response is one of projection; he paints the portrait of the Monster in terms of the image of the beast lurking in himself that he wants to destroy: "It's a thing of violence—to whom death would be—a merciful release." Yet it is Nina who persistently spars with the doctor, using intellectual arguments and her small, deformed frame to obstruct his intentions. It is intriguing that Nina unequivocally shares Talbot's thoroughgoing condemnation of the Monster as evil. Her own physical deformity does not make her sympathetic to the Monster's plight; it renders her more unforgiving.

Night falls, and Miliza, elegantly dressed, sits at the piano, playing "Moonlight Sonata" as the baron makes his appearance. She flirtatiously asks the vampire if he likes the piece; he replies affirmatively, then reminds her that that very piece was playing at the concert at which they had earlier met. She recalls that and seems puzzled by the resurgence of memory. Suddenly, her fingers, seemingly of their own volition, fly across the piano keyboard, composing an unfamiliar, dissonant melody, wild and demonic. "I've never heard this music before—yet I'm playing it!" she exclaims, unsettled.

The vampire's hypnotic gaze is fully upon her. "You're creating it . . . for me."

The ensuing conversation is again the language of erotic victimization, rendering Miliza the impaled object of the vampire's gaze, tempted by the promise of immortality through sensual death. One intriguing facet of this seduction is that Dracula combines the elemental power of music—an art often associated with feminine turbulence and passion (as opposed to the masculinized art of clean lines and controlled contours, sculpture)—with the most masculinized (least sensually rooted) faculty of vision. Yet music is only a means through which images become visible to the victim. The music Miliza appears to create is not of her own volition; its function is to conjure the images that will capture Dracula's intended erotic prey.

Just as Miliza's doom seems sealed, she reaches for a small crucifix, hung on a chain around her neck. She begins to snap out of the trance, and the music returns to "Moonlight Sonata." When Dracula commands her to continue playing, she counters by attempting to follow the doctor's instructions to get a blood sample from the vampire. It is as if the memory of Edelmann's bidding serves partially to block Dracula's directives. The rivalry between the two (apparent) saviors over Miliza's soul again reveals itself. Dracula relentlessly focuses his hypnotic gaze on her, his voice seductively low: "My world is waiting for you. . . . Forsake the Cross so you can join me there." But Edelmann's entrance interrupts Dracula's attempted seduction; ultimately, Nina, Edelmann, and Talbot, through concerted effort, manage to save Miliza from the vampire. But Edelmann does not escape unscathed: the vampire manages to shoot some of his own blood into the doctor, while he has lain unconscious during a transfusion.

Later, Edelmann is transformed into his own *doppelgänger*, as the evil he thought he had destroyed resurrects itself in his own body. What follows next in the film is a phantasmagoria wildly unfolding in Edelmann's mind, framed by a whirling cloud pierced by electrical gadgets. The nightmare begins with Dracula moving toward him, pointing ominously. The gesture is ambiguous, and verges in between an accusation of betrayal, an acknow-ledgment of sameness, and a foretelling of the future. Then, Edelmann's face suddenly becomes transformed into his evil self; the two versions of the doctor argue over the inert body of the Monster, and it is the "good" doctor's face that disappears. The scene again dissolves to reveal the Mon-ster being dispatched by the cackling, evil Edelmann to attack innocent townspeople; the familiar Whale shot of Karloff's Monster pushing over a papal figure in a cemetery is also embedded in the montage. The scene again shifts to focus on the doctor's instruments, then on himself and Mil-iza operating on Nina, to culminate in the lovely nurse's descent upon some steps, proudly bearing her new body devoid of its hump. However, the evil Edelmann's clawlike hands hover above the camera ominously as the dream sequence ends. Nightmare and reality melt into an ominous whole. The evil Edelmann rushes off to his laboratory to animate Frankenstein's Monster. For a moment, the narrative potentially shows how the Ego and the Mon-strous shadow are linked, rather than oppositionally related. However, in-stead of effecting a rapprochement, Edelmann (now depicted as completely Monstrous) and the vampire have become one, combining scientific/me-chanical and hypnotic power in the effort to bring the parthenogenetic myth to its completion. Nina interrupts the evil Edelmann's experiment, who reverts back to the good Edelmann, à la Hyde to Dr. Jekyll, just in time to prevent harm to Nina.

After the operation, Nina leaves the task of comforting the embittered Larry to Miliza. Interestingly Miliza uses Dracula's words of seduction to soothe her anxious lover, and Larry's words unconsciously resonate with her own near brush with immortality-death under the spell of Dracula's hypnotic gaze. "Miliza: Try to see the night as something beautiful. Larry: (sounding bitter) Until the moon turns it into a thing of ugliness and hor-ror." Miliza finally momentarily prevails by reassuring Talbot that her "heart" tells her that his suffering will soon end. Miliza is obviously a very competent medical assistant, but ultimately, when Larry doubtfully asks her for her reasons in being so certain that he is cured, she falls back, not upon the (masculine) scientific mode of reasoning in which she has been rigorously trained, but upon an unabashedly feminine intuition. Miliza's role is that of supporting the central male characters; unlike Nina, she unquestioningly follows Edelmann's orders, and she is unable authorita-tively to use the language of (masculine) science in treating the patient whose vulnerability touches her.

Like a cat stalking its prey, Edelmann surprises Seigfried, his faithful gardener, and then fixes the vampire's hypnotic gaze upon his old friend with a sadistic leer before he kills him. The evil Edelmann runs from Seig-fried's body, but the police and villagers are hot on his trail. After eluding them for a considerable period, he runs through a cemetery, leaping ener-getically over headstones (again symbolically referring to his fusion with and overcoming of death as a supernatural creature), and then proceeds to climb the gate wall of his own estate when he finds the door locked. As Edelmann jumps from the top of the wall on to the roof of a small building, he slides off and loses consciousness momentarily. The transformation again begins. Larry, still sitting from his perch, watches curiously as the doctor rises slowly and painfully, realizing what has transpired.

After Edelmann, at Nina's prompting, exonerates Larry from the suspicion of having murdered Seigfried, Talbot gently extracts a confession from his savior-father that his blood has been contaminated with the vampire's. Now, like Talbot, he, too, is consumed by "some nameless horror—a lust which changes me into the thing that killed Siegfried tonight." Edelmann requests Talbot's silence, not to preserve himself, but to give him time to operate on Nina. He assures Talbot that he will destroy himself once that is accomplished; using his paternal tone, he gazes deeply into Larry's eyes and exacts the promise that if he were to fail to kill himself, then Larry should do it for him. The scene reinforces the paternal-filial relationship binding both men, and again shows the radical exclusion of the women from critical spheres of decision making. Edelmann bequeaths his secret to Talbot, whom he knows will not oppose him, rather than Nina, who has consistently done so with quiet strength.

Larry is cured, but Edelmann reverts back to his evil self and sneaks off to his laboratory and succeeds in awakening the Monster. When the evil Edelmann promises to grant the Monster "the strength of a hundred men," a cry of protest bursts from Nina's lips, who has been silently watching. She reminds him of his earlier promise to her not to reawaken the Monster. The evil Edelmann, whose persona seems to merge with that of the vampire, now accuses Nina of spying on him. He fixes his hypnotic gaze upon her, and as she moves toward him in a daze, advances menacingly: "I don't like people who see what they're not supposed to see." This statement links this scene with the earlier attempted seduction scene, where it is Nina's spying that reveals the vampire's identity and intentions. Larry, Miliza, and the policemen hear Nina's bloodcurdling scream, and rush into the laboratory. Even under the evil Edelmann's hypnotic influence, Nina maintains enough independence to protest against the violence done to her.

Edelmann is shown grasping Nina by the throat; he thrusts her to the floor, and she rolls into a trap door like a discarded ragdoll. Miliza clings on to Larry's arm as the evil doctor leers at them. Larry picks up a gun dropped by one of the policemen and fires twice; Edelmann's face reveals a feeble smile as he slumps to the floor, acknowledging a debt to a Monstrous son he has converted into a manifestation of his former self, the Ego. As a mob bursts into the laboratory, Talbot warns them of the Frankensteinian Monster; they flee while he and Miliza escape. In a poor rendition of one of Whale's final images, in which the Monster is imperiled by burning crosslike structures, the Monster is impaled by a burning rafter as an inferno rages about him. Mank expresses dissatisfaction with one particular dimension of the film: "The one happy blessing of the film is its liberation of Chaney's Talbot from his curse of lycanthropy. This blessing is unsatisfyingly counterbalanced by the pathetic demises of Stevens' Edelmann and Jane Adams' Nina. Both have managed to make the audience care about them in the film, and it seems unfair to have Chaney escape clutching the lovely Miss O'Driscoll while both Stevens and Adams are ruthlessly destroyed."[119]

The doctor's death is necessary insofar as Edelmann's schizophrenic split reveals the dark face of technology; its promises of salvation and utopia are shown to be lies, and for that, he must be destroyed. Mank remarks on the particular viciousness of Nina's death: "It seems overly sadistic to have her strangled in the finale, her deformed body rolling over the laboratory floor and into a pit with a most unlady-like tumble."[120] Yet Nina's character concentrates the complex ambivalences of the parthenogenetic myth. She is a female Fritz who is at once devoted servant, groupie, daughter, mother, and (potential) lover. She seems the force that grounds the "good" Edelmann, yet in providing that moral guidance, she reifies patriarchal values through her unproblematic condemnation of the Monster as evil. As a beautiful hunchback, she combines the shadows of feminine-as-monstrous and female monster, and unveils the attraction-repulsion at the heart of these shadows. Like Miliza she is an object of erotic desire, yet her physical deformity both suppresses and magnifies this status. Unlike Miliza, despite her adoring stance, she is capable of resistance, and occasionally rises beyond the status of daughter to mother. The tensions in her character and form—as powerful and vulnerable, compliant and defiant, adoring and critical, beautiful and grotesque—are incapable of resolution within the patriarchal narrative. Her violent death appears to be the only way in which the parthenogenetic myth may harness its borders.

CLOSING REMARKS

The Universal film series definitively establishes the Frankensteinian myth as an enduring film narrative. However, its reworking of the face/s of the monstrous in relation to gender and technology moves from more complex revisionings, in which a tight tension holding the tragic and comic in fragile conjunction exists, such as in Whale's first two films, to more caricaturesque depictions, such as in Kenton's films, in which Frankenstein's Monster is no more than a ritualistically slaughtering and slaughtered automaton. Not only is the original creature robbed of its eloquence and intelligence; just as significantly, it is increasingly rendered even more invisible in a medium where visibility constitutes epistemological weight. The novel's frame-tale structure, after a hesitant and strategic use of it to get around censorship policing, is discarded in favor of an omniscient point of view that flattens the narrative and generates stock characters. Absent-present female characters in the book, such as Caroline, Elizabeth, and Justine, are either completely absent or thoroughly domesticated. Victor's and the Monster's ambiguous sexuality in the novel become unproblematically sexed as male. In other words the Universal series sets up the shift from the novel's fascination with the creature to the obsession with the mad scientist (rather than the haltingly Promethean medical student). Ultimately the Universal series sets into motion the increasing repression of the feminine shadow through techniques of excision and domestication, the increasing hyperbolization of the Monstrous shadow through progressive dehumanization and demonization, and the ruthless extermination of any conjunction between the feminine and Monstrous shadows. The creative agonism between the competing and imbricated myths of Baubo's *anasuromai* and Dionysus's thigh birth are replaced by a hysterically insistent parthenogenetic myth in which scientific gadgets take the place of Zeus's thigh as the site of reproductive and erotic power. These are thematic strains the Hammer series picks up and capitalizes upon.

NOTES

1. Janice Hocker Rushing, "Evolution of 'The New Frontier' in *Alien* and *Aliens*: Patriarchal Co-Optation of the Feminine Archetype," *Quarterly Journal of Speech* 75 (1989): 1–24.

2. Ibid., 5.

3. Ibid., 6.

4. Gregory Mank, "Production Background," *Frankenstein*, ed. Philip J. Riley, Universal Filmscripts Series, Classic Horror Films, Vol. 1 (Absecon N.J.: MagicImage Filmbooks, 1989), 22–23.

5. Dennis Fischer, *Horror Film Directors, 1931–1990* (Jefferson, N.C.: McFarland and Company, 1991), 714–715.

6. See Mary Shelley, *Frankenstein* (New York: Bantam Books, 1991), 127.

7. Janice Hocker Rushing and Thomas Frentz, *Projecting the Shadow: The Cyborg Hero in American Film* (Chicago: University of Chicago Press, 1995), 176–177.

8. William Veeder, *Mary Shelley and Frankenstein: The Fate of Androgyny* (Chicago: University of Chicago Press, 1986), 82.

9. Mary Shelley's mother was Mary Wollestonecraft, an ardent feminist and writer of *A Vindication of the Rights of Women*.

10. William Godwin was Mary Wollestonecraft's lover-turned-husband, and the father of Mary Shelley.

11. Veeder, 82–83.

12. See Shelley, 150.

13. Anne K. Mellor, "Possessing Nature: The Female in *Frankenstein*," in *Romanticism and Feminism*, ed. Anne K. Mellor (Bloomington: Indiana University Press, 1988), 224.

14. Fischer, 714.

15. Steven Earl Forry notes the complex doubling and rivalry of Henry and Victor in John Balderston's revision of Peggy Webling's play, from which the composite script of Whale's *Frankenstein* was derived. "Balderston's conclusion carries the doubling even further when after Henry Frankenstein's death Amelia [Elizabeth in the novel] seeks shelter in the arms of Victor Moritz, exclaiming 'don't leave me, don't ever leave me.' (Frankenstein in this version has after all stolen the heart of Amelia from Victor, to whom she was originally engaged.)" See Steven Earl Forry, *Hideous Progenies: Dramatizations of Frankenstein from Mary Shelley to the Present* (Philadelphia: University of Pennsylvania Press, 1990), 99.

16. Garrett Fort and Francis Edwards Faragoh, *Frankenstein*, Screenplay, Universal Pictures Corporation, August 12, 1931; *Frankenstein*, ed. Philip J. Riley, Universal Filmscripts Series, Classic Horror Films, Vol. 1 (Absecon N.J.: Magic-Image Filmbooks, 1989), 30.

17. Veeder, 125, 144.

18. Fort and Faragoh, 47.

19. Michael Weldon, Charles Beesley, Bob Martin, and Akira Fitton, *The Psychotronic Encyclopedia of Film* (New York: Ballantine Books, 1983), 256.

20. Fischer, 720.

21. Mank, 37.

22. Ibid., 40.

23. Jay Robert Nash and Stanley Ralph Ross, *The Motion Picture Guide: E-G, 1927–1983* (Chicago: Cinebooks, 1986), 928.

24. Fischer, 719.

25. Mank, 22–23.

26. Ibid., 22.

27. Fort and Faragoh, 71.

28. Weldon, Beesley, Martin, and Fitton, 255–256.

29. Fischer, 718; Nash and Ross, 928.

30. Fort and Faragoh, 1.

31. Ibid., 5.

32. Martin Tropp, *Mary Shelley's Monster* (Boston: Houghton Mifflin, 1976), 94.

33. Rushing and Frentz, *Projecting the Shadow*, 70.

34. Fort and Faragoh, 29.

35. Tropp, 89.

36. Ibid., 93.

37. Ibid., 90.

38. Donald Glut, *The Frankenstein Legend: A Tribute to Mary Shelley and Boris Karloff* (Metuchen, N.J.: Scarecrow Press, 1973), 121.

39. See, for example, "The Bride of Frankenstein," *The Variety Film Reviews 1934–1937*, Vol. 5, May 15, 1935.

40. Paul M. Jensen, *The Men Who Made the Monsters* (New York: Twayne, 1996), 43.

41. Ibid., 3.

42. Quoting Lanchester, Jensen remarks on a shift in Whale's personality as a result of this breakup and a growing bitterness. " 'I don't think he liked humanity very much,' she concluded, and this seemed particularly true of women." See Jensen, 7.

43. Glut, 123.

44. See Sir William Crookes, quoted in E.E. Fournier d'Albe, *The Life of Sir William Crookes* (London: Fisher Unwin, 1923), 365.

45. Emily W. Sunstein, *Mary Shelley: Romance and Reality* (Baltimore: Johns Hopkins University Press, 1991), 121.

46. Ibid., ix.

47. John Polidori, *The Diary of Dr. John William Poldori, Relating to Byron, Shelley, etc.*, ed. William Michael Rossetti (London: Elkin Matthews, 1911).

48. Shelley, x–xi.

49. Refer to Lucy Madox Rossetti, *Mrs. Shelley*, Eminent Women Series (London: W.H. Allen, 1890), 28.

50. See Stephen Behrend, "Mary Shelley, *Frankenstein*, and the Woman Writer's Fate," in *Romantic Women Writers: Voices and Countervoices*, ed. Paula R. Feldman and Theresa M. Kelley (Hanover and London: University Press of New England, 1995), 69–87.

51. For a detailed account of the various rhetorical battles waged over *Frankenstein*'s (im)morality, refer to Forry, 3–11.

52. As both Jensen (42–43) and Everson (45) point out, a historical anachronism plagues the transition from prologue to the main action. The prologue is set in the nineteenth century, and yet the story begins in our century. Whale gets around this difficulty a bit by framing it as a (futuristic) tale told by Mary Shelley, existing in an uncertain timeframe that naturalizes the elaborate laboratory equipment and treats the telephone as simply another "electrical device." See also William K. Everson, *Classics of the Horror Film* (New York: Citadel Press, 1995).

53. Jensen points out how the original script called for a rat "quivering in a crevice between the stones." Because the Hays Office objected to this on the grounds that the use of a rat "has in the past proved offensive," Whale simply improved the script by using the impassive owl. Jensen, 44.

54. Alberto Manguel, *Bride of Frankenstein* (London: British Film Institute, 1997), 22.

55. Jensen strengthens the connection between this figure of death whom Elizabeth foresees and Dr. Pretorius with the remark: "To Minnie, Pretorius declares that he has come 'on a secret matter of grave importance,' which the servant reports to her master as 'on a secret grave matter.' Aside from being an amusing pun, this phrase—coming when it does—further connects the intruder with death." Jenson, 45.

56. Tropp, 99.

57. Tropp locates the film historically and conjectures that Pretorius's obsession is fixed upon creating the perfect weapon, rather than the perfect human being, and symbolically aligns Pretorius's experiments with Nazi experiments in eugenics. Ibid., 99–103.

58. Jensen, 42.

59. Manguel, 30.

60. Jensen, 47.

61. Manguel, 34.

62. *New York Times Review*, May 11, 1935.

63. Jensen notes that the original script had set up very different imagery. Originally the Monster was supposed to encounter a huge figure of Christ crucified and

"sees it as a human being tortured as he was in the wood. He dashes himself against the figure, grappling with it. The figure is over-turned. He tries to rescue the figure from the cross." As if to reward his sympathy, the fall of the statue reveals an underground crypt, which saves him from the angry mob. However, because the Hays Office again objected to this scene, Whale substituted the papal figure, and reinterpreted the Monster's interaction with the statue as attacking it rather than identifying with it. Instead of being a haven, the underground crypt became reinterpreted as a chamber of death, where the Monster declares his love for the dead and hatred for the living. An irony emerges: "In its hypersensitivity, the Hays Office had converted a moment that was pro-Christ into one that is starkly anti-Church" (49). Yet the revision, serendipitous as it may have been in its inception, is very much in keeping with the lugubrious and darkly parodic tone of *The Bride of Frankenstein*.

64. See Glenn Erickson, "The Bride of Frankenstein," in *Magill's Survey of Cinema*, First Series, Vol. I, ed. Frank Magill (Englewood Cliffs, N.J.: Salem Press, 1980), 224.

65. Jensen, 51.

66. Erickson notes that the creation scene is steeped in "phallic and orgasmic overtones." Erickson, 224.

67. Manguel, 46.

68. William K. Everson, *Classics of the Horror Film* (New York: Citadel Press, 1995), 48.

69. *Variety*, May 15, 1935.

70. Glut, 128.

71. Jensen, 47–48.

72. Ibid., 48.

73. Manguel, 14–15.

74. Ibid., 18.

75. Glut, 131.

76. See "Bride of Frankenstein," *Variety Film Reviews 1934–1937*, May 15, 1935.

77. Manguel, 55–56.

78. Everson, 49.

79. *The Encyclopedia of Horror Movies*, ed. Phil Hardy, Tom Milne, and Paul Willemen (New York: Harper and Row, 1986), 71.

80. Peter Brooks, "What Is a Monster? (According to *Frankenstein*)," *Body Work: Objects of Desire in Modern Narrative* (Cambridge, Mass: Harvard University Press, 1993), 206.

81. Everson, 52.

82. W. Scott Darling, *Ghost of Frankenstein*, ed. Philip J. Riley, Classic Horror Films, Vol. 4, MagicImage Filmbooks (Atlantic City, Hollywood: Universal Filmscripts Series, 1990), 15.

83. Ibid., 21.

84. Everson, 52.

85. Darling, 24.

86. Ibid., 36.

87. Ibid., 46.

88. Ibid.

89. Ibid., 52.

90. Ibid., 68–69.

91. Arnold Mindell, *Dreambody: The Body's Role in Revealing the Self*, ed. Sisa Sternback-Scott and Becky Goodman (Santa Monica, Calif.: Sigo, 1982), 158.

92. James Hillman, "Abandoning the Child," *Loose Ends* (Spring 1985): 147.

93. Ibid., 105.

94. Ibid., 106.

95. Ibid.

96. Glut, 160.

97. Gregory William Mank, "Production Background," *Frankenstein Meets the Wolfman: The Original Shooting Script*, ed. Philip J. Riley, Universal Filmscripts Series, Classic Horror Films, Vol. 5 (Atlantic City, Hollywood: MagicImage Filmbooks, 1990), 17.

98. Ibid.

99. Ibid., 18.

100. Curt Siodmak, "Wolf Man Meets Frankenstein," *Frankenstein Meets the Wolfman: The Original Shooting Script*, ed. Philip J. Riley, Universal Filmscripts Series, Classic Horror Films, Vol. 5 (Atlantic City, Hollywood: MagicImage Filmbooks, 1990), 61.

101. Ibid., 64.

102. Mank, "Production Background," 23.

103. Siodmak, 101.

104. Ibid., 104.

105. Ibid., 117.

106. Because of Lugosi's health problems, the unbilled Eddie Parker substituted for him, particularly for the strenuous scenes in the climax of *Frankenstein Meets the Wolf Man*. Cf. Glut, 161.

107. Leslie Halliwell, *The Dead That Walk: Dracula, Frankenstein, the Mummy and Other Famous Monsters* (New York: Continuum, 1988), 162.

108. See Glut, 167.

109. Ibid., 7.

110. Ibid., 23.

111. Ibid., 24.

112. Ibid., 39.

113. Ibid., 40.

114. Ibid., 83.

115. "House of Dracula Review," *The Hollywood Reporter*, November 29, 1945.

116. "House of Dracula Review," *Variety*, November 29, 1945.

117. Dorothy Masters, "House of Dracula Review," December 22, 1945. University of California Film Archive file on "Frankenstein Meets the Wolfman."

118. Gregory William Mank, *It's Alive! The Classic Cinema Saga of Frankenstein* (San Diego and New York: A.S. Barnes, 1981), 145.

119. Mank, *It's Alive!*, 149.

120. Ibid.

CHAPTER 3

―――∞∞∞―――

The Hammer Series

Despite cult following and the undoubted brilliance of Karloff's Monster, for many it is Hammer's colour revival which has given the screen its definitive Frankenstein, even if his monsters change from film to film. The colour Frankenstein belongs as firmly to Peter Cushing as the first Universal Monster belongs to Karloff.

—Alan Frank, *The Movie Treasury: Horror Movies,*
Tales of Terror in the Cinema

REVEALING THE (UN)REAL

Hammer's eruption into the horror movie scene occurred as a result of Sir James Carreras's (the producer) desire to capitalize on the $3 million profit of *The Quartermass Experiment* (1955), which was released as *The Creeping Unknown* in the United States. He conceived of the idea of remaking the "classic" horror films of the thirties and forties, but this time in vivid and graphic color. Carreras's reading of popular tastes proved accurate. But even if audiences eagerly consumed their low-budget productions, critics at that time, for the most part, treated the Hammer movies with sneering derision, outraged disgust, or amused and ironic detachment. For David Pirie critical condemnation could not have been more unanimous: "One suggested a new certificate 'SO,' 'For Sadists Only,' another reviled Hammer, 'a sickening and nauseating way to make a living,' and C.A. Lejeune, in the *Observer*, put it 'among the half-dozen most repulsive films I have encountered.' "[1] Peter Hutchings returns to the same reviews and reads them very differently. "The virulently negative reviews were far outnumbered by reviews that were, on the whole, either indifferent to or amused

Still from *Frankenstein Created Woman* appears courtesy of the Academy of Motion Picture Arts and Sciences. 20th Century-Fox, 1967.

by the film. Of the twenty-three press notices available in the BFI archives, only five could conceivably be described as 'outraged.' "[2] Nevertheless, critics in general found the Hammer films gory, explicit, and excessive. Of Hammer's maiden "screamiere," *The Curse of Frankenstein, The Film Daily*, dated June 25, 1957, writes: "Filmed in WarnerColor by Jack Asher, the footage features a preponderance of blood and gore, including several individual scenes of severed eyes, hands, etc., that should send those with weak stomachs heading for the exit and provide nightmare material for the kiddies in the audience." Even Donald Glut, a contemporary authority on the historical and critical reception of monster and horror films, comments in a similar manner: "Unlike Universal's attempts to imply rather than show physical representations of horror (i.e., blood, isolated organs), Hammer dwelled on them in the most detailed close-ups—always shown in vivid, bloody color—along with a generous roster of well-endowed servant girls and barmaids who spilled out of their low-cut dresses."[3]

Although I agree that the sexuality merely hinted at in the Universal films becomes explicit in the Hammer series, I disagree with the notion that the Hammer films, particularly the early ones directed by Terence Fisher (who directed five out of the seven movies) indulged in gory excess. Particularly in *The Curse of Frankenstein*, Fisher keeps much of the invasive cutting into corpses below the line of sight, and keeps the camera focused on the expressions upon the characters' faces. The contrast between Victor Frankenstein's (Peter Cushing) impassivity and Paul Krempe's (Robert Urquhart) revulsion as the sound of the chain saw cutting through bone permeates the room is disquieting, even if the actual dismemberment is not shown. This is not to say that Fisher flinched from showing dismembered parts, as in scenes when Frankenstein goes about collecting "materials" for his experiments or the scenes showing the spurting forth of blood, such as when Krempe's bullet enters the creature's skull. But Fisher uses such scenes sparingly, and reserves them for moments of heightened cinematic and emotive impact.

Nevertheless, one distinctive attribute of the Hammer films is their attempt to stay within the realm of the real, even when their subject matter contains elements of the supernatural. Fisher was not attracted to the abstraction of German Expressionism, which had shaped the atmospheric aesthetic of the Universal series. Instead, he sought a down-to-earth quality. He was interested in engaging the audience in the emotional conflicts of the characters, and reversed the hierarchy of Universal's settings. Fisher substituted lush Victorian settings and less ambitious laboratories for Universal's Gothic castles and ruins, which served as backdrops for its magnificent displays of scientific power. "Gone are the forced perspectives and larger-than-life laboratories of the Universal films: instead, there are the glass spirals, tubes, retorts and umbilical electrical wiring of a Victorian laboratory."[4] Paul Jensen holds a similar view concerning Fisher's directorial prerogatives:

Fisher was equally intent on establishing the physical reality of the characters' world. Many of his films are set in a concretely realized Victorian milieu created by Hammer's masterful production designer, Bernard Robinson. Fisher described that period as a time "when superstitions still had all their power. The fantastic was an everyday affair," and so it existed as a facet of physical reality. In this light, Fisher's determination to show, as explicitly as possible, the staking of a vampire or Baron Frankenstein's surgical procedures becomes understandable.[5]

Hammer's "realism" and colored vividness have often been praised as the studio productions' principal cinematic virtues, as well as its most nauseating weakness. Yet as Hammer's most distinctive traits, these characteristics problematize the films' relationship to Mary Shelley's novel. Because of copyright restrictions, Milton Subotsky's original script, *Frankenstein*, had to be completely reworked; Jimmy Sangster was forced to build his own script from the novel, which had long been in the public domain. Yet many of the crucial characteristics of the novel, such as its problematization of narrative perspective and its fluctuations across the realms of the natural and the supernatural, the scientific and the alchemical, and the seen and unseen, end up flattened out or simplified in the films. By assuming either an omniscient/objective authorial voice, or a narrative framed purely by Victor Frankenstein's account, the Hammer films create an illusion of realism that camouflages its mythic dimensions. By appearing to literalize the myth of Frankenstein, the films appear to submerge their allegorical content, which intensifies, rather than dilutes, their mythic force. Ironically, precisely by attempting to break away from the Universal series, the Hammer films constitute a natural continuation. They continue the heightening of the parthenogenetic myth, the misogynistic repression/demonization of Baubo's *ana-suromai*, the splitting of the "feminized" and "monstrous" shadows from the Ego, and the ruthless destruction of the feminized-monstrous shadow in the unfolding of the Frankensteinian narrative.

REMAKING THE FACE OF FRANKENSTEIN

Production histories of the genesis of *Curse of Frankenstein* begin with Jimmy Sangster being charged with the task of producing a script, and a lot is made of the fact that the film was shot in color. Yet the original script, *Frankenstein*, was hastily put together by an American writer, Milton Subotsky, and was meant to be shot in black and white at the breakneck speed of three weeks.[6] Part of the reason for the total revamping of Subotsky's script is because *his* script bears an unmistakable kinship with the Frankensteinian narrative as crafted by Universal. When Universal threatened to sue, Sangster was hired to begin a script from scratch; one of his legalistic innovations was to use the term "creature" rather than "Monster." In addition, because the Monster makeup that Jack Pierce had designed was also copyrighted by Universal, Phil Leakey literally had to hastily throw together the creature's new look, resulting in a very different image. In this section I highlight some of the significant differences in the transformation from Subotsky's original conception of the Frankensteinian narrative to Fisher's interpretation of Sangster's script, as well as various exploitative attempts by Hammer both to establish a difference from, as well as a continuity with, the Universal series. The method I use is diachronic, weaving across Subotsky's original script and Fisher's direction, which in turn, is a revision of Sangster's rewriting of Subotsky's script. I juxtapose Subotsky's script and Fisher's film as they both chronologically unfold, occasionally intersecting, but often diverging. Such attention to genealogy will enable us to catch sight of often invisible sites of tension in the transformation from script to film.

Subotsky's script, like Whale's *Bride of Frankenstein*, begins with a depiction of the setting that produced *Frankenstein*. Subotsky's script is more historically accurate; he includes Mary's half-sister, Jane (Claire) Clairmont, and Byron's physician, Sir John Polidori, in the scene. However, whereas Whale's film maintains Mary's ambiguous status as the powerful author of the tale who identifies most closely with the narrative's most powerless creature, the female monster, Subotsky's script renders Mary Shelley as simply another character in the unfolding narrative. The stress is less on the gendered politics of authorship than on the tale's potential for cinematic exploitation. Mary's voice is silenced and an omniscient voice speaks, rendering Mary, herself, the object of the filmic gaze.

The differences in the shift from Universal films to Hammer productions are further accentuated by the flashbacks that provide the narrative threads of both the script and the film. The script shows Victor bidding his father, Henri, and Elizabeth good-bye. The script repeatedly emphasizes Elizabeth's emotional vulnerability, as it is she who kisses Victor "hard and hungrily" before she whispers "good-bye" softly against his cheek.[7] In turn, it emphasizes his relative emotional independence as he easily gets distracted and looks forward to the journey once it is underway.

Even more hyperbolically detached, the film's Victor Frankenstein's account of the beginning of the entire affair begins with a smug affirmation of his intelligence. "Where did it all begin? I suppose it was when I was a boy at school. I always had a brilliant intellect." From a dismissive tirade concerning his first tutor's stupidity, Frankenstein explains that he inherited his mother's fortune, which granted him independence. It is clear that the adolescent Victor (Melvyn Hayes) thinks little of social convention, is cut off from intimate relations, and is supercilious and haughty when he is dealing with in-laws. The film's Victor is extremely self-possessed, despite his tender age, and is neither gauche nor awkward, as he hires the amused Paul Krempe (Robert Urquhart) as his next tutor: "You were to be engaged as my tutor subject to the Baron's approval. You will take up the position. You will be paid as arranged."

The parthenogenetic myth achieves its clearest instantiation in the figure of Frankenstein, who is now an imperious, brilliant, and amoral force.

The script shows Victor's gradual and reluctant rebellion against his teachers; in contrast the film reveals Victor's brilliant overcoming of Krempe. It takes Victor only two years to learn all he can from Krempe; nevertheless, the two go on with their experiments together, ostensibly as equals. A time lag is implied, and the mature Victor Frankenstein (Peter Cushing) now stands alongside Krempe, with the barest hint of silver in his hair. It is now clear that Frankenstein is Krempe's superior in every sense. When Krempe reaches over to touch the puppy that they have been attempting to animate, Frankenstein slaps his intellectual father's hand away, pours liquid over the puppy, and then checks for a heartbeat with the stethoscope. The camera lingers over Frankenstein's face as his eyes widen slowly and he murmurs, with characteristic British understatement, a version of the line Colin Clive histrionically immortalized: "Paul, it's alive." Krempe now reaches for the dog, which begins to stir, and Frankenstein allows himself a moment of joyous agitation: "Paul! Paul! We've done it!" But the differences between the Universal and Hammer depictions of Frankenstein are deeper than superficial changes. Frankenstein, in many of the Hammer versions, is a character in control, whose ability to fluctuate across numerous realms—the legal and the criminal, the rich and the poor, the boyishly appealing and the paternally forbidding, the coldly passionate and the brilliantly obsessed—is constitutive of his charisma. One could argue that in the baron's figure, the mythic kinship of Dionysus and Apollo becomes forged into a charming, satanic whole. As R.D. Stock writes, "I should like us to recall . . . that Dionysus and Apollo are closely related. They shared the shrine at Delphi. . . . Apollo may be the aristocratic Olympian and Dionysus the cthonian. . . . But the Olympians themselves came of earth, and Dionysus was sired by the Olympian Zeus. . . . Thus they are inevitably antagonists; as often, perhaps, they are collaborators."[8] What results, through the Frankensteinian transmutation, is the emergence of a radically self-enclosed force obsessed with the dream of immortality through the appropriation of the power of (self) birthing.

Cushing, reflecting upon his portrayal of the baron, admitted that he patterned his character after the real-life anatomist Dr. Robert Knox of Burke and Hare infamy. Yet Cushing hyperbolizes many of the scientist's traits, rendering Frankenstein a simultaneously more attractive and repulsive character. As John McCarty writes, "In his quest to create life—to duel, as it were, with God—Cushing's baron seems instead much like Herman Melville's equally obsessed and pitiless hero, Captain Ahab, whose hatred of the white whale that has bested him sparks Ahab's long voyage of vengeance."[9]

The script, unlike the film, repeatedly draws attention to Victor's frailties. Victor attempts to steal the brain of the recently deceased Professor Waldman. But the young man who fiercely declares himself devoid of superstitious fear is tense as he digs up the body and harvests the brain; his efforts prove futile when, startled by the sound of a church clock tower striking midnight, he drops the velvet bag containing the brain, sending shards of glass through it. Later, Krempe welcomes Victor back to the university but makes the mistake of calling Victor's experiments "ridiculous." Again the centrality of the rivalry between intellectual father and son is emphasized. Victor proudly declares that Krempe will witness the success of his experiments very soon. Another brain harvesting sequence follows. But, in a section that mimes the Universal scripts, the brain Frankenstein obtains belongs to a man who had been confined to a state asylum for the insane.

In contrast the interaction between Krempe and Frankenstein is extremely different in the film. Fisher's treatment of the creation scenes veers radically away from Whale's handling of it, both formally and thematically. In Whale's *Frankenstein*, Fritz obeys Frankenstein's orders and cuts down the body from the gibbet. In Fisher's *Curse of Frankenstein*, Victor himself cuts down the body while Krempe prevents the horses from bucking as the corpse drops into the wagon. Whale emphasizes the act of scavenging for parts; Fisher is more concerned with the construction of the creature. Although Fisher barely reveals the deformities of the corpse, and keeps the surgical operations below the camera's line of sight, Fisher consistently maintains a realistic approach, emphasizing the physical messiness and emotional dislocation in which Frankenstein indulges in order to satisfy his cold passions. When Frankenstein finds out that the eyes of the corpse have been eaten away by birds, he dispassionately takes a scalpel, cuts off the head, and disposes of it in a vat of acid. Unlike the script's Victor, he feels neither the need to give his actions verbal justification, nor to hide his actions from his mentor-turned-student; every move he makes is calculated, cool, and elegantly confident. He is certain that he will spawn the perfect being, who will possess his erudition, as well as the aesthetic creativity he does not. The parthenogenetic myth, with its hubristic desire to generate a son who is simply an idealized extension of the father, reifies itself. There are indications that in the original film version, Fisher's camera does not shy away from showing the severed head that Frankenstein proudly displays like a trophy as he walks over to the acid bath. Instead, probably mainly due to the concerns of the board of censors, current prints simply alternate between Krempe's revulsed expression[10] and Frankenstein's impassive face as he carries the covered head to its fluid grave. In decapitating the corpse, Frankenstein reduces the male body to the level of physical materiality, a feminized position; the brain, the anatomical part that will restore the creature's masculinity, is to be reserved for last.

When Krempe begins to resist his charm, Frankenstein feminizes/disowns his adopted/surrogate father by refusing to treat him as an equal. Victor refuses to reveal the reason behind his sudden departure, and charges Krempe with the less than masculine task of being a laboratory nanny, seeing to the well-being of the monstrous son they are gestating/resurrecting: "Oh, and Paul, better not touch our friend here while I'm gone. Let him rest in peace while he can."

In the script, at this time, the usual attempt at animation occurs, but Victor is far from his egocentric and self-assured filmic counterpart. The creature is animated by accident, rather than as a result of his efforts. He is hysterical when Krempe pays him a visit and faints, like a stereotypically overwrought woman, into Krempe's arms.

In contrast the film moves into a series of subplots that further defer the awakening of the creature and emphasize Frankenstein's unassailable and irresistible masculinity. Again the Frankensteinian mythic themes resound: Victor forms a close kinship with Paul, while he alienates, or at least keeps at a safe distance, the women in his life. It is significant that when Elizabeth unexpectedly appears, she and Justine are wearing the same colors—a combination of black and white. Although Elizabeth wears a fashionable travel outfit, she and Justine wear clothes that are similar in color composition (shades of black and white), slating their roles to be mirror-imaging ones. She, too, is slated to be Victor's servant. The cinematic Elizabeth is conscious of her status as chattel for economic transaction; the most disturbing thing is that she romanticizes this condition, and sees subjection to Victor as a noble rather than demeaning situation. What is equally striking is that the filmic narrative supports Elizabeth's delusion; her tragic nobility and chaste domesticity are part of her charm, and the narrative frames this perspective without ironic distance. Once again the repression-domestication of the feminine shadow is the movement that parallels the hyperbolization of the parthenogenetic myth. What is frightening is that the film aestheticizes the repression of the feminine shadow as beautiful, and the displacement from feminine bodily reproduction to masculine technological production as inevitable.

In the film, the scene shifts abruptly to reveal Victor and Justine kissing passionately in a dark hallway. Justine admits that she is jealous of Elizabeth, and is fearful that the other woman is Victor's mistress. Victor glibly replies that Elizabeth is meant to be Justine's mistress, not his (thus being truthful in a twisted way since he intends to make Elizabeth his wife, and not his mistress). The camera, which had earlier used a shot-reverse shot sequence, equalizing their perspectives, lingers on an angle that privileges Victor over Justine, and shows her with her back vulnerably exposed to the camera's merciless gaze. Justine is yet another instantiation of the feminine-as-monstrous. In her body the scandal of the expression of female erotic desire is imprinted; this body is exposed, glorified, and visually besieged very early in the film.

Jensen remarks on the complexities of victimhood and victimization in the interaction between these two characters, and shows how the narrative is already set up implicitly to show how Justine's terrible fate is one that she has created and therefore deserves. "The affair itself is quite consistent with Frankenstein's character; he is no Lothario of the laboratory, but he is a man and Justine satisfies his physical needs with fewer complications than someone from his own class. He uses her, but no more than she *tries* [italics mine] to use him. A social climber, she has her calculating eye on marriage."[11]

In contrast, when the scene shifts to reveal Victor about to leave the house, his interaction with Elizabeth is instructive. When he inquires concerning her unhappiness, she replies that she would "like [his] assistance" with settling household bills. He immediately reverses the hierarchy of power and laughingly conjectures that soon Elizabeth will be asking to "help" him with his experiments. Elizabeth's eyes shine fervently as she replies that that is her dearest wish. Victor, like his novelistic counterpart, touches her chin—a gesture curiously paternal—and treats her as one would a favorite pet or daughter. Unlike the novel, however, Elizabeth, by virtue of staying safely within the realm of the feminized shadow, survives. Perhaps the fact that she remains not only chaste, but also devoid of any hint of motherhood, and thus the unruly powers of Baubo, assures her salvation.

As the film narrative continues, the camera stays interestingly below the level of faces as Victor goes through the motions of bribing a worker at a charnel house for a pair of eyes. It is as if the camera participates in the shameful, furtive nature of the exercise, and refuses to reveal faces. The contrast between its subtlety and the explicitness of the next scene is effective as the camera focuses closely on Frankenstein's eye as he peers through a magnifying glass at the specimens he has just acquired. We become jarringly aware of the camera as an eye that itself peers with the same clinical efficiency as Frankenstein does at his harvested eyes.

The dynamics of the camera are equally instructive when Victor and Elizabeth entertain the distinguished genius, Professor Bernstein (Paul Hardtmuth). Interestingly Victor and Elizabeth do not sit together; rather the professor and Victor sit beside each other on the couch, visually marking who is Victor's momentary victim-object of desire. In addition such an arrangement allows the camera to frame the two men together, emphasizing both their intellectual kinship, as well as their personal differences. In the shot–reverse shot sequences in which Frankenstein and Bernstein discuss the ethics of scientific experimentation, Victor is visibly shown as smug and disbelieving while the professor speaks with quiet but earnest conviction. Elizabeth uses the occasion charmingly to voice her complaints concerning Victor's devotion to his work, and Bernstein takes her side. Victor's remarks are not only quintessentially misogynistic, but they again underline the rivalry between erotic attachment to Elizabeth and erotic attachment to his work. "Women, Professor, you see? How cleverly they twist our words to suit their own ends. She'll only be happy if I give up my work entirely." On that note he kisses her hand with polished gallantry—the only time he shows her affection of that sort.

Victor sets up the professor's murder as an accident and offers the family vault as the professor's final resting place. Frankenstein arrives furtively to harvest the professor's brain. Paul attempts to wrest the brain away from Victor, and in the ensuing struggle, the brain is smashed against a wall, sending glass shards through it. This continues the filmic mytheme of the damaged/"criminal" brain which the Universal series started. Victor blackmails Paul into collaborating with him by threatening to "introduce Elizabeth to the world of science." Paul's erotic and paternal interests in Elizabeth are established early in the film; he repeatedly refers to her youth and her (female) incapacity to comprehend the nature of their experiments as reason to shield her. However, it turns out that Paul's assistance (and even Victor's efforts) are unnecessary. As in the Subotsky script, in their absence a stray lightning bolt sets the equipment spinning, and when Victor hears glass breaking, he rushes into the laboratory alone. He finds a bandaged figure standing, which then whips away the strips covering its face. This is the first time the camera reveals what the being looks like, and it is far from both Karloff's interpretation of it, as well as from the novel's depiction.

Critical reception concerning Hammer's visual interpretation of the Creature seem unanimous in their denouncement. The *Los Angeles Times*, dated July 18, 1957, scathingly remarks: "Instead of that hulking, stone-faced brute (which on occasion could make even film critics catch their jaded breaths) we have only a scarecrow."[12] Archer Winsten sardonically writes:

This monster, to come right out with it, is too darn vulnerable to be much of a threat. If one small pistol shot in his eye can lay him low, who's going to shiver at the prospect of meeting him? When you add to this mortal frailty the monster's slowness afoot, his poor eyesight, his bad circulation . . . and a balance about as good as that of a one-year-old child, it shouldn't require an athlete to best him.[13]

Indeed, the creature's (Christopher Lee) appearance violates every expectation that had been associated with Karloff's Monster. Karloff's Monster was a hulking embodiment of power; Lee's creature is gaunt and frail. The principal impetus for the change in the image of the Monster was legalistically based. Universal, fearful of declining profits from its monster releases, threatened a lawsuit if the creature's makeup resembled the Monster's in any way. To top things off, Phil Leakey, the makeup artist, had very little time in which to reconceive the creature's appearance. He remarked, "We really needed months—or at least weeks—to experiment with different materials and try different approaches."[14] Instead he was given the tight leash of twenty-four hours, resulting in the idea that "we would just try sticking lumps of flesh on a skeleton or skull and stitch it all up."[15] Marrero details how "Leakey applied wax, rubber, wool cotton, several repugnant coloration aides, and other materials directly on Lee's face."[16] The result was a grotesque collection of peeling tissue lashed by vivid yellows, greens, and reds, topped by a luxuriant mop of black hair styled in a Beatle cut. David Pirie argues that *Curse*'s depiction of the creature actually "conforms extremely closely to Mary Shelley's description: " 'His yellow skin scarcely covered the work of muscles and arteries beneath. His hair was of a lustrous black and flowing. But these luxuriances only formed a more horrid contrast with his watery eyes, that seemed almost of the same colour as the dun white sockets in which they were set, his shrivelled complexion and straight black lips.' "[17] Faithful or not to the novel, Lee was repulsed by the makeup he was compelled to wear. He alternated between calling it the makeup of a circus clown[18] and "a walking road accident."[19] Both Fisher, the director, and Lee conceived of the creature as ill coordinated and childish. Thus the actor reasoned that "I had a damaged brain so therefore I walked slightly lopsided . . . , [that his] hands must have an independent life," and "movement must be spastic and unbalanced."[20] In this first of the Hammer series, the alienation of the monstrous shadow intensifies. Not only is he robbed of his eloquence and intelligence, even his physical prowess is taken away from him. He no longer partakes of the wild grace of nature; he is indeed simply a "creature created by man and forgotten by nature," as the Warner Brothers' advertisements proclaim him to be.

From the moment of his awakening, despite his physical frailty, Lee's creature is an insane, homicidal maniac—the most infernal expression of the demonized technological shadow. He wraps his large hands around Victor and is on the verge of strangling him to death when Paul arrives and attacks the creature by breaking a chair over its back.

In contrast the Subotsky script's creature is very much Shelley's fallen Adam, rendered dangerous by its hostile environment. When it hears faraway strains of music, it utters glad sounds and moves in the direction of music, where peasants are dancing and children are playing a game of hide and seek. Subotsky resurrects the Maria-Cloestine character in the figure of an attractive little girl who, while she is attempting to hide, slips and falls down a bank into the river. The creature wades into the river and rescues her; when the little girl awakens, she screams in fright. The creature, attempting to communicate like Karloff's Monster in *Bride*, after he has rescued the shepherdess from drowning, growls and shakes his head as if to say "No." Yet all this proves futile, and once again the creature is hunted and tortured before it flees.

Still in Subotsky's script, the scene shifts to reveal a remake of yet another scene from Whale's *Bride*: the encounter between the wounded creature and the blind man. Although the old man in this case makes no attempt to teach his mysterious guest his own language, this script underlines the kinship the old man shares in relation to the Monster, as an outcast from the realms of beauty and youth. He speaks of his granddaughter, for whom "everything must be new and perfect. She does not understand an old, blind man and avoids me." The blind man accidentally discovers the wound upon the creature's forehead and binds it; in gratitude the creature sinks to its knees and puts its head trustingly in the old man's lap. But the two lonely beings' happiness is not meant to last; the discovery of the creature leads to his accidental killing of the blind man's son-in-law and the creature's eventual capture. So far the miming of Whale's *Bride* is evident, minus the brilliantly disturbing parallels drawn between the persecuted creature and the suffering Christ.

Victor, safely ensconced within his room, watches, appalled, as the creature is brought into town. What follows next in the Subotsky script again imitates Whale's, with an unnamed woman acting the part of Minnie. Yet though she possesses Minnie's comedic relief and sharp tongue, all of Minnie's ambiguous mythic references are effaced; she is no longer a parodic Cassandra, nor a comic female Pontius Pilate. Thus when the first woman, who approximates Minnie with her taste for the hyperbolic, says, after looking at the creature, that she will surely bolt her door tonight, the second woman, replies: "Humph! And what would anyone want with you!" The pseudo-Minnie then walks away from the second woman with an exaggerated show of hurt pride.

In contrast, in the released film, the creature's innocence has long been lost; it has never known naïveté because it has a damaged brain from the start. The movie resumes with a shot that pans a forest, resplendent with the colors of autumn. The creature shuffles into the clearing where a blind old man is sitting, awaiting his grandson's return. The blind man recognizes an alien presence and asks who it is as he gropes for the creature's face. The creature, which suddenly seems to realize the vulnerability of the old man, breaks the old man's cane viciously, and lurches toward his terrified victim. This creature is probably one of the loneliest and most subhuman of the beings spawned by the filmic interpretation of the Frankenstein myth. The momentary communion enabled by the trustfulness of De Lacey in the novel, the blind old hermit in Whale's *Bride*, and the numerous Maria and Cloestine figures in various Universal films is savagely rent. The alienation and demonization of the overdeveloped or Monstrous shadow is at a peak, just as the hyperbolization of the parthenogenetic myth is at its extreme.

Various modifications from script to film are important. Not only does the film sunder the relationship between Victor and Clerval (Krempe's character, modified into a mentor-collaborator, rather than inspirational friend), but like Whale's *Frankenstein*, it also reduces their relationship to a conventional heterosexual rivalry over Elizabeth's love. But the film exaggerates Victor's hubris and his unremitting quest for appropriating the powers of God, with their control over life and death. Victor aspires to becoming more than just a scientific Prometheus; he aims to become Zeus himself, a self-generating source. As McCarty writes, "[Victor's] single-minded purpose is not just to steal the secrets of the gods, but to *become* God by creating a man in his own image."[21]

In contrast, in the Subotsky script, events have taken a different turn. As Victor lies asleep on his bed, a shadow comes progressively closer till Victor awakens with a start. The script in effect feminizes Victor by placing him in the position of the vulnerable sleeper in Fuseli's *Nightmare*. Yet the shadow turns out not to be of the creature, but of his father, who gently urges Victor to come home and to marry the long-suffering Elizabeth. The creature's pursuit is initially implied through its shadow, then shown metonymically by its feet; then it is visualized as moving in the same direction as the coach. The visualization of the creature's pursuit is significant because the segments that precede the appearance of the whole monster in effect distill the essence of the creature, which has by now become no more than an ominous shadow and unstoppable automaton.

Later Victor gives in to the creature's demand of creating a mate under the threat of harm to everyone he loves. When the creature arrives to ensure that Victor keeps his promise, a series of intended shot-reverse shots (because this is the script and not the released film) magnifies the battle of wills, and Victor rebels, vowing not to keep his promise. He viciously and repeatedly slashes the female monster's inert form (which is not described at all) as he cries, "This is how I break our unholy bargain! Forever!"[22] This scene continues the following trends: (1) it renders visibly invisible the female monster's form; (2) it visualizes the misogyny that contours Victor's destruction of the female creature; and (3) most significantly, it replaces Victor's fevered and panicked rationalization of his decision to rip open the monster's intended bride—an act once again resembling a violent rape—with a heroic rebellion against blackmail. Furthermore, whereas the novel's focus is on showing how Victor envisages the threatening specter of a woman physically stronger than a man and in control of the power of reproduction, the script replaces that with a conflict based on a patriarchal bargain struck between a father and his monstrous son. Once again, similar to Whale's *Bride of Frankenstein*, the female monster is ruthlessly destroyed while the male creature's motivations for revenge become humanized and understandable.

In comparison the released film returns to the issues of misogyny and broken promises, but does so very differently. In this version Justine in effect occupies the position of the feminine-as-monstrous—voluptuous, unapologetically passionate, unabashed about using her sexual power, ambitious despite her lowly station. As the film continues, Justine interrogates Victor on whether he intends to marry Elizabeth. He laughs as he acknowledges that he had never intended to keep the promise he had made to marry her, and she threatens to kill him as she lunges at him.

The balance of power shifts, and even Justine's tenuous independence is undercut. Justine loses her ferocity and cries out like a little girl that he is hurting her as he parries her physical assault of him. As she leans against a door, looking trapped, she cries out hysterically that he has to marry her because she is carrying his child. Victor comes closer to her and in effect calls Justine a whore by claiming that if she chose to claim any other man in the village as the father of the child, she would probably be accurate. Justine, desperate, now loads threat after threat: She threatens Victor with revealing his paternity of the child she bears in her womb to Elizabeth. More alarmingly, she threatens to reveal the nature of his experiments to both Elizabeth and the authorities. So far, Justine has flourished because indulgence in her powers of erotic pleasure has been safely demarcated from her potential capacity for reproduction; once that line has been violated, coupled with the threat of undermining Victor's illicit parthenogenetic activities, her fate is sealed. Unlike the male creature in the script though, the film does little to enable sympathy for Justine. From the start she is established as a social climber and ambitious whore—an uppity maid who deserves to be thrust into her proper station.

The scene shifts to reveal a darkened stairway. Justine, like Ilonka, has her hair down (again signifying the unrestrained and passionate female sexuality associated with Baubo). She tiptoes about in a low-cut white nightdress that again, like Elsa Lanchester's bride, resembles something in between a bridal gown and shroud—thus associating eroticism with death in this instantiation of the feminine-as-monstrous. She roves about curiously in Victor's laboratory, and the camera shares her gaze, implying her active status as the subject of the filmic gaze at this point. Then she enters an inner door and plays with mice, with her back turned to the camera. She does not yet know that like the experimental mice, she has just stepped into a cage, and a deadly experiment is about to commence. The camera suddenly veers back, now revealing a hand in shadow behind her. Victor, however, locks the door shut and puts his ear to the door, as if to witness, through sound, Justine's violation and murder. The creature's shadow, followed by its hand, is shown close to the camera as it zooms in for a tight close-up on Justine's terrified face. She screams. Victor, as he listens, has a shadow covering his face as well, as if he himself were imperiled. Yet when he hears her scream, he closes his eyes, and his relieved face is fully lit. The danger that threatened him came from Justine, and now that she is safely disposed of by the creature that is simply executing his own desires, he can again breathe more easily. Once again the audience is voyeuristically and vicariously implicated in this event. Much as the murders of the young boy and his grandfather are set in an autumnal wood where the visual composition maximizes the effect of green and gold, Justine's murder, though it occurs in a dark laboratory, is aestheticized by making her appear as both virgin and whore, victim and would-be victimizer, sacrificial victim and punished transgressor in her revealing white dress and alluringly released hair.

Fisher seems to share Whale's quirky dark humor because without warning, he cuts from this grim murder to a scene of total domesticity. At a sunlit breakfast table, Victor sits with his intended wife, Elizabeth. As Frank summarizes the effect of that juxtaposition, "Frankenstein finishes buttering a piece of toast and asks politely 'Pass the marmalade!' The deliberate incongruity of this scene and the horror of the girl's death before it sets the audience laughing."[23] It also diffuses the audience's collaborative guilt established through the earlier scene, and draws the audience closer to Victor's bipolarities as he glides easily from elegant Victorian drawing rooms to disreputable charnel houses and a laboratory that houses body parts, and back.

In contrast the treatment of the relationship between Victor and Elizabeth is very different in Subotsky's script. Similar to Shelley's novel, both Victor and Elizabeth are distracted and fearful as guests congratulate them. Unlike Shelley's novel, the script emphasizes their passionate love for each other as they kiss hungrily, away from the prying eyes of guests. Unlike the film, therefore, the script grants the relationship binding Elizabeth and Victor together a more genuine, full-blooded dimension. In so doing, however, it lessens the complexity of the parthenogenetic father-son tie to become one of simple rivalry.

The film, in contrast, continues with Paul's late arrival at the abandoned wedding feast. He has come to toast the new couple, but arrives only to find Victor eager to demonstrate his experimental progress. In a remake of Whale's *Frankenstein*, Victor commands the shambling and jerky creature to approach them, then once it has gone the length of its chain, to sit down. Krempe is scathing as he remarks that "this animal" is far from the creature of superior intellect and perfect physical being Victor had envisaged. Victor again uses his trump card: He points out that the creature's damaged brain is Krempe's handiwork. Again, the film makes it clear that despite the romantic rivalry between Paul and Victor over Elizabeth, the pivotal relationship here is between both men. Despite the bitter break between Paul and Victor, it is to his former tutor, and not to his faithful wife, that Victor immediately reveals his most recent experiments. Victor still appears to be attempting to win back Paul's admiration and devotion, and when it is clear that he cannot regain that, he appears viciously bent on proving his intellectual superiority over Krempe.

The final scenes in the film show how Elizabeth, curious about the sounds emanating from the roof, carries a lamp to the roof and is attacked by the creature. Frankenstein fires his gun, accidentally shooting Elizabeth, who faints and is dropped precariously on to the edge of the roof by the creature who has also been shot by Victor. Victor attempts to command the creature to get back, but when that fails, he grabs the lamp Elizabeth had set down and flings it at the creature. The monstrous being ignites and lets out an infernal howl as it topples into the acid bath as the film fades back into the prison cell where Victor remarks with regret and pride: "My life's work destroyed. Destroyed in a moment. And by the same hand that gave it life." The film's Victor acknowledges the dark eroticism and drive to domination at the heart of the parthenogenetic myth, but it exaggerates it, effectively re-creating the face of the Monstrous. It is Victor Frankenstein who is now the Monster, not the nameless creature; as such Victor now becomes the demonized Other in the narrative—the scapegoat upon whom the audience may dump all the traits of the technologized shadow and deny, rather than acknowledge, as a part of themselves.

Victor's frantic and pitiful tone in the final scenes of the Subotsky script is maintained in Fisher's film, despite the obvious incongruity between the later Victor's groveling and his earlier imperturbable imperiousness. The priest is silent despite Victor's urgent pleas to believe his story (which ironically still indicts him of the murder of Justine). Victor is beside himself with joy when Krempe comes to visit him. Affectionately and desperately addressing Krempe by his first name and calling him "my dear friend," Victor attempts to extract corroborative evidence concerning the reality of this creature, and its guilt in the murder of Justine. But Paul is now the one aloof, and it is clear that he now possesses Elizabeth's loyalty. As Frankenstein is led through the corridor, the guillotine's descending thud is heard in the distance.

One of the striking aspects of Fisher's films is that beauty (particularly visual) is linked with the horrible. Frankenstein's impeccable charm and dandyesque attention to elegance emphasize his magnetic appeal for women, whereas Krempe's staid and bourgeois protectiveness appears emasculated in contrast. Although the power relations are reversed in the end, the equation still holds. Victor, now humanized, looks disheveled and unkept; Paul, neatly and elegantly dressed, replies with the coldness so characteristic of Frankenstein in the earlier scenes. It is certainly true that the narrative justifies Paul's detachment as righteous vengeance, yet it does underline the hidden kinship binding the two men/types of masculinities together.

Despite their radical differences, both script and film render Frankenstein's voice as the vessel of the narrative. The focus has now changed: The parthenogenetic myth has taken an even more pernicious turn. The monstrous son fades in comparison with his father; the creature to be resurrected in each film sequel is Victor Frankenstein, with all the rest of the characters, the creature included, essentially dispensable. *Curse of Frankenstein* also opens a gap between female reproductive power and feminine erotic wiles. This is potentially a sphere for enabling the resurgence of an attenuated version of the myth of Baubo. The film initially hints that there is narrative room for female erotic pleasure and power, as sundered away from the tyranny of domesticity. Yet even this weaker iteration of the myth of Baubo is savagely rent. The film implies that female reproductive power can be appropriated or harnessed to suit patriarchal aims as in the case of the demure Elizabeth, and that feminine erotic wiles may be teasingly indulged in for pleasurable purposes, but ultimately ruthlessly destroyed, as instantiated in the mutilated body of Justine. The myth of Baubo, with its transgressive linking of reproductive power with sexual energy, is again silenced. This movement, as I have shown, accompanies the strengthening of the parthenogenetic myth, as instantiated in the creation of a more ruthlessly charismatic Frankenstein.

VENGEFUL REINCARNATION

Given the resounding success of *Curse*, Hammer could not resist a sequel, which was initially advertised as *The Blood of Frankenstein* (and eventually released as *The Revenge of Frankenstein*) while *Curse* was undergoing its record-breaking run. To the problem of saving the baron who was destined to be guillotined at the end of *Curse*, the ever-present producer, Carreras, flippantly replied, "Oh we just sew his head back on. It's fascinating!"[24] Off the cuff as his reply may be, it underlines the overt identification between creature and creator, which is characteristic of the Hammer movies. More importantly, the parthenogenetic myth shifts from stressing the Otherness of the son to painting the fractured image of the father as both noble and evil, capable of flitting to and from the worlds of bourgeoisie socialites and the alienated poor. Although this version unconceals the dark underside of the parthenogenetic myth—the Ego's splintering against itself—that splintering appears both amoral and even desirable because the baron's clinical detachment from the superficial civility of the upper classes, as well as the animal-like rawness of the impoverished and uneducated, is a crucial component of his charisma. Far from drawing the Frankensteinian myth's three shadows into the light, this account pushes them further into the realms of darkness, rendering them inevitable and naturalized features of the narrative landscape. The feminized shadow (in the figures of Countess Barscynska and her daughter; Margaret, the fashionable do-gooder; and the disease-ridden poor in the hospital), the monstrous shadow (as instantiated in the two Karls), and the feminized and monstrous shadow (vividly exemplified in the mortally wounded and deformed cannibal into which Karl has degenerated) simply constitute the backdrop against which the parthenogenetic myth unfolds with a certain tragicomic grandeur. Correspondingly, the myth of Baubo's *ana-suromai* is silenced. The women in this movie are either earnestly bereft of the powers of transgressive laughter and reproductive power (as in the figure of Margaret, who is twice-bound by her status as a pastor's daughter and socialite), or attempt to wield these powers so unsuccessfully, as in the case of Countess Barscynska and her daughter, that they become the butts, rather than the bearers, of the joke.

Revenge of Frankenstein was also directed by Terence Fisher; its script was penned predominantly by Jimmy Sangster, with some dialogue provided by Hurford Janes. Jensen conjectures that several instances revealing the cool wit of the baron, such as when Dr. Kleve (Francis Matthews) stumbles while descending a flight of steps and Frankenstein, catching him, remarks: "It would be a pity to lose you—so soon," are probably contributions of Janes because humor was not one of Sangster's strong qualities as a scriptwriter.[25] Nevertheless the baron (Peter Cushing) in this version loses his pleading and groveling tone even as he is led to the guillotine as a bell tolls in the distance. The condemned man is lead by the priest who has refused to become his mouthpiece, and flanked by a strange, deformed man (Oscar Quitak) who exchanges meaningful glances with the masked executioner. The priest begins intoning an *Ave Maria* as the guillotine descends, cutting the scene abruptly.

At a tavern, a seedy-looking man (Michael Ripper) is attempting to convince his equally disheveled companion (Lionel Jeffries) to help him pull off a grave robbery. After the body is uncovered, Frankenstein's voice rings out, masterfully introducing himself, as he and the deformed man are revealed in a dramatic shot. One robber flees; the other suffers a stroke, and falls appropriately into the coffin. Frankenstein is now set up as a mythic character who manages to cheat death, at least in terms of his own person. Although his attempts at infusing life into his creatures eventually prove abortive, there can be no doubts concerning his self-resurrections. Again, a more concentrated and yet more refractory version of the parthenogenetic myth is created. Insofar as Frankenstein's self-resurrections are flawlessly executed, parthenogenesis as self-birthing, in which the distinction between Self and Other, or Father and Son, disappears, emerges in a starker form. And yet, contrastively aligned with his failures at resuscitating healthy parthenogenetic sons, it reveals this unproblematic conflation between Ego and shadow (yet another iteration of the parthenogenetic myth's masked will-to-domination) to be a lie.

The story shifts forward by three years, and we find the Carlsbruck medical council agitatedly expressing their discontentment with the popular practice of an unknown but highly successful "Dr. Stein." The shadowy doctor's virility is emphasized contrastively with Dr. Molke's (and the medical council's) effete manhood; Molke is implied to be a (potential if not actual) cuckold, and his inability to control his wife (one of Stein's avid customers) not only emasculates but also feminizes him.

Dr. Stein, unsurprisingly, turns out to be Victor Frankenstein, who fashionably places a flower into his buttonhole before he opens the door, smells the air as if in recognition of a familiar scent, and coolly welcomes Countess Barscynska and her daughter, Vera. It turns out that Dr. Stein had long pronounced Vera to be healthy, but the countess's remarks make it clear that the cure both mother and daughter seek has not (yet) been delivered. The countess strategically points out how all of her wealth is destined to be inherited by her only daughter, implying that Vera's mysterious lack of animation and his financial instability have one simple solution. When Frankenstein uses a stethoscope, rather than his ear, to listen to the young woman's heart, she protests, saying that it is too cold. At the countess's prompting, the doctor gives in, and places his ear against Vera's chest as the young woman smiles, satisfied. Despite the fact that Frankenstein is shown giving in to the women's whims, his masculinity is far from compromised. Ironically his virility is reinforced through this scene, which emphasizes his desirability, as well as an apparent nobility that is not compromised by women's wiles. Yet this detachment from petit bourgeois concerns of economics and matrimony also insulates him from genuine compassion as he works with the poor; Frankenstein's civilized veneer hides his parasitism. In the same way he bleeds rich, hypochondriac women for money, he harvests limbs from the poor in order to further his parthenogenetic quest.

The scene shifts to reveal Dr. Stein attending to a very different clientele. Fritz (Richard Wordsworth), the janitor of the poor ward, announces the impatient arrival of three gentlemen. Unperturbed, the doctor has them wait in the poor ward, where the stench of poverty and sickness assails the nostrils and sensibilities of the medical delegation. Frankenstein veers in between scorn and politeness as he turns down the doctor's invitation to join the medical council, recalling how the council had attempted to stop him from setting up his practice earlier. Repeatedly, Frankenstein's unassailable masculinity is emphasized; his manner is equally and effectively imperious with the street rabble as it is with the privileged class, which in this case, represent two different types of masculinities, which are feminized in relation to Frankenstein.

Later, harking back to *Curse*, Kleve reveals himself to have been a student of the ill-fated Professor Bernstein, whose body was buried in the family crypt of Baron Frankenstein. When Frankenstein finally reveals his identity, Kleve reverently and enthusiastically presents himself as Frankenstein's pupil. Again, despite the fact that Frankenstein is initially in a weaker position under the threat of potential blackmail, his masculinity is never compromised. It is Frankenstein who sets the terms of the contract as he circles Kleve, drying a knife as he remarks, "Uncertainty is one of life's fascinations, isn't it?" Ironically it is upon Kleve's shoulders that the responsibility for proving his trustworthiness falls, and it is only after he has detailed his credentials that Frankenstein accepts him as a protégé, cautioning his newly found assistant-son to address him as "Dr. Stein."

Frankenstein leads Kleve to his laboratory, which is hidden in a wine cellar. There he introduces his other assistant, Karl, who is feeding Otto, a chimpanzee. Frankenstein dazzles his new student with displays of scientific power. Kleve is enthused, but Frankenstein is unimpressed, and finally unveils his "revenge"/reinstatement: a perfect male body wrapped in bandages enclosed in a misty tank, thus reifying the central parthenogenetic theme of the Frankensteinian narrative.

Frankenstein confirms that his work at the poor ward has provided him with a very fruitful supply of limbs, but that he needs only a living brain to complete his experiment. Kleve shows the first qualms of conscience and inquires if this would surely entail murder. Frankenstein blandly informs him that he has a volunteer willing to donate his brain, and Kleve flinches, as the horrible thought briefly crosses his mind that apprenticeship with Frankenstein entails becoming part of his experiment. Frankenstein laughs and indicates that it is Karl, and not Hans, to whom he had been referring. How Frankenstein earlier had escaped the guillotine is now explained: in exchange for saving Frankenstein from the guillotine, Karl had been promised a new body. Kleve is concerned about the state of Karl's brain because of his partial paralytic condition, but Frankenstein reassures the younger doctor that these problems, caused by a minor blood clot, can easily be fixed by a surgical operation. Karl expresses absolute faith in the success of the experiment, and in reply to Kleve's doubting Thomas question, Frankenstein utters the godlike pronunciation: "The operation will be a complete success." Karl thus continues the role of supplicant-servant-monstrous son first given form by *Frankenstein*'s Fritz. The tension of differentiation, between parthenogenetic father and son, master and slave, is yet to manifest itself.

The entrance of Margaret Konrad (Eunice Gayson), who makes the startling declaration that she is going to work at the poor ward, disrupts the all-male enclave. She asserts with the forcefulness of one accustomed to having her way: "Well, my father is the minister. Dr. Stein has been informed. I shall read to the sick. Shop for them, you know, get them things like tobacco, writing paper, soap." Margaret, as a socialite-do-gooder and pampered spoiled brat, who relies upon the authority of her absent father, is immediately set up as a potential source of trouble. When Karl proves too embarrassed by his deformity to shake her hand, her potential power of rivaling Frankenstein in commanding adoration is hinted at. She appears a much-attenuated manifestation of Baubo: a woman of arresting beauty and strong will, though all too bourgeoisie and self-righteous, who becomes a Pandora-figure in her later naïve interference in Frankenstein's plans, resulting in disaster.

As the two doctors prepare themselves for the operation, Karl gazes upon the body he is going to inherit. When Karl turns around to eye the instruments they are preparing, Frankenstein, in one of his few moments of gentleness, paternally advises Karl to keep looking at his future body instead. In the background the camera shows the chimpanzee lurking, forming a foreshadowed parallelism with Karl; the camera also shares Karl's gaze as it pans desirously down the body enclosed in its misted, glassy womb. Again, save for the brain dripping blood as it sits in a glass container filled with clear liquid, details of the operation are not shown. The camera stays at a level slightly above their hands, evoking rather than revealing the procedure, though it repeatedly links the confined and tormented Karl to the agitated animal, which rattles its cage ominously. In so doing the film hints that the demonization of the technological shadow is linked with its descent from the human to the bestial or animal and, therefore, subhuman.

A few weeks pass, and Frankenstein is shown unwrapping the bandages around Karl's head. The new Karl (Michael Gwynn) awakens and looks at the straps that bind him; Frankenstein apologizes and reassures Karl that these constitute temporary measures. Left alone with Kleve, Karl first inquires when he may finally see his new body—a question that again aligns him with the "feminized" in a twofold sense, insofar as (1) Karl's new identity is entirely bound up with his new body, and (2) Karl's sense of self can only gain concreteness with making himself the object of his own gaze via the mirror, that is, the new Karl has not escaped the feminized realms of the bodily and the specular, despite his acquisition of a perfect male body. Karl next inquires about his intended future, and Kleve, without thinking, blurts out Frankenstein's and his plans for the new Karl: he is to be displayed beside his old body as proof of the success of the procedure to the medical and scientific community. Karl realizes that even by acquiring a new body, he has not escaped the status of a "freak"; he is still destined to be an object to be stared at, and he turns his head away from Kleve in distress. The younger doctor senses that his words do not have their intended effect upon the patient, and gives Karl another sedative, treating him like a potential (feminized) hysteric, whose agitated emotional outbursts must be suppressed.

The camera at this point cuts in between the events in the attic and concurrent events in the poor ward, where Kleve and Fritz converse. Kleve is shown in a white laboratory coat, vigorously cleaning instruments as the unkempt Fritz scratches himself. Fritz humorously mounts a vigorous defense in favor of keeping his fleas as a means of keeping himself healthy. The realms of masculine and scientific activity versus feminized and animal activity are sharply demarcated, with Kleve cleaning instruments and Fritz ineffectually plying a broom and scratching himself. In the meantime, Margaret, earlier led secretly by Fritz to the new Karl, sympathetically loosens the straps that bind the young man, inadvertently setting into motion a chain of events destined tragically to destroy the new Karl.

Fritz continues his lecture on the health benefits of having a layer of dirt as protection against disease. He draws a direct parallel between himself and animals in the jungle, and to drive his point home concerning the Edenic state of animals, points out the difference between human and monkey eating habits. Humans cook their food, while monkeys simply reach out for a banana, having no craving for meat. Kleve is struck by a sudden thought and rushes to the laboratory, where he finds Frankenstein feeding Otto raw meat. Kleve finds out that Otto had eaten his "wife"—another chimpanzee—soon after his operation. Frankenstein coolly remarks that he made no attempt to correct the condition, given that the monkey had "been through enough and . . . [is] perfectly happy and in good health." The female chimpanzee's violent death is of no concern to him; what matters is that he has rebirthed Otto through giving him a new brain.

In the attic, Karl, who is now alone, has managed to free himself from the straps. He tests his limbs and seems satisfied, though he appears to walk in a manner similar to the old Karl. He escapes and reenters the laboratory to dispose of his old body. But he is destined for yet another rebirth in this laboratory. The caretaker spies Karl, and Karl attempts to defend himself but ends up being sadistically beaten by the caretaker. However, the next punches no longer seem to affect Karl at all, who is now pale, disheveled, and wild looking. Karl falls upon the caretaker and strangles him. In the aftermath Karl sees Otto eating a piece of raw meat, begins to drool, and realizes that he, too, now has Otto's cannibal urges. With a cry of terror, he flees from the laboratory, scourged by understood but undesired urges—a figure both pathetic and fearsome, simultaneously feminized and monstrous—yet another fallen Adam. The vision of the Monstrous as a cannibal rather than a grotesque and misshapen being was Sangster's. Sangster's idea also provided a legal loophole for Hammer, which had hastily flung together the creature's (Christopher Lee) "roadkill" appearance; the horror of the second monster would depend less on its appearance, than its deeds.[26] This is the only time the visualization of the creature in which the same-Otherness of the creature is overt. Its "sameness" lies in its recognizably human form; its "Otherness" in the scandal of its cannibalism.

At Countess Barscynska's stables, Margaret, who is the countess's niece, feeds the ponies after her fashionable horseback riding. She coaches the horses to take sugar cubes from her hands with the words, "Hello, my lovelies, how about a piece of sugar? Piece of sugar from a woman?" Margaret plies her power as a woman who tempts and nurtures with care. Yet this power, as we shall see, is carefully circumscribed. It is no surprise, therefore, to see that the disheveled Karl, who has now sunk to the level of the animal and subhuman, has come to her for help. Like the horses he is immediately tamed by Margaret. She offers to bring him to Dr. Stein for medical help, but Karl displays such terror and then rises so menacingly that she promises not to inform Dr. Stein. Nevertheless she exacts his promise that he will stay to await her return. She rushes off to fetch Kleve, who hesitates concerning whether to inform Frankenstein. At Margaret's prompting he decides against seeking out Frankenstein—an act Frankenstein bitterly takes as treachery.

At a park, an adolescent boy and girl are having a less than successful date, at least in the young woman's eyes. They've spent the past half-hour staring at ants, and the young woman obviously thinks that "getting on with it" rather than "sitting around all night" is indicative of learning what is essential. Gerta, the young woman, thus marks herself as an aggressive sexual creature; when she leaves the young man in an irritated huff, she is pounced upon by the salivating Karl. The narrative marks her as a natural (and justifiable) victim by aligning her with the animal realm of untamed eroticism (a facet of Baubo's genitalia-revealing *ana-suromai*). Unlike Margaret, whose nunlike and fashionable chasteness tempers her strong-willed aggressiveness, Gerta is a virgin willfully longing for devirginization, and that renders her the perfect victim within the confines of the Frankensteinian myth.

Back at the countess's home, Margaret, dressed in a becoming white gown, stands at a lighted balcony. In a parodic rendition of Romeo and Juliet, the degenerative Karl looks longingly and piteously at her as she disappears back into the house. His hand has reverted back into being a human claw, and he walks away despairingly.

Frankenstein arrives unexpectedly at Countess Barscynska's party, imperiously corners Margaret, and inquires into Karl's appearance and whereabouts. Before Frankenstein is finished with his interrogation, Karl breaks through the fashionable glass windows—a monstrous eruption into the bourgeois world of refinement and civility. Karl initially heads for Margaret with an ambiguous expression on his face, but then he spots Frankenstein and staggers toward him, the familiar limp all too evident. With a piteous cry, he calls Frankenstein by his real name and implores for his help as he collapses into his creator's arms and dies. It is never completely clear whether the erotic/cannibalistic drives do battle with Karl's desire for help when he approaches Margaret, yet when he does turn to Frankenstein, his motives appear simpler: he asks unambiguously for deliverance. Thus, salvation and destruction are inextricably intertwined in the figure of the feminine. Genuine deliverance appears to lie solely in the realm of the masculine and parthenogenetic.

The final scene is set at Harley St. W, London, where a Dr. Franck has an office. The camera focuses on a pair of hands being washed in the sink; it lingers over the elaborate tattoo of a pickpocket's former hand. It then pans up to the individual's face, revealing it to be Frankenstein, who has grown a beard. He looks in the full bloom of health despite his fatal encounter with the enraged inmates, who had found out how he had been using their limbs. The master thief's hand has been stolen by the greatest thief of them all. Frankenstein, reborn through the surgical procedure he has created, looks upon his mirror image with a satisfied air and congratulates Hans (and himself) with the words: "You were an excellent pupil. This scar will hardly show." In an ending that harks back to the beginning, Dr. Franck inserts a flower fashionably into his lapel before he puts on a monocle and expansively welcomes another society matron and her daughter. Kleve closes the door with a knowing smile. Frankenstein's revenge is complete; he can never be killed. He has become his best creation; the parthenogenetic myth symbolized by the emblem of the snake swallowing its own tail, a self-generating source, reifies itself. Although creatures and assistants are expendable, his monstrous immortality is assured.

PROBLEMATIZING THE FACE OF EVIL

The next sequel, *The Evil of Frankenstein* (1964), is generally decried as one of the least impressive in the series. Stephen Jones describes it as "the third and probably the weakest in Hammer's Frankenstein series";[27] Leslie Halliwell sighs over its plot line, writing, "Alas, *Evil* was not particularly interesting despite a considerably improved budget";[28] and Howard Maxford apologetically says this third film in the cycle is "by no means the best entry in the saga."[29] Six years had elapsed since *Revenge of Frankenstein*, and because Terence Fisher's *The Phantom of the Opera* (1962) had proven to be a financial flop, this project was handed to Freddie Francis, "Britain's second but far less inspired horror specialist."[30] This assessment is echoed by David Pirie, who writes, "*The Evil of Frankenstein* . . . turned out to be a most disappointing film whose only real merit was that it indicated, beyond a shadow of doubt, how great Fisher's contribution to the series had been."[31] Francis's directorial strengths certainly did not lie in traditional monster tales, and Jensen, on a more even-handed note, declares, "Francis lacks Terence Fisher's fascination with physical sensation and the stern morality of good confronting evil. His forte lies elsewhere, with stories of mood and suggestion, with atmospheric films that evoke the unseen terrors of someone victimized by his own obsessions or those of others."[32]

Glimmers of Francis's talent with creating mood and atmosphere may be seen in the film's opening sequence. The camera roves, tilting past a lake to focus upon a dilapidated cabin, from which an elderly couple, dressed in black and bowed in grief, emerge. A savage wind howls through the trees. Suddenly, in the extreme foreground, a man's hand, grasping the gnarled outgrowths of a dead tree limb, invades the visual space; the camera moves into a medium shot, revealing the body of the man, dressed in black as well, who follows the departure of the old couple with his eyes. The camera moves in for a close-up, then the man moves toward the cabin, where the camera pans across the inert body of a youth spread out on top of a table, with a crucifix laid close to his feet. The door opens, and a young girl looks into the room as the candles flicker and die out. Jensen does an excellent job of detailing how Fisher ricochets in between objective/ omniscient and point of view/diegetic perspectives as the drama unfolds.[33] The girl screams and runs through the woods; the wind howls even more fiercely through the trees as the camera shares her terrified gaze. She runs into a figure dressed in black, who turns out to be Frankenstein (Peter Cushing). Like his monster, the scientist ambiguously holds out his hand— a gesture both potentially friendly and threatening—to the young girl, who screams once again and runs away.

Frankenstein, more so than in previous films, is shown grimacing from the effort of extracting the heart as vividly colored liquids bubble in the back while an overhead lamp sways precariously. Hans (Sandor Eles), at Frankenstein's prompting, attempts to set two large and intersecting wheels to move by pressing a switch. When the switch fails to turn the machinery on, Frankenstein impatiently grasps one of the wheels and, like Atlas, shoves it forward as Hans joins him. Frankenstein succeeds in reviving the heart but his victory is short-lived. A priest from the earlier scenes forces his way into the laboratory, sanctimoniously exclaiming, "In the name of God, out of my way! Blasphemer! Foul desecrator of tombs!" The clergyman, with a wild gleam in his eye, uses his cane to smash the tank containing the beating heart. The film problematizes the characters of both Frankenstein and the priest. Both are dressed in black; both are driven by an obsessive and uncompromising ethical system. Both are equally concerned with themes of redemption and damnation; both view themselves as heroic saviors, with the other being "evil." The authority of both men is undermined.

Yet in some ways, Frankenstein emerges as a more heroic figure than the priest. The priest's wild and demented look, in contrast with Frankenstein's ironic reserve, tends to depict the clergyman in an unsympathetic light. Frankenstein, in contrast, shows a wider range of human emotion, inclusive of despair; his physical exertions also provide a markedly human dimension to his characterization. His efforts at reanimating life are shown to be precarious at many levels; his powers as a scientist and baron are shown to be limited. The dark underside of the parthenogenetic myth momentarily reveals itself, showing that the promise of the unhampered ease of masculine self-generating sufficiency is a lie.

At Karlstaad, a beautiful redhead (Katy Wild), dressed simply in a dark coat, begs for alms. It is clear that she cannot speak as she gestures plaintively with her hands without uttering a word. When bullies grab her begging bowl away from her, she pounces on one with the unruly force of a desperate animal and bites his hand. The incident underlines the young woman's ambiguous status as a possible instantiation of Baubo's *ana-suromai*: As a beggar and a mute, she is an outcast, yet her beauty draws others, however predatorily, toward her; she is a mere slip of a girl, yet she has the survival instincts of a wild animal. Nevertheless, overall, she is radically weaker than Whale's bride, who displays the ambiguous and exotic beauty of death intertwined with life, as well as Fisher's Justine, whose unharnessed sexuality and verbal forcefulness render her, alongside the bride, problematic embodiments of female power. That the mute woman is never even given a name in the movie reduces her to the less than a "?"— the designation originally assigned to Karloff's monster, which eventually became transferred to Lanchester's female monster. Her muteness infantilizes her, and her physical beauty is not a source of power but a potential for vulnerability. Baubo, as the embodiment of sexual and reproductive power and the disruptive power of laughter, is kept tightly regulated in this version of the Frankensteinian narrative, even if its version of the parthenogenetic myth hints at its impossible hubris.

The vulnerability of the baron is emphasized even more when the pair finally arrive at Frankenstein's chateau. The chateau is not only in disarray, its floor littered with leaves, but also its walls and rooms are empty. The paintings, carpets, and beds Frankenstein had boasted of have been looted. Frankenstein in this narrative is more a victim than a would-be victimizer. Hans inquires into Frankenstein's banishment from and harsh treatment at Karlstaad. The narrative employs a flashback and voiceover to frame the embedded narrative of Frankenstein's birthing of the male monster, which is, like Whale's bride, covered from head to toe in bandages. Its first sign of life is not of its fingers fluttering, however, but of its eyes opening. Like the bride this creature loses consciousness and slumps precariously close to a flight of steps immediately after its awakening. Unlike the bride it is dressed in unattractive sackcloth when it wakes up, and its decidedly unattractive boxlike head is a crude reconstruction of Jack Peirce's makeup for Karloff's monster. The references back to Universal's monster movies were not only deliberate, but they also had legal backing from Universal Studios, which had signed on to release *Evil of Frankenstein*, and had thus loosened its strictures concerning copyright.[34] Yet these changes only served to underline the differences between Hammer and Universal, and Kiwi Kingston's (a New Zealand wrestler hired for his build rather than acting ability) appearance and performance as the creature is universally decried as the film's weakest component.

Kingston's makeup was conceived by Roy Ashton, who had wanted the creature to look like something sewn together from different corpses. Glut vividly describes the failure of this attempt: "Resembling a young amateur's attempt to imitate Jack Peirce, the square-headed creature was a sloppy pasted together affair, with clear lines separating the putty from Kingston's real face. The hair was stringy and sparse. And the actor lumbered about on raised boots. [That] had none of the impact of Lee's make-up and aroused many giggles from young members of the audience."[35]

Within the flashback the creature is shown pulling out and devouring the fresh organs of a dead sheep—a depiction that is reminiscent of the cannibal in *Revenge of Frankenstein*, but lacks the former's sympathetic depiction and dramatic pathos. Like the degenerative versions of the Universal series, there is something seriously wrong with the creature from the start. Its instincts are toward violence and bestiality, and even the official excuse of having a defective brain is not used, rendering the Monstrous shadow an even more alienated force. There is no attempt to understand why the creature is monstrous; it simply is. The final shot of the flashback shows the creature, chased by the usual mob as it climbs a cliff, and falling as the sound of a gunshot rings out, implying its demise.

The return to the contemporary scene reveals Frankenstein, with his head buried in his hands in agony. His sentence was banishment. Penniless and alone he worked tirelessly as a common laborer to hoard money so he could continue his experiments. Strangely enough the baron's final remarks mirror the medieval fervor and obsessive singlemindedness he deplores: "One failure after another and always hounded by these *disbelievers* [italics added]. I'm not beaten yet. It's only a matter of time till I prove my theory."

The scene shifts back to the carnival, where cameo appearances of various freaks are featured. A voluptuous white woman, dressed as an Indian girl, is pressed against a backboard; her form constitutes a strange dartboard, and is outlined by knives thrown by a man dressed as a cowboy. Once again mingling all too human elements, Fisher shows how the woman flinches as the knives land with a thud close to her flesh; but this type of portraiture is reserved for female characters. A white man dressed in a Turkish attire brings a torch close to his hand, and allows the flames to lick at his flesh, unperturbed. A boy preens himself with a gigantic python coiled around his neck. As if to underline her kinship with these outsiders, the camera reveals the mute redhead, who wanders around the carnival, hungrily eyeing the lavish displays of food. Frankenstein and Hans enter the scene, also spurred by hunger. Hans again worriedly asks whether "it is safe" and Frankenstein amusedly banters, "What? The food?" The use of humor is instructive in relation to the baron because even if it reveals a more human Frankenstein, it also underlines his self-confidence, which verges on the arrogant. The unsettling power of transgressive laughter, tied up with the myth of Baubo's *ana-suromai*, is appropriated and transplanted on to the figure of Frankenstein, to shore up his disintegrating authority.

Nevertheless, to appease his assistant, the baron purchases two masks, and thusly concealed, they enter a pub. There Frankenstein recognizes two of his enemies: the burgomaster and the chief of police sitting intimately with several attractive women dressed fashionably and provocatively. The camera lingers over the view of one of the women's lush breasts as the burgomaster drapes his arms around her. Comically, the camera, depicting Frankenstein's point of view, zooms past the display of breasts and focuses on a ring on the burgomaster's hand. Again, in an unusual display of emotion, Frankenstein seems to forget himself and raises his voice, accusing the burgomaster of being a thief. The commotion causes the chief of police to recognize Frankenstein.

Fleeing from the resultant mayhem, Frankenstein and Hans slip into a tent where Zoltan (Peter Woodthorpe) is shown exerting his power over a hapless man. In every instance the (feminized) victim unfailingly obeys, and, satisfied, Zoltan releases him from the hypnotic spell as the admiring crowd applauds. Zoltan singles Frankenstein and Hans out for the next act. Before Zoltan can attempt to exert his powers over the masked baron, however, the police close down the show and arrest Zoltan, declaring that the hypnotist does not have a license. Zoltan is incensed, but his loud protests prove futile. The kinship between Frankenstein and Zoltan, at this point, begins to be set up: both men seek thoroughgoing power, but both are crippled by their common status as disreputable outcasts.

In another memorable sequence that pokes fun at human vanities, the burgomaster is shown vainly preening himself in front of a mirror. Frankenstein, no longer wearing his mask, bursts into the burgomaster's bedroom, demanding the return of his property. Again a note of humor creeps in, which Jensen astutely details:

In anger, [Frankenstein] . . . rushes about the room identifying items stolen from him ("My chairs—my desk—my carpet—"), then looks into the bedroom and adds, "even my bed!" The statement is not in itself amusing, but Francis' composition juxtaposes Frankenstein's face with the bed containing the Burgomaster's young wife, and this prompts a viewer to notice [yet again] how oblivious Frankenstein is to the voluptuous woman, which provokes at least a chuckle.[36]

The chief of police unexpectedly comes to the rescue of the burgomaster and Frankenstein shuts himself in the bedroom with the young burgomaster's wife, who gazes upon him, not with fear and horror, but with excited anticipation. Frankenstein rips the sheets off her body and fashions a rope from it. He ties one end to the bed, and before he leaves, bids the still expectant lady a gentlemanly good-night. As the force of his descending weight pulls the bed across the floor, the burgomaster's wife appears to enjoy the ride.

The joke is a complicated one, and to dissect it is to spread it out, etherized, upon a table. Yet it is necessary to get at the gendered dynamics at work in the sequence. The fulcrum of the joke lies in the young woman's unexpected (sexual) receptiveness to Frankenstein, which serves to underline his vigorous and appealing masculinity, compared with the effeminate and effete masculinity of the aging burgomaster. Yet part of the joke also hinges upon Frankenstein's imperviousness to the voluptuous woman's enticements (which constitutes a masculine refusal of a certain type of feminine power included in Baubo's *ana-suromai*), as well as the woman's reduction to no more than being a body marked for sexual conquest. Laughter, in this case, is used to reinforce, rather than unsettle, gendered categories of power.

Frankenstein goes in search of Hans, and the two escape to the wintry mountains. Despite his youth, Hans is unable to keep up with Frankenstein, and begs for a break—once again underlining the older man's virility. A storm threatens, and the mute young woman appears serendipitously and beckons to them. With the agility of one used to the mountains, the fleet-footed young woman leaps over rocks as they follow her. Again the young woman's individuality is carefully circumscribed. Although she saves Frankenstein and Hans from the wrath of the storm, her muteness, animal agility, and deafness underline her essential inferiority (and linkage with the animal/subhuman) in relation to them. Her offering of bread seems more motivated by a domesticated desire to please rather than a genuinely benevolent gesture extended by a gracious hostess. She invites the two men into her private space, maintaining their hierarchy of power, assenting to Frankenstein's dominance over Hans and herself.

To be fair, though, Frankenstein himself is less forceful than in earlier Hammer versions. For example, in this iteration, as if to underline Frankenstein's humanity, the baron only stumbles across the body of his creature accidentally. He does not actively seek it out, and it is through the mute young woman that he makes his discovery. Nevertheless his authoritativeness returns quickly, as does the gender hierarchy. What follows next is a quick succession of brief clips: Frankenstein and Hans carry the monster's body down as the mute woman leads; the two men bend over the laboratory instruments as the woman watches, wide-eyed; Frankenstein gently attends to the creature's inert body, again silently observed by the mute woman; the two men finally turn on the instruments and restore life to the creature, with the woman as the passive voyeur. Although the camera shares some of her gaze, it objectifies, rather than subjectifies her gaze. The expression of wonder on her face, combined with her deafness and muteness, render her an object acted upon, rather than a coparticipant in the proceedings.

The experiment proves to be only a partial success. Although they succeed in biologically resuscitating the creature, its brain is dormant. In a remarkable parallel to Whale's Dr. Pretorius, Frankenstein craftily solicits Zoltan's help by baiting him with a challenge. Zoltan bristles at the thought that anyone could evade his powers, and declares, "There's never been a man born of woman whom I can't put under." Again, appropriating a line from Pretorius, Frankenstein remarks, "Then this experiment could prove very interesting," the double entendre lying in that the creature is not a man born of woman.

Frankenstein brings Zoltan to the chateau, where the hypnotist successfully commands the creature to awaken, which it does, screaming in frenzied pain from the wounds of the brain operation. It becomes increasingly clear that as glimpses of Frankenstein's frailties are shown, Zoltan's character expands to fill the mythic void that Frankenstein's humanization leaves. Zoltan aspires to take over Frankenstein's position as parthenogenetic father. Zoltan's usurpation of that role is based on a mental rather than physical conquest: a version of the myth of male self-birthing that is even more pernicious because it promises the jettisoning of the maternal messiness of bodily birthing, a reality associated with the "feminine."

Alone with the creature, Zoltan instructs it to rob the village church of its gold. The creature fulfills his command successfully, with only a disreputable drunk accidentally witnessing the crime. Unsatisfied, the inebriated Zoltan sends the creature back to "punish" the burgomaster and the chief of police—the two men who are responsible for banishing him, and, incidentally, Frankenstein. The creature obeys its orders, resulting in another darkly comedic set of murders, which depict the burgomaster and chief of police as effeminate dandies in relation to the creature.

Frankenstein sees the creature's bloody hands and realizes what has happened. He imperiously commands Zoltan off, but Zoltan returns, exerting hypnotic control over the creature. The creature initially attacks its biological parthenogenetic father but then breaks free of its hypnotic father's grasp, kills Zoltan instead, and flees. The mute woman sympathetically attempts to make the creature drink wine to ease its pain. It, like Zoltan, begins to drink heavily as the mute woman looks on, horrified—yet as another Pandora figure, like Margaret in *Revenge*. Her good intentions prove to be the catalyst that provides the justification for the creature's violent demise.

Frankenstein arrives to find the creature running wild, smashing objects in the laboratory and taking heavy swigs mistakenly from a chloroform bottle as his father-creator protests in vain. An explosion signals the deaths of Frankenstein and his creature as Hans, fleeing with the mute woman, looks back and says, "They beat him after all." The air of defeatism that pervades this particular film allows glimpses of the dark side of the parthenogenetic myth. Yet its virtual effacement of the shadow as feminine/ woman (as in the burgomaster's wife), its reduction of the monstrous shadow to an unthinking killing machine, and its severe truncation of the monstrous female to a vulnerable animal-angel (in the figure of the mute and deaf woman) ultimately reinforce the power structures of the parthenogenetic myth. This is a trend that continues and eventually culminates in the figure of the "Angel" in *Frankenstein Must Be Destroyed*.

(RE)CREATING WOMAN

In 1958 Anthony Hinds wrote a screenplay, *And Frankenstein Created Woman*, in parodic mimicry of the then popular *And God Created Woman*, starring Brigitte Bardot.[37] Eight years later Hammer dusted off the script. The press exploited every opportunity they had to publicize the fact that Susan Denberg, a twenty-two-year-old Austrian *Playboy* "playmate" (August 1966), was cast as the female monster. The *Daily Mirror* printed a photo of Denberg with the caption: "Susan, the monster's girlfriend. One of the many nice things about mini-skirts is the way they enable young actresses to attract attention simply by wearing them."[38] Not to be left behind, the *Evening Standard* printed the same picture a day ahead, proclaiming, "Susan: The Creature in the Mini-Skirt. Twenty-two-year-old Susan—who has just finished filming *Frankenstein Created Woman*—chose her corduroy mini-coat, mini-skirt and Beatle cap for a flight to New York."[39] And the *Daily Sketch* conjectured (referencing the same outfit): "Frankenstein, it seems has created a vastly different version of delightful Miss Susan Denberg. One with similar beauty but with the brain and mind of a monster."[40] Critics seem divided on Denberg's performance. Robert Marrero evaluates her performance as a seductive and possessed character as "believable."[41] Yet the majority of critics seem to think Denberg was chosen because of her "bodily curves than her acting abilities,"[42] leading to the exploitative use of "misleading cheesecake advertising, which is presumably what the studio wanted."[43] The specific reference is to certain publicity shots, one of which features the baron (Peter Cushing), with his sleeves rolled up, either holding the bound hands of his female creature (Susan Denberg)—who just happens to be wearing a cross between bandages and a bikini—against a mechanical contraption. In another publicity shot, he is shown lifting her up as she gazes upon him and he gazes at the camera; in yet another, he is looking up into the camera, which gazes down from overhead at him as he stands beside the gracefully and seductively posed body of Denberg, whose eyes remain passively and acceptingly closed, as she lies upon a structure that looks like a dissecting table, and yet is framed to resemble something in between a bed and a scientific altar. Gregory William Mank reports that "apparently scenes were filmed (or at least posed for publicity purposes) of the Baron becoming so attracted by his creation's beauty that he raped her on the operating table."[44] Although these scenes are not in the released film version, the sexual undercurrents in the Frankensteinian myth are here made overt. However, the convincing exploration of problematic androgyny—of a righteously vengeful man's "spirit" trapped in an alluring woman's body—is not sustained. In addition, at first glance, Frankenstein's character seems comparatively less clinical and cold, and, at times, even vulnerable in this version. He even seems to recede from the narrative's center, fulfilling the function of a catalyst and a bystander, rather than the active orchestrator of events. Yet, ultimately, the Frankensteinian narrative reifies itself.

Although the fulcrum of the narrative appears to be Christina Kleve (Denberg), whose deformed body Frankenstein has fused with her dead lover's spirit (Robert Morris), she never concretely gains a voice or identity. Even her apparent assertion of sexual independence is instigated by her worshipful obedience to Hans, whose commands she obeys. The only avenue for freedom for her appears to be suicide, and the narrative justifies her destruction as it sympathetically traces, not her watery demise down a waterfall, but the baron's back as he turns away from the cliff. Although the film has the potential of demystifying the feminine, monstrous, and monstrous feminine/female shadows, it instead absorbs these elements back into the grand design of strengthening the parthenogenetic myth and repressing the myth of Baubo's *ana-suromai*. Woman, in this narrative, is no longer purely a (potential) bride; she is also the child birthed parthenogenetically, whose dangerous sexuality requires that she kill herself. Nevertheless critics generally hail *Frankenstein Created Woman* as one of the most compelling of the Hammer *Frankenstein* offerings. David Pirie writes, "It is not as intellectually satisfying as Fisher's two earlier Frankenstein films [*Curse* . . . and *Revenge* . . .], but in one respect—the sheer beauty and poetry of its images—it certainly excels them."[45] Hanke holds a similar view: "As it stands, *Frankenstein Created Woman* is still second only to *Revenge of Frankenstein* as the most intellectually stimulating entry in the series. Had its makers only been as good artists as they were craftsmen, it could have been one of the all-time great genre-transcending horror films."[46]

The film begins with an inebriated prisoner (Duncan Lamont) being led to the guillotine by two guards. Yet the prisoner grows sober when he realizes that his son, Hans, is watching the execution. The boy calls out "Papa!" as the relentless blade descends and is raised, now crimson with fresh blood. This scene sets both the atmosphere of the movie—with fluctuations across dark humor and poignance—as well as its thematic focus. The execution of Hans's father triggers and is mirrored by Hans's own execution, which in turn triggers, and is mirrored by, Christina's revenge for her murdered father (Alan McNaughton) and lover: a cycle that can be broken only by Christina's second death.

Hans Baumer (Robert Morris), who has now matured into a young man, stops running momentarily to gaze upon the rusted instrument while the memory of his father's final desperate words resounds. Hans hurries into Dr. Hertz's (Thorley Walters) ramshackle house, where Hertz is in the middle of an experiment that requires precise timing. Hans assists in prying open the cover of a coffinlike structure to gaze upon the inert figure of a man dressed in black, frosted over, with his black gloved hands covering his face. Hertz gently extricates the hands from the face, and the camera reveals the face of Baron Victor Frankenstein (Peter Cushing), whose eyes are closed. Hertz feels for a pulse; when he does not find one, he shakes his head. He and Hans struggle to reinfuse life into the baron's body. A look of relief floods Hertz's face, and he utters a version of the all-too-(in)famous "It's alive!" line Universal had popularized: "Yes, yes! He lives!" The allusion to Whale's *Frankenstein* is interesting as it partially reverses the power relations in the former: Frankenstein is now the object of his own experiments, and he is dependent on both Hertz and Hans for his reawakening/rebirthing. This tendency to render the baron more vulnerable and to show his parasitism upon his assistants is more characteristic of Hammer offerings than Universal productions. Yet there are limits to the extent to which Hammer offerings may reveal the hidden side of the parthenogenetic narrative.

Nevertheless, when Frankenstein regains consciousness, there is no doubt of who is in charge. His first sentence is both imperious and genteel: "Kindly take that foul-smelling stuff away, please!" Hertz is evidently ecstatic as Frankenstein rises, massaging his stiff limbs. The resultant conversation strongly mimes Christ's dialogues with his disciples, and his authoritative exhortations for faith. "Hertz: 'He lives. See, Hans, he's alive!' Frankenstein: 'Of course, I'm alive. Did I not tell you I would be?' Hertz: 'Yes, but . . . ' Frankenstein: 'I am constantly surprised at your lack of faith in my work, Hertz.' "

It appears Frankenstein had been dead for an hour, and yet he had been successfully resurrected, implying that somehow his soul had remained trapped in his body, though he was dead. Frankenstein thoughtfully conjectures on why and whether he could trap souls himself but Hertz breaks in, jubilantly insisting on a celebration. Frankenstein, still clinically in character, thinks they are celebrating the success of his experiment, but Hertz corrects him and says that they are celebrating Frankenstein's safe return. The conversation draws out the contrast between both men: Frankenstein, whose immense intellect innures him to emotion, and Hertz, whose great gift lies in his compassionate sensibility. Both men are dependent on each other: Frankenstein is unable to perform his experiments alone because, as we see later, he has damaged his hands; Hertz genuinely adores Frankenstein too much to abandon him, unlike his knowledge-hungry predecessors. Again it is a sign of the suppression of the myth of Baubo that the nurturing/maternal/affective role is given to an adoring male pupil, rather than a female of equal wit and daring.

Hans arrives at a deserted café and wanders into the kitchen where a young woman works, chopping food, her back to the camera. Hans calls out her name, and Christina Kleve (Susan Denberg) spins around awkwardly, then her hands quickly fly to her face to use her hair (which is currently a chestnut brown) as a veil over a mark that disfigures her otherwise beautiful face. It appears they are secret lovers. Christina is worried that her father would return and find them together. Christina's father arrives in the interim and sharply interjects. Hans displays an angry look when the door swings open as if to show that there are worse types than Hans, revealing three "bloods"—well-dressed swains who arrogantly think they own the place. Hans lingers and watches amusedly as Kleve bustles about, trying to make the three young men at home. The bloods each take a table and comfortably prop up their feet as Anton (Peter Blythe), the ringleader, impudently orders a bottle of the best red wine, and sweetly threatens Kleve with the unspecified threat of his father's (the police chief's) authority if the wine proves inadequate. Yet when Kleve begins to move toward the tables to serve the wine, Anton demands that Christina, his "lovely daughter," serve the wine. Anton and Johann (Derek Fowlds) mockingly and roundly praise her "beauty," and Christina pleads that they not tease her. Hans watches angrily, restrained by Kleve, as Christina hobbles from one table to the other, barely able to keep her composure and balance as she serves the wine, dutifully trying to keep her father from losing his license. When Christina accidentally spills wine on Anton, he loses his temper, and a fight ensues, ending with Anton's acquisition of a nasty head cut, inflicted by Hans, whom the dandy had called a "spawn of a murderer."

The web of interactions reveal fascinating fluctuations of gender and power. In relation to Kleve as Christina's father, Hans is in effect rendered effete and cowed. Yet because Kleve has to pander to the commands of the three bloods, for fear of losing his license, Hans regains his independence and masculinity in relation to Kleve. The three bloods, who are depicted as feminized dandies, are also sadistic bullies, and are revealed to be petulant children when they cannot have things their way. The only character who remains stable is Christina. Although the action of the scene revolves around her (it is she who Hans comes to see; it is because of her that a conflict exists between Kleve and Hans; it is because of her that the three bloods come for amusement; it is because of her humiliation that Hans initiates a fight), she remains passive and powerless throughout. She is locked in the roles of the dutiful daughter, ugly beloved, and fascinating freak. Even when she has been rebirthed as the "new" Christina, she will not transcend these roles.

Christina's physical imperfections, particularly as she is a woman, render her doubly alienated; she is "other" because she is both woman and not what woman is supposed to be: beautiful without blemish. Yet her ugliness is also the reason why men are both fascinated and repulsed by her. Hans appears to identify with her, as he caresses the scar that mars her face, and remembers his scarred status as the spawn of a murderer; the bloods appear to define their problematic masculinity and sexual desirability in contrast with her imperfect womanhood. Peter Hutchings remarks:

As the film makes clear, this scar—conventionally a sign of castration, especially when used to mark the female body in horror films—does not stand for castration and sexual difference *in itself* but rather signifies *only in relation to a male perception of it* [italics mine]. This is clear from the response of the town "cads" to Christina, which is part fascination, part repulsion, their apparent need constantly to return to her suggesting that their own masculine identities are (re)established through an awareness of the difference represented by her.[47]

At Hertz's attic-laboratory, Frankenstein moves rapidly across the humming, throbbing machinery as the doctor tries to stay out of his way. Frankenstein manages to harness the energy of the mountainside rocks—a feat Hertz calls "magic." The baron allows himself a slight smile as he responds: "Everything we don't understand is magic. Until we understand it . . . and master it." As if to contradict him, a connection springs loose, generating sparks. Frankenstein moves rapidly to the malfunctioning equipment and tries to correct the error with gloved hands. When he is unable to do so, he rips off his gloves impatiently, but that does not do much good as his hands are charred and raw. He finally calls out to Hertz: "Help me, man! Hurry!" Then, solicitously, he tells his assistant to "mind [his] hand." The small sequence reinforces the interdependence binding both men; despite Frankenstein's talk of "mastery" and his obvious intellectual dwarfing of Hertz, he is helpless without his seemingly bumbling assistant.

Finally, Frankenstein, speaking like a half-impatient Sherlock Holmes to his less mentally agile sidekick, Watson,[48] tries to explain how what they have done is tantamount to the overcoming of death. (Naturally, the audience, too, is just as bewildered as Hertz, and identifies more with the humble and confused doctor rather than the confident and opaque baron.) The baron reveals his reasoning in the following steps: (1) They have proven that the soul does not leave the body at the instance of death; (2) Since they have built an impenetrable force field, this same shield should prevent anything from leaving it; and (3) If Frankenstein can trap the soul with his apparatus, repair the damaged body, and transfer the soul back, then he will have conquered death.

Hans is arrested for the murder of Kleve while Christina is out of town. What ensues is a dramatically shot sequence that underlines intricacies binding gender and power. The mayor/judge (Philip Ray) is a kindly but not very bright man, while the chief of police (Peter Madden), who leads the prosecution, is depicted as cold and calculating, casually throwing in "like father, like son" and calling his first witness before the judge can protest. Using Hans's heated words, "I'll kill you for that," and the fact that Hans was seen wearing Hertz's coat on the eve Kleve was killed, the prosecutor builds a convincing case. Yet when Frankenstein is called to the stand, the balance of power shifts. Jensen astutely observes how the camera visually records the struggle for power between the two men.

Fisher intercuts two reverse-angle medium shots of both men. In one, the three youths who are really guilty can be seen in the background, between the protagonists; in the other, the jury occupies that position. When one of the youths heckles Frankenstein, Fisher uses the first angle, and when a statement of Frankenstein draws laughter from the jury, he uses the second shot. In this way, the director keeps both principal characters prominently and continually in visual opposition.[49]

As the sparring heats up, the camera veers in closer. When Frankenstein is forced to admit that it is "extremely unlikely . . . but not impossible" that the defendant could commit murder, the camera zooms in for a tight close-up of Frankenstein, then on Hans, whose initially hopeful face falls. Anton's enthusiastic testimony hammers in the prosecution's case, and Hans's sentence is pronounced: death by guillotine at dawn.

Frankenstein, in a matter of fact fashion, divulges that he intends to transfer Hans's soul to another body. Alarmed, Hertz asks whose body Frankenstein intends to use, and the baron's reply, with a shrug, is instructive: "Bodies are easy to come by. But souls are not." Again the Frankenstein narrative reifies its misogynistic twist: the precious soul they trap is a male entity; but the disposable body they eventually fix in order to infuse it with this rare soul is female. Christina commits suicide when she, like Hans, witnesses her beloved's execution. Her deformed body becomes the raw material Frankenstein surgically perfects to render it the adequate vessel for Hans's spirit.

In the original script from which the film barely diverges, there is a scene in which Frankenstein tries to undo the bandages but cannot because of his injured hands. Hertz takes over. When the bandages are undone, we simply see Hertz's face cloud but we do not see what he sees. Frankenstein is unmoved and dispassionately declares, "Too soon yet. But she's healing. Another month or so."[50]

However, in one of the significant departures from the script, the film shows a figure all covered in bandages lying on a bed. Hertz snips off the ribbons from the face, and the first masklike protective layer is removed, revealing blond, rather than dark, hair. Hertz's hands are shown slowly peeling off the bandages until the new Christina, in her blond and physically perfect splendor, is shown. The departure is significant, as the script version details the struggle against possible failure, which the movie excises. The baron's success in conquering not only death, but also ugliness, is complete. As Mank quips, "Christina's face was hideously scarred, due to the make-up created by George Partleton, and her hair was black. It would take the scientific genius of Baron Frankenstein to bring out her Playmate beauty."[51] More importantly the baron steals the ambiguous power of the womb and female sexuality by birthing a sexually desirable woman whose soul is male.

Christina, though she has been resurrected devoid of physical imperfection, still occupies the status of the domesticated female grotesque as a Cinderella, Sleeping Beauty, laboratory rat, and potential evil witch. Her body is ambiguously marked as a site of triumph and potential destruction. Her sexual desirability is barely kept harnessed by her infantilization; her reproductive power is never hinted at in the movie. Once again Hammer's revisioning of the myth of Baubo severs the connection between female reproductive power and feminine erotic pleasure. In this case, because Christina's status as pure child and dangerous seductress preclude the idea of pregnancy, this aspect of Baubo's *ana-suromai* is simply excised.

Frankenstein decides that it is time for an experiment. Despite Hertz's misgivings he brings the blindfolded Christina to the guillotine. The camera veers in for tight shots of the guillotine and Christina's face as she screams, in a child's voice, "Papa!" and then loses consciousness. The baron is excited, exclaiming, "He remembered; he remembered his father on the guillotine." When Hertz questions the use of "he" in referring to Christina, Frankenstein leads the doctor to the only conclusion possible: that Hans's soul inhabits Christina's body—but only at times. Frankenstein is eager to try more tests, but Hertz, the compassionate (and maternal) one, prevails upon his overzealous colleague to give the young woman some rest.

In the evening Christina tosses and turns in nightmarish sleep; she awakens and looks about her darkened room with a bewildered gaze. As she begins to undo the ribbons of her white nightgown, implying the shedding of her status as pure child and domesticated daughter, the camera abruptly cuts the scene. One by one, Christina-Hans, like a vampiress, seduces and stalks the three bloods who are responsible both for her father's death and Hans's execution. These erotic and violent scenes are intercut with images of domesticity, in which the pigtailed Christina cleans, cooks, and with the barest hint of violence, chops wood in an unsuccessful attempt to win the affection of this narrative's recurring object of desire—the distant father figure, Frankenstein. The contrast marks the similarity-difference between the infantilized and domesticated Christina, who strives to please her father figures, and the seductive and untamed Christina, who strives to use men's sexual desires against them, but only in accordance with her desire to please yet another male figure: Hans, whose soul not only occupies, but also dominates her body. Christina's body is but a projection of male fantasy and fear; her identity is even more sharply circumscribed once she has a perfect body and face, given to her by a distant father who is interested only in using her for experiments. Baubo's gesture of *ana-suromai*—of claiming reproductive power and sexual independence—is impossible even for the rebirthed Christina. From the start, her role fluctuates between child and *femme fatale*, neither of which allows for carving out a genuinely independent identity from the sphere of men. Pirie merges images of Keats's Lamia and the archetypal vampiress in discussing the new Christina's (apparent) power: "Like Keats's Lamia, she is formed from her true hideous shape. . . . In scene after scene of cloying beauty, Christina stalks and lures her victims with a kind of vampiric power continually acting out the fears of all sexual fantasy by metamorphosing into a vengeful beast at the moment of intercourse."[52]

With the guillotine again in sight, the frenzied Johann desperately hails the carriage heading for Innsbaad. As he gets in and heaves a sigh of relief, a feminine voice asks, "Are you traveling far, sir?" As a gong suddenly sounds, the camera abruptly reveals Christina, who is sitting in the coach, now wearing a black coat and red skirt, along with striped black stockings—the outfit rendering her a strange mix of distinguished lady, formidable dominatrix, and alluring whore.

Like a magnificent beast of prey, Christina lures the mesmerized Johann into the forest. They sit facing each other with Johann being obviously the smaller of the two, his olive-green trousers seeming to blend into the grass, while Christina's taller figure dressed in black seems a visual assault on the peaceful looking scene. Christina reveals her full name, and repeatedly plunges a dagger into the screaming Johann.

The baron finally bursts upon the scene to see Christina holding her dead lover's head. From her lips, Hans's voice emerges: "You have done what you had to do, Christina; you may rest in peace." Frankenstein calls out her name, but she flees from him to the edge of a cliff. For the first time, Frankenstein speaks soothingly and pleadingly to Christina. But Christina's mind is already made up, and she proudly states that she knows who she is; nevertheless she still asks his forgiveness before she plunges into the water, drowning herself a second time. Frankenstein cries out her name as she disappears into the water, but he later shrugs and walks away. The camera frames his face from below the cliff before it shows him turning and leaving in one of the most eloquently understated horror movie endings.

Nevertheless the narrative makes Christina's second suicide—her only genuine act of "self-determination"—seem like an inevitability. Thus the ending naturalizes the prison of tyranny and violence that has enveloped her, both as a deformed and ugly woman, and as a perfect and sexually alluring one. Her "rebirth" has been naught but a cycle, and like and unlike the male creature, death is her lot—but she is compelled to choose it willingly. As Hutchings remarks, "Like the Baron, the filmmakers cannot save Christina. Having provided a sensitive and sympathetic portrayal of her plight, with this involving a representation of the difficult existence of female subjectivity in a patriarchal world, they are . . . unable to transform their insights into the more radical investigation of gender identity . . . that Christina's survival would have necessitated."[53]

Interestingly enough, like Whale's monstrous bride, Christina is a cipher. Although her desire to know her identity is touching, she remains, for the most part, a beautiful shell. The relation between the "new" Christina and

Hans is confusing, as it appears she is not possessed by his spirit, but is simply obeying his orders when she hunts down, seduces, and kills the three bloods. Her fluctuations across domesticated daughter and wild seductress do not seem to bewilder her, and her character, overall, remains undeveloped. As Hanke comments, the film has great potential, but ultimately fails to portray "the implications of a man's soul using his new-found female body to sexually amuse himself with the very men responsible for his own death prior to killing them."[54] Yet even that analysis points out how Christina is interesting only insofar as Hans occupies and uses her body. In an intriguing twist, though this female monster is eloquent, she never speaks her own voice—until the very end, when death is her only "free" choice. Within the strictures of the Frankensteinian narrative, suicide is the only form of "self-birthing" to which she can resort.

ATTEMPTING TO KILL THE BARON

Frankenstein Must be Destroyed is generally hailed as one of Hammer's (and Fisher's) finest *Frankenstein* productions. Despite its nihilistic tone and return to the gritty physicality of brain transplants, rather than the "poetic abstraction"[55] of soul transferences, praise was generally positive when it was newly released on June 8, 1969. As Tom Johnson and Deborah Del Vecchio recount, "The British Film Institute's *Monthly Film Bulletin* (June) [wrote]: 'The most spirited Hammer horror in some time'; *The Kinematograph Weekly* (May 24) [stated]: 'The period atmosphere and lowering settings keep the excitement at a fine active simmer'; *Variety* (June 11) [declared]: 'There's nothing tongue in cheek about Fisher's directing'; and *The London Times* (May 22) [asserted]: 'As nasty as anything I have seen in the cinema for a very long time.' "[56]

The lone dissenting critical voice I have come across is Ken Hanke's, who pejoratively writes, "About the only positive thing that can be said about *Frankenstein Must Be Destroyed* is that the gloves are off as concerns Frankenstein's character."[57] And, indeed, the character of the baron (Peter Cushing) in this version is more ruthless than charming: he actively murders a passerby in order to harvest fresh organs as the film opens, and he later coolly rapes a young woman, Anna Spengler (Veronica Carlson), in order to "discipline" her, even though he exerts complete control over her through the threat of blackmail he holds over her and her fiancé, Dr. Karl Holst (Simon Ward). Interestingly, Fisher, Carlson, and virtually everyone on the set, were firmly against shooting the rape, which was hastily written up to satisfy Carreras's demand for a more graphic sex scene. The rape scene was crassly composed and reluctantly flung together, yet turned out well acted and directed, though everyone but Carreras regarded the scene as degrading at that time. Jensen reports the following: "As Veronica Carlson recalls, 'Terry argued at length to keep it out, but was overruled, so we had to shoot the scene.' . . . Five years later, Fisher still felt incensed. 'It was dragged in . . . to follow the trend.' He then declared, with unexpected passion, 'I'm not going to talk about this, because I thought it was diabolical.' "[58]

Fisher's and Carlson's objections to performing the rape scene lay not in the fact that it was a rape scene. Rather, both felt that it was inconsistent with character development. Carlson felt her character had been undermined because by then, her later scenes had already been shot, with no clear reference to the fact that she had been raped (though she consistently shrinks and cringes, which viewers are apt to interpret as in keeping with her rape). Fisher, on the other hand, would have preferred to shoot a scene of Brandt-in-Richter's-body (Freddie Jones) raping his own wife, Ella (Maxine Audley), when she rejects him because of his new body. In retrospect he said such a scene would have been both "tremendous" and "justifiable," revelatory of a "human situation"[59]—again indicative, nevertheless, of the tenacious justifications within the resilient Frankensteinian narrative for violence against the feminized shadow.

Nevertheless the film's emotional focus this time is Brandt-Richter's monster, whose pathetic gestures for help are misinterpreted by Anna as an attempt at rape and whose hiding behind a screen to prevent his wife from seeing him stir genuine sympathy. The scenes in which the dying Brandt-Richter struggles to return home, and weeps when he gazes upon his sleeping wife, evoke pathos, and create an emotional complexity with which even Frankenstein cannot compete.

The film opens with the murder of a Dr. Heideke by a man with a ghostly, kabuki-white face. The white pockmarked face is ripped off, revealing it to be a mask worn by Frankenstein. By then, the identification of Cushing as the baron had become so institutionalized that the script needed no overt introduction of his character. Nevertheless the clear association of Frankenstein's character with the hideous mask and his ruthless gathering of body parts lends the Hammer Frankenstein series a new viciousness. In a manner similar to the way the Universal series progressively demonizes the Monster and eventually reduces it to no more than a mechanical brute, the Hammer series progressively moves towards recreating Frankenstein as a monstrous monomaniac, rendering his charming and gentlemanly manner increasingly a strategic veneer rather than a complex dimension of the character. The earlier Frankenstein was a figure simultaneously sympathized with and feared, with his ambiguous rebel status that enabled him to straddle the worlds of the bourgeois and the criminal. This Frankenstein leaves little room for compassion with his iciness and cruelty. His darkened hair and unencumbered physical agility (as opposed to the frailty shown in, for example, the character's burned hands in *Frankenstein Created Woman*) signal his rebirth as the genuine monster of the tale.

Inspector Frisch (Thorley Walters) and a police doctor (Geoffrey Bayldon) are assigned to the case. The two emerge in their relationship to each other, as parodic versions of Sherlock Holmes and Dr. Watson. Yet both display Holmes-ian characteristics, with the doctor possessing Holmes's intellectual acumen, and the police inspector displaying a buffoonish exaggeration of Holmes's imperviousness to manners and sensitivity. Interestingly enough the film is littered with doctor characters, both as hunter and hunted and as objects of violence or active subjects perpetrating violence. Even the police doctor, through his ambivalent admiration for the invisible murderer's intelligence, is not a completely noble character. His ambivalent spectation of the results of Frankenstein's predation mark him as someone who vicariously shares in the exhiliration of the hunt as he aids the police inspector in tracking down the killer.

Meanwhile Frankenstein alights from a carriage and rings the bell of Anna Spengler's boardinghouse. The attractive blonde ushers him in, and he signs in the register as a "Mr. Fenner." As she leads him up the steps, she assures him that she has only four other guests, and that he will find the house a quiet place. As if ironically to undercut that statement, the scene shifts abruptly to reveal a woman screeching as though she were possessed. It is an asylum, and a young and handsome doctor, Karl Holst (Simon Ward), injects the screaming woman with a sedative as two uniformed men pin her down. The woman suffers from delusionary spells of believing that spiders are running all over her body, and these attacks render her hysterical—a fact of symbolic and narrative significance as the story unfolds. The juxtaposition of Anna's quiet mastery over her boarding home contrasts sharply with the hysteric's helplessness. Yet that superficial difference is soon to be shattered, as Anna finds herself progressively enmeshed in a situation that results first in her rape, then in her murder. Anna's independence, which is a result of her absent/unseen mother's illness, is tightly circumscribed even from the start. She rules purely within the domestic realm, and she remains financially dependent upon her fiancé, Dr. Karl Holst, who steals drugs from the asylum to sell them off at the black market in order to help Anna pay off her hopelessly sick mother's medical bills. Yet even the partial autonomy of the feminized shadow is soon to be ruthlessly appropriated by Frankenstein. The narrative justifies Anna's (as yet another feminine-as-monstrous figure) destruction by revealing that she is a willing accomplice to her fiancé's crime, and also uses a noble trait she possesses—an unwillingness to abandon Karl—further to cement the inevitability of her violent sacrifice.

At the hallway of the asylum, Holst inquires of a certain Dr. Brandt's condition. Dr. Richter, Holst's superior, sounds despondent, and speaks with frustration of the difference between an abscess in the brain that can be removed, and a sick brain, which cannot be cured simply through surgery. This is a distinction Frankenstein, the brilliant sane-mad explorer in search of preserving the immortality of minds, is to challenge later. The scene is steeped in an air of hopelessness, saturated by images of Dr. Brandt (George Pravda) staring off mindlessly into the distance, as Richter's voice resounds, "A terrible, terrible waste." Ironically, Frankenstein, the restorer of Brandt's sanity, blurs the line between sanity and mental sickness by rendering the outside world simply an extension of the asylum's workings; Brandt, soon to be locked into Richter's body, is reborn not as a new Adam, but as a fallen demon, who lusts for revenge. Frankenstein, as well, is not free from his own sickness, which is his consuming obsession with obtaining Brandt's knowledge concerning how to freeze or preserve brains. His actions are motivated not by the altruistic desire to restore sanity to his former collaborator, but by the determination to gain access to his medical secrets.

At the boardinghouse, the four boarders speak dismissively of Frankenstein's lack of social skills. The interaction marks them as bourgeois as they sit around, smoking pipes and reading newspapers while playing chess. It also feminizes them by characterizing them as akin to the caricature of gossipy women who have nothing better to do. As Frankenstein enters the conversation shifts to the decapitation reported in the newspapers and the general sentiment that madmen are loose on the streets. Yet when the conversation turns to a discussion of Brandt's mad collaboration with a Bohemian baron concerning brain transplants—a business they dismiss as "claptrap"—Frankenstein suddenly flares up and says rudely that "stupidity always brings out the worst" in him. He takes his leave curtly by insinuating that the person he directly addresses has not progressed beyond the caveman stage because he has greasy lapels—a detail that is indicative of his lack of proper gentlemanly manners. The interaction again underlines Frankenstein's aristocracy, which adds another dimension to his stature as an outcast. Yet this time, in place of the complex fluctuations across the bourgeois and criminal worlds characteristic of, for example, *The Revenge of Frankenstein*, is a thoroughgoing damnation of a Machiavellian monomaniac who uses the appearance of gentlemanly behavior to mask his less than civil inner self. The hideous pockmarked mask that Frankenstein rips off in the earlier sequence is his true face; the youthful and aristocratic demeanor he projects is the mask. Interestingly enough his monstrosity bears all the marks of traditional marginalization: His status as a baron is cancelled by his status as a foreigner; he has lost his wealth and social station as a result of his being expelled from his native Bohemia. The only thing he has left is this burning ambition to appropriate the secret of preserving brains, which is what precisely defines his identity as monstrous. The baron's almost reverential worship of (intelligent) brains also underlines his indifference to the body, which is mythically associated with the feminine archetype. To him, it is only an outer casing, which may explain why images of body parts as disgusting and dispensable proliferate throughout the film.

Frankenstein finds out about the drugs Karl is illegally spiriting away and blackmails Karl and Anna. With the young couple now under his control, Frankenstein takes over the house. As the other boarders are forced to leave, Frankenstein emerges from the top of the stairway, signaling his sinister usurpation of Anna's limited domain of freedom. As Hutchings eloquently phrases it, "As a demonstration of his mastery of the house, the baron then appears, Dracula-like, in a commanding position at the top of the stairs during the eviction."[60] The baron's invasion leaves no room for compromises. In the same way his domination requires the removal of all (feminized) men who accept Anna's authority, he exacts both the loss of Karl's self-respect as a doctor, and the rape and murder of Anna. Like a vampire who parasitically feeds upon the blood of his victims and contaminates them with his own blood, Frankenstein exploits and undermines the young couple's love, and turns them into reluctant extensions/versions of himself.

Under the cover of fog, Frankenstein and Karl pierce through the asylum's security, with the baron viciously knocking out a guard. The camera sharply juxtaposes images of the mad woman's face, which grows increasingly alarmed, as Frankenstein and Holst struggle with Brandt, who shows an unexpected alertness and strength. As they begin to overpower him, the woman begins to scratch her body, emitting piercing screams. Frankenstein and Holst are forced to flee hurriedly as the woman's screams function not only diegetically to alert the guards to what has happened, but also symbolically to represent the violence of Frankenstein's invasion of the asylum. The madwoman with her disheveled and unbridled hair is monstrous in a twofold etymological sense: Not only does she point to (*demonstrare*) and warn against (*monere*) Frankenstein's mad invasion of the asylum, but she also undercuts her position as herald precisely by being marked herself as a monstrous object. Her womanhood marks her as prone to hysteria; her face seems to dissolve into nothing but a screaming mouth and cascading hair—again marking her as a feminized and monstrous shadow, whose madness reveals a strange sanity in its recognition of Frankenstein's violation. Frankenstein and Karl manage to dump Brandt's unconscious body into a carriage, whose reins are held by Anna—an act that now marks her as an active, even if unwilling, collaborator.

At the boardinghouse, Karl returns to find out that Brandt has suffered a massive heart attack. Undeterred, Frankenstein coolly picks out Dr. Richter's body—yet another brilliant surgeon—as the ideal home for Brandt's brain. This particular rendition of the Hammer series is interesting because it is littered with the bodies of surgeons or doctors, who are objects of violence perpetrated by fellow doctors or surgeons. It is their intelligence that renders them appealing as prey to the baron, who seems to thrive upon harvesting their parts for experiments (rendering them pure body—and thus, feminized shadows) or using them as reluctant extensions of his own will (making them tools or mechanized shadows, as in the case of Karl).

Based on production history, we know that the next scene, the infamous rape, was tacked on for commercially exploitative reasons. Nevertheless it was well acted and directed, and brings the baron's cruel domination of Anna to a new pitch. As he passes by, he glimpses, through the partially open door, the young woman undressing. The scene is shot provocatively, with the camera dwelling upon the image of Frankenstein's hands ripping through Anna's pink nightgown, and the image of Anna's terrified and protesting face. The scene partakes of the disturbing aesthetic of Fuseli's *Nightmare*, and aestheticizes brutality and cruelty. The vividness of color, and the careless poetry of wrinkled white bedsheets, alongside Anna's pretty face, partially covered by her blond hair, establishes a curious kinship-difference to the madwoman in the asylum, and invites a politics of the gaze similar to Delacroix's *Death of Sardanapalus*, with its visual lushness and thematic violence. Anna's identity as a reluctantly monstrous female, whose beauty enslaves Karl, and is the cause for their being black-mailed, has long been established. Her increasing participation in Frankenstein's violent activities renders her impure. The Frankensteinian narrative's parthenogenetic structure demands the eradication of all female independence and power; it justifies her violent disciplining by showing her complicity, however unwilling, with Frankenstein's monstrous schemes.

Brandt's wife forcefully demands to see the baron, and in order to avoid a commotion, Frankenstein smoothly draws her into the house, introduces himself, then glibly claims that he had intended to call on her, and that she has saved him a trip. To prove the veracity of his claims, he leads her down and asks the veiled form of Brandt-Richter to respond to questions of an intimate nature. The baron suavely ushers her out, urges her not to speak of the matter to anyone, and promises her husband's return in a week's time.

The scene, which displays the baron at his best as a gentleman and miracle worker, is sharply undercut as soon as Mrs. Brandt has left. Frankenstein shuts the door after her, turns, and in a tight close-up, orders the couple to pack for a quick departure. An abrupt cut then shows "the macabre spectacle of Brandt in a carriage at night being fed through a tube,"[61] forcing a confrontation with the complex moral ambivalences surrounding Frankenstein's status as ruthless life-giver.

At the hideout Karl realizes that he and Anna are meant to be Frankenstein's sacrificial pawns. He sends Anna to fetch the hypodermic needle and chart from the patient's bedside and to meet him at the stable, where he will be preparing the carriage for a swift getaway. When she inquires what he needs these for, he replies that based on these, he will be able to calculate exactly when Brandt-Richter is regaining consciousness, and they can then make good their escape because Frankenstein will be absorbed in extracting the secret of freezing brains from the patient. There is something that rings rather falsely in his reply, for he could just as easily simply watch Frankenstein, and take note of when the baron would descend to the cellar. Perhaps he, too, desires some access to Frankenstein's medical secrets, and decides to use Anna to obtain the information. Karl has become very much Frankenstein's proverbial son, who carries on the sins of the father. Nevertheless the narrative moves too swiftly to render clearly what Karl's motivations are. What is clear is that it is his instructions that inadvertently lead to Anna's death.

The creature now regains consciousness. Paradigmatically his fingers twitch to indicate his awakening. His hands, which then move to explore his face, rip off the bandages. Brandt-Richter, whose only physical grotesqueness lies in the crudely stitched suture around his head, then snatches up a bowl, whose reflective sheen reveals to him what has happened. Freddie Jones, the actor who played the monster, reflected upon the challenge of depicting a character who finds himself imprisoned in another's body:

Incredibly, I recall the logical sequence I followed: fearful headache, therefore a desire to touch and perhaps discover some things. On its way up to the head, the hand naturally came into view. *Shock!*—as the hand was instantly unfamiliar! More spontaneous perfunctory investigation and then, I notice the shiny surface of a kidney-shaped bowl—a mirror! And the truth. I don't recall any role making a greater demand.[62]

Unlike Christina (*Frankenstein Created Woman*), whose tragic self-awakening occurs much later, Brandt-Richter immediately recognizes his situation for what it is: an entrapment posing as a miraculous rebirth. He staggers about the room as if he were in severe physical pain and emotional torment. When Anna unsuspectingly enters the laboratory to retrieve the notes and the syringe, the scene is dramatically set for pathos. Brandt-Richter, speaking haltingly and walking toward her with a clumsy gait, tries to assure her that he means her no harm, and inquires concerning the whereabouts of the baron. Anna fearfully stabs him in the stomach with a scalpel. Although the earlier rape scene was tacked on, it lends credibility to the impression that Anna mistook the creature's approach as a sexual attack. Brandt-Richter flees, leaving behind a trail of blood.

The baron roughly interrogates the catatonic Anna, who still clutches the bloody scalpel as she sits against the wall upon the steps, staring blankly into space. When he finds out what has happened, the enraged Frankenstein stabs her and runs after his patient. The manner in which Frankenstein murders Anna is sexually suggestive and reminiscent of the earlier rape: He roughly embraces her, then presses her own hand, bearing the scalpel, into her own body. Anna's transmogrification, from independent and bourgeois boardinghouse matron to slavish and criminal scapegoat, is complete. That she physically holds the instrument upon which the baron impales her signifies her lack of innocence; she is guilty of complicity and, therefore, both her rape and death seem natural consequences. The patriarchal structure of the Frankensteinian narrative justifies her destruction, and shifts the emotional focus of the story back to the male creature.

Mrs. Brandt awakens to find a note sitting beside the lamp close to her bed. Yet even as she reads the letter in a bewildered manner, Brandt-Richter's voice wafts from behind a screen, where he has carefully hidden himself so as not to alarm her. To prove his identity to his incredulous wife, he recounts the conversation they had in Anna Spengler's basement before he leaves for his study. As Brandt-Richter throws out books and rediscovers his notes in the library, his irrepressible wife mounts a ladder and sneaks through an opening in the ceiling. The camera moves in for another tight close-up of the creature's face, sharing his wife's horrified glance. Interestingly, at the moment of his discovery, he bears two lamps— a parodic reenvisaging of the classic Promethean pose of fire-giver. Like the Prometheus who dared to defy the gods, Brandt-Richter chooses to defy death; like Prometheus who finds himself chained to a cliff, his self-reconstituting liver continually devoured by an eagle, Brandt-Richter finds himself locked in a stranger's body, his torment intensified by his wife's adamant refusals to accept him, which seals his murderous resolve for revenge against Frankenstein.

The creature now begins dousing the house with gasoline. When he spies Frankenstein's arrival, he coolly instructs his wife to leave via the back staircase. His wife leaves without a backward glance. Her salvation is striking alongside Anna's violent demise, and it is premised upon her refusal to transgress the boundaries of the domestic and the bourgeois. Despite her heroic traits, Ella is defined in no other way than as Brandt's wife. Her ruthless eagerness to kill off Brandt-Richter is resonant with her desperate attempt to separate the spheres of madness and sanity, unlike Anna, who shares in Frankenstein's fluctuations across these realms. Her unhesitating abandonment of Brandt-Richter frees him to indulge his vengefulness.

Like the original novel's monster, Brandt-Richter is cunning and articulate. He calls himself the spider and identifies Frankenstein, who is momentarily taken aback, as the fly he has trapped. The baron attempts to appeal to the fraternal collaboration that bound them, but Brandt-Richter cuts through his pretensions. When Holst suddenly bursts in on the scene and attacks the baron, Brandt-Richter shoots the young man, determined that no one is to interfere with his plans of revenge. The creature then hoists the semiconscious baron over his shoulders as he reenters the house he has set on fire. This is the only Hammer production in which both creature and creator perish in a cataclysmic end; its overall temper bears an unremitting nihilism that wreaks its cruelty particularly upon the figure of Anna, who occupies the intersecting spheres of woman of monstrous beauty and reluctantly complicitous female monster. Hutchings eloquently traces how the resurrection of Frankenstein's virility in this version demands the aggressive hyperbolization of his masculinity to monstrous dimensions alongside the thoroughgoing sacrifice of feminine self-determination.

> While the earlier *Frankenstein Created Woman* presented a tentative exploration of the possibilities—and eventual impossibility—of female subjectivity within the cycle's constitutive structures, *Frankenstein Must Be Destroyed* stands as a reaction against this, a self-destructive implosion by which the certainty . . . which had largely been dissipated in *The Evil of Frankenstein* and *Frankenstein Created Woman*, is restored, but only at the cost of the explicit destruction of the woman.[63]

Once again the exaggeration of the parthenogenetic myth demands the murderous covering over of the myth of Baubo, with an ending that returns to Whale's *Bride of Frankenstein*.

DEATH THROES OF A RELUCTANT RESURRECTION

Frankenstein and the Monster from Hell, which was released in May 1974 in the United Kingdom, and in October of the same year in the United States, was Hammer's final *Frankenstein* offering. It was also Fisher's final film to direct, and the last film in which Peter Cushing played the baron. The movie was far from a box office hit, and critical reaction was split, as Johnson and Del Vecchio report: "*The London Times* (May 5, 1974): 'Efficiently horrible'; *The Daily Express* (May 3): 'Dr. Helder should learn a trade'; *Cinema TV Today* (May 11): 'Peter Cushing's Baron throws a cloak of elegance over the gruesome malarkey'; *Variety* (June 26): 'An economy of filmmaking that is missed in more ambitious efforts'; and the *New York Times* (October 31): 'Chock full of the old horror film values we don't see much of anymore.' "[64]

What is clear is that this film paradoxically combines a restraint in color with a more graphic depiction of violence. Images that Fisher usually evoked rather than showed, such as sawing open a head and extracting a brain, were made visible, rather than kept below the camera's line of sight. Nevertheless the gray that seems to seep into every scene, predominantly set against the claustrophobic setting of an asylum, offsets this, and provides the narrative frame with a distanced, almost objectivistic, perspective. Hanke echoes this observation: "Absent are the usual scenic locales and warm colors of the previous [Hammer *Frankenstein*] entries. In their place we have the cramped, inhuman confines of a grey [*sic*] asylum and cinematographer Brian Probyn's almost clinically detached view of the proceedings."[65]

Nevertheless the film is rich in symbolism and irony, rooted in John Elder's script, and visually elaborated upon through Fisher's direction. The baron is now ensconced in the high temple of medical (mal)practice appropriate for his activities: an asylum, where he is registered as a deceased patient, yet in which he reigns supreme through blackmail. Again the complexities of the baron's (Peter Cushing) character emerge. He fulfills a paternal role, protecting the asylum's inmates from the asylum director's and warders' cruel and exploitative urges. Yet he just as spontaneously has no problems with using selected patients as sources for body parts. He takes Sarah, "the Angel" (Madeline Smith), as his special assistant to protect her from her father's/the director's lascivious designs; yet he does not hesitate in proposing that he use her to mate with the monster in order to "recreate" the creature in the "normal" way. Nevertheless this is a Frankenstein who seems a degenerated and senescing version of his former self. As Phil Hardy, Tom Milne, and Paul Willemen observe, "[Frankenstein] is presented as a somewhat cultural boor, guffawing at a bad joke, unable to solve mathematical problems or to appreciate music. His hands, burnt in the previous film [Frankenstein Must be Destroyed], have become useless for surgery."[66] Like the baron in The Evil of Frankenstein, the Frankenstein in this version has become vulnerable, and despite his ambivalent swings between ruthlessness and civility, he has become a partially sympathetic character in his fragility. Jensen conjectures on the biographical link between Fisher's aging years, and his consistent coupling of frustrated creativity with decreased vitality in the figures of Frankenstein, and the monster who is coupled from Durendel's brain, Tarmut's hands, and Schneider's body (David Prowse). According to Jensen, Fisher's depiction of both Frankenstein and his creature reveals a "purity" and "sensitivity" that reveal his empathy with someone whose former creative powers now bear visible signs of dimunition.[67]

This film, in essence, constitutes Fisher's farewell to the Frankenstein series and his work as a director; it also signifies the death throes of the Hammer Frankenstein offerings, which were soon displaced by the far more sensationalist thrills of The Exorcist, more visceral big-budget spectaculars like The Omen and Alien series, as well as low-budget, splatter spine tinglers like The Texas Chainsaw Massacre, Halloween, and Friday the 13th.[68] With its tight visual economy and lurid rendition of the Frankensteinian narrative, Frankenstein and the Monster from Hell, like Whale's Frankenstein (1931) and Bride of Frankenstein (1935), hyperbolizes as well as ironically undercuts the myth of parthenogenetic birthing; however, it fails to reinvigorate the myth of Baubo's ana-suromai. Like the other madwomen in the asylum, Sarah, "the Angel," is an image of severely circumscribed femininity, as evidenced in her muteness, her unquestioning devotion to Frankenstein, and her intended role as bride of the monster, and mother-to-be of the creature's offspring.

Dr. Simon Helder (Shane Briant) is found guilty of "sorcery" because of his attempts to replicate Frankenstein's experiments and is committed to an asylum. From the start the arbitrariness of the border delineating the sane from the mad in the asylum is made clear. Helder momentarily tricks Director Adolf Klauss (John Stratton) into thinking he is a visiting doctor who has come to inspect the premises. When the director attempts to hand Helder a glass of wine, he finds the young man shackled and comes to the horrified realization that the man whom he has been treating as an authority is a mere inmate under his control.

Ernst (Philip Voss) and Hans (Chris Cunningham), two warders, decide that it is time to subject the haughty young man to an initiation rite: a bath inflicted with a fire hose. They gather the rest of the inmates, who mill about in anticipation of the forthcoming spectacle. Interestingly, the warders feminize both the inmates (by calling them "my pretties") and Helder (by dramatically ripping off his shirt to give the leering audience a "show"). Helder's "bath" is loaded with sexual overtones. The women, with the exception of "the Angel," shriek like banshees when they see his shirt stripped off forcefully—an act that makes the scene a hybrid of an enforced striptease and visual rape. The crowd howls with sadistic delight as the powerful gush of water first momentarily blinds Helder, then creates welts in his back, and finally causes him to slump forward, momentarily losing consciousness. The madness of the scene is punctuated by the madwomen's soothing interjections of clichés such as: "My mother used to say that cleanliness is next to Godliness," and "Oh, that's nice isn't it? He's going to be nice and clean." In sharp contrast are Sarah's dismayed and compassionate looks. From the very start, her difference from the rabble is conveyed: "The Angel" immediately moves away from an inmate who tries to grope her; she does not share in the base, carnal desires of the other inmates and warders. Nevertheless her mute stance of protest and difference are futile; she can only look on helplessly until a figure dressed in black suddenly appears.

The figure, who is simply addressed as "Doctor," by Ernst, immediately assumes control. He orders all the inmates back to their rooms, instructs Sarah to tend to Helder's wounds, and stomps off to the director's room. From the moment of his introduction, the doctor's imperious manner, and his savvy manipulation of others around him (not to mention the close association between Peter Cushing and his screen identity as Frankenstein) tip the audience off regarding who truly defines the fluctuating borders separating the "mad" and the "sane" in the asylum.

Helder shrewdly confronts Frankenstein concerning his identity, and the older man acknowledges it. The young man then becomes Frankenstein's medical assistant. The subtle rivalry over control of Sarah is made explicit from the start, yet "the Angel" appears oblivious to such earthly matters. Her function as a ministering "angel" is simply to obey orders, and it does not seem to matter to her who plays God. The various patients they visit at the asylum illustrate not only the arbitrariness of the borders separating the sane from the insane, but also the frailty of lines separating the empowered from the disempowered. Herr Muller (Sydney Bromley), who believes he is God, presses his body against the wall as though he were crucified. He says that "God is always fine," but replies that Herr Muller is feeling sore, and like a child, bares his wounded arm trustingly to Helder as Frankenstein looks on. Muller's delusion of being God contrasts sharply with his actual circumstances as a frail old man committed to an asylum. His despairing statement of having created "man in his own image" mirrors the absurdity of Frankenstein's ambition of creating the ideal man (in his projected image of what the ideal man should be like). Like Muller, Frankenstein is essentially as trapped in the madhouse as everyone else is, despite his constant threats to leave; it is the only place where he can finally proceed with his experiments unimpeded by external authorities, and where he can define what is "mad" or "sane."

As they pass a corridor, Frankenstein mentions that his "special" patients are localized in this area. It turns out that the first room is empty, though the window bars are bent and mangled. Frankenstein speaks with mingled awe and fascination for the "more animal than human" Schneider, who possessed such sheer strength and willpower that he wrenched the window bars apart and for days clung on to life despite his intense agony. Schneider possessed the body of a Neanderthal, and suffered from homicidal tendencies; he liked stabbing people in the face with broken glass.

The next patient, Professor Durendel, is playing a hauntingly beautiful violin piece inspired by "the Angel" as they enter; Helder is touched by it, but Frankenstein, confessing to his being tone-deaf, is unable to appreciate it. Sarah, the object of veneration, keeps her face down as the professor acknowledges that the piece is dedicated to her. The walls of the cell are filled with chalk scribblings of mathematical equations and geometric shapes. Durendel asks if Helder appreciates pure math, and is disappointed slightly that the young man is unable to share his pleasure in something "more beautiful even than music and nearly as beautiful as my little Angel here." As he utters the last words, Durendel uses his bow to touch Sarah gently, who does not recoil from the contact. Durendel's remarks and gesture again underline Sarah's ambiguous status as both empowered and disempowered, embodied and disembodied, daughter and madonna. By using his bow as an extension of his hand, he physically and symbolically touches her body while treating her as a disembodied muse—an Angel who inspires composition in one of the most sensual and the most abstract of the arts, music.

The final inmate they visit is Tarmut, a craftsman who used to sculpt pieces of exquisite beauty, as evidenced by numerous pieces lying around him. Tarmut's dangerousness is tied up with his creativity; when his brain atrophied rapidly, he became both harmless and incapable of further creation. Just as the three are about to leave, Tarmut suddenly seems to have a lucid moment, and he hands over a statue of an Angel to Sarah. "The Angel" smilingly accepts his gift of veneration, but does not return his gaze for very long and hurries out. The two men follow, and unlike the three characters, the camera looks back, to reveal a dejected and lonely Tarmut with his arms held out beseechingly. Sarah's status as "Angel" is upheld by her distance from the suffering inmates who worship her; though she is in a position to understand them and ease their sufferings, she cannot seem to bear intense emotional intercourse, and shrinks from its physical expression. In that sense she is truly Frankenstein's daughter, as she partakes of a version of his clinical detachment. Later, in the hallway, she seems absorbed in contemplating the angel sculpture, yet obediently pays attention when Frankenstein gives her instructions. She then shyly exchanges glances with Helder—an indication of the possibility of an emotional breakthrough, yet even this potential liberation is problematic because the young man shares Frankenstein's propensities for mastery and domination.

Above the din of madwomen's cries and a storm, Helder hears animal cries and in tracing their origin, discovers Frankenstein's secret laboratory, where a furry Neanderthal with a massive physique, the supposedly deceased Schneider (David Prowse), is held behind special bars. Both David Prowse, who played the part of the creature, and Fisher were strongly opposed to the Neolithic mask and hairy body suit designed by Eddie Knight and Les Bowie. Prowse's objections were based on the physical discomfort of wearing the outfit: "I could only wear the costume for short periods. It was warm and thirsty work. The costume got terribly hot after a time working under all those studio lights, and, for part of the day, I couldn't see where I was going as the mask covered my eyes."[69] Fisher was adamantly against the use of excessive makeup because he believed it would interfere with the emotive potential of the creature. However, because the contract with Paramount hinged upon the creature's characterization as a hairy and grotesque beast, Fisher had to content himself merely with toning down the makeup. This constitutes another example of how the technological shadow, at this point in the unfolding of the Hammer series, had become mythically enshrined as the site of the exaggeratedly grotesque and bestial. Subtlety could no longer be employed particularly in its physical depiction, as the exaggeration of the parthenogenetic myth requires the radical Othering of the technological shadow.

Helder delicately poses the issue of the crude quality of the surgery on the beast, as evidenced by the creature's scars, and Frankenstein reveals both his burned hands and the fact that it has been Sarah who has been performing the surgery under his supervision. Helder, now emboldened, reveals that he, too, is a trained surgeon and volunteers to assist Frankenstein with his next operation. In so doing Helder unwittingly displaces

Sarah from her invaluable position as Frankenstein's hands—a replacement that is to cost the young woman dearly, because she then moves from the realm of indispensable to dispensable in Frankenstein's utilitarian calculus.

The next scene overtly illustrates the parthenogenetic myth. Frankenstein, masterminding the operation, watches carefully as Helder repairs a damaged peripheral artery connection. The original film appears to have contained a scene in which Frankenstein helps hold a blood vessel with his teeth because his burned hands are useless, but this was cut from the American release.[70] Instead the remaining version simply has him wiping his mouth, as he proclaims his satisfaction with the result of the operation. Sarah, unsurprisingly, has not actively participated in the proceedings and has simply been hovering about, as an "angel" should. As the operation occurs, shots of both her concerned, and at times averted face, link her with the monster, whose passivity mirrors hers. As "Angel"/ "Beauty" and "Devil"/ "Beast," the feminine and technological shadows possess a kinship: they are both potentially seductively perilous and the embodiment of imperilment themselves.

The camera dissolves into a blurry haze, and we realize that we are peering through the awakening creature's eyes at the backs of Frankenstein and Helder working together at a bench. The creature shrugs Helder aside, but Frankenstein breaks a bottle containing the sedative into a coat. He then drops the shards upon a table, preying upon Schneider's weakness for broken glass; while the creature is distracted, he jumps on top of the hulking figure and throws the coat, which has the gaseous sedative trapped in it, over its head—once again attesting to Frankenstein's greater virility over Helder.

Rather conveniently the professor, the only one with a brain suitable for Frankenstein's project, commits suicide. In a series of quick close-ups, the camera moves from an image of evocative poetic power to one steeped in the macabre and brutal: first it roves over a violin without strings lying on top of disheveled music sheets—a powerful image of wasted creativity—and then rapidly to a tight close-up of the professor, with his neck bloodied, his mouth gaping open, suspended from the ceiling. Helder finds out that Frankenstein had planted a document stating that the doctor was "incurable," meaning that Durendel would never be allowed to leave, which must have driven him to take his own life. Frankenstein, despite his protests to the contrary, is effectively the professor's murderer. This is the first time Simon Helder, the rock upon whom Frankenstein meant to build his scientific kingdom, shows a sign of wavering.

Nevertheless all is brushed aside as the stage is set for the final segment of the parthenogenetic birth. The birthing sequence acquires a new twist, as it appropriates the myth of Athena's birthing from the head of Zeus. The professor's brain is going to be transplanted into Schneider-Tarmut's body to create the new Adam. The birthing of the ideal man through the ministrations of the father-son pair can only take place through the re-placement of (feminized) bodily birthing with mental/intellectual resurrec-tion via (masculine) surgical transplantation. All these are visualized by Fisher in sordid, detailed form, as if to emphasize that the attempt to escape from the bodily, with its fluids and cavernous spaces, is doomed to failure.

After the operation Frankenstein stands by the monster with his hands forming a halo around its head, and fervently utters, "If I've succeeded this time, then every sacrifice will have been worthwhile." The language and pose are close to that of a prayer, yet if Frankenstein is praying, it is to himself: he construes himself as the scarificial lamb whose suffering could result in the birthing of the perfect man—again, another iteration of the parthenogenetic myth. That Helder performed the operation, actually with very little supervision this time, is not significant; Helder is simply an ex-tension of himself, and yet another proverbial son of Frankenstein.

The awakened Durendel-Schneider-Tarmut edges toward a violin lying close to the bed. With shaking hands, he attempts to pick it up but fails. He tries again, but in frustration, crushes it with his bare hands. The scene underlines how Frankenstein's "perfect man"—with the brain of a genius, the body of a hulk, and the hands of a sculptor—is simply a nightmarish parody. What emerges from the discombobulated bits is a confused amal-gam that possesses qualities Frankenstein himself possesses: a keen intellect (Durendel), the ability to persevere amidst great pain (Schneider), and the ability to compensate for an infirmity (Tarmut, prior to going over the edge). Frankenstein, the parthenogenetic father, has indeed created the monster "in his own image and likeness."

At the laboratory Frankenstein urges the professor to practice coordi-nation and to exercise his brain, despite the creature's obvious frustration. A cut reveals the hulking figure writing a mathematical equation on the chalkboard. The creature then begins to write at a downward slant. Frank-enstein sharply inquires why this is happening, and the creature grunts, "hungry"—implying the dominance of the bodily over the mental, and the subversion of the masculine appropriation of the myth of Athena's birth from the head of Zeus (i.e., a birthing of pure intellection by a father of a son, rather than a masculinized daughter).

The romantic component of the film gains momentum, yet it is striking that it does so within a very strict hierarchy of power. At no point does Sarah possess any genuine power; her poses are all vulnerable, whether asleep or awake, and Helder fluctuates across treating her like a fragile jewel, a sickly child, and a divine being. Again, as in *The Evil of Frank-enstein*, the myth of female disruptive power, instantiated in Baubo's *ana-suromai*, is radically domesticated; Sarah is "the Angel" precisely because in her figure, the "obscene" has been carefully shorn away from the "di-vine."

The monster attacks Helder, implying its sense of sexual ownership over

Sarah. Helder is once again saved by the older but more virile Frankenstein. Ecstatic over the fact that both brain and body are still functioning well, albeit antagonistically, Frankenstein proposes a new experiment: to "capture the essence of the man . . . [reborn] in the normal way, by mating." Helder is thunderstruck, and inquires with whom Frankenstein intends to mate the creature. Frankenstein calmly replies "Sarah."

In reply to Helder's bewildered and shocked queries, Frankenstein first assures him that she would be a suitable mate because "she is not subnormal either physically or mentally." Her inability to speak was caused by the traumatic shock of her father attempting to rape her, and Frankenstein nonchalantly says that another shock could arbitrarily cause her power of speech to return. For now he smugly proclaims: "Her real function as a woman could be fulfilled." Frankenstein's treatment of Sarah reveals her true status: she is not only "the Angel," she is also both the female-as-monstrous, and the monstrous female, whose potential for self-liberation and reproductive power must be further harnessed through her rape and impregnation by his grotesquely "ideal man."

Desperate, Helder heads for the inner room, and attempts to warn Durendel of Frankenstein's plans for him and Sarah. But the creature merely grunts and says, "Hungry." Helder gives up and tries to kill the creature, which overpowers him and is on the verge of a lethal blow when, in a tight close-up, the camera whirls to reveal Sarah scream. She then calmly says, "Let him go," to the creature, who obeys. Despite the return of Sarah's voice, she is ultimately unable to transcend her status as potential mate of the monster and feminine shadow, as I demonstrate.

As the film builds to its climax, the strain caused by the negation of the feminine and technological-demonized shadows builds tension within the narrative, and foretells their vengeful rupture. As a storm rages, the monster screams. A madwoman cackles, muttering, "He's angry now. He wants revenge. . . . You shall have it, my beauty!" The madwoman's disheveled appearance, witchlike laughter, and ironic reference to the monster as "my beauty" aligns herself and the creature with the demonic.

After the Monster kills Klauss, Sarah's father, because it remembers the director's rape attempt upon his own child, the creature lurches into the asylum as the inmates mill about excitedly. Ernst and Hans shoot the creature, which staggers forward and, upon glimpsing Sarah, reaches out to its Angel with a bloody hand. In one of the two self-determined acts she displays throughout the film (with the earlier act consisting of saving Helder from the creature), Sarah breaks free of Helder's restraining grasp and moves close to the wounded Monster. It touches her hair gently as she gazes upon it sympathetically. The crowd suddenly grows alarmed. Thinking that the Monster intends to harm their Angel, they attack the wounded creature and dismember it. What is interesting is that though the original motivation for the inmates' behavior may have been in preventing violence, they readily lose sight of this and engage in a frenzied melee, tearing out the creature's organs while laughing maniacally. The film's potential for healing the rift between Ego and its shadows is sundered. Ironically, the crowd becomes the insistent enforcer of the line delineating the mad from the sane, the healthy from the sick, the demonic from the Angelic. Instead of wreaking revenge upon Frankenstein, they destroy what frighteningly resembles them, as if in an effort to negate the asylum's characterization of what they are. Sarah's attempt to cross the line from Angel to monstrous woman, and to reveal their kinship, is too disturbing, and must be reabsorbed into the logic of the parthenogenetic narrative.

The wounded Frankenstein rushes in and imperiously commands order, but it is too late. The creature is dead, its innards gaping, with its various organs strewn about the room. Yet the movie does not end with this scene. In the next, we see the baron simultaneously bandaging himself and reading a book. It appears the baron has flung himself back into his experiments and has come across a different tack: less reliance on surgery, and more on biochemistry. Helder significantly does not move to assist Frankenstein in dressing his injury even when the older man asks him to do so. When Helder does not respond, Frankenstein gets up and begins sweeping the room clean of broken glass, implying a return to the process of assembling the ideal man from scratch. Both Sarah and Helder remain frozen, as the camera moves away, and reveals the massive outer structure of asylum cast in darkness. The ending leaves little room for optimism; it is clear that both Sarah and Helder are fully in Frankenstein's control, and the dissolve to the impregnable looking exterior of the madhouse is eloquent testimony to their entrapment in a world where the standards of sanity are determined by someone mad. The ending makes it clear that the Hammer films had run full circle; though the movie left itself open-ended, the narrative integrity of the Frankensteinian parthenogenetic myth is undercut by glimpses of its dark, nihilistic underside. The triumphant dream of the masculine birthing of a world devoid of the realms of body, the irrational, and the feminized exacts so much strain that it unveils its subterranean counterpart: the ruthless harnessing of the refractory power of the feminized, technologized, and femininely monstrous shadows.

CONCLUDING REMARKS

The Hammer series renders overt much of what remains repressed within the Universal series. The uncompromising version of the parthenogenetic myth is progressively undercut; Frankenstein now seems capable of ironic self-appraisal (*The Evil of Frankenstein*), is dependent on others because of physical infirmities (*Frankenstein Created Woman*), and even subjects himself to the vulnerable position of being an experimental object (*Frankenstein Created Woman*). Peter Cushing's Frankenstein, unlike many of the

Universal series versions, is a genuinely charismatic and terrifying character. As such, it is his face that replaces Karloff's iconic representation of the creature as the visage of the monstrous. The shift signifies a displacement in the identification of where the monstrous or overdeveloped shadow lies. Unlike the Universal series, where it was linked predominantly with the Monster, it now becomes grafted on to the ever-resurrected baron-doctor. Yet like Universal's monstrous creatures, who degenerate into mechanical killing machines, Hammer's Frankenstein eventually becomes no more than a madman, whose repulsiveness wipes out any sympathetic identification earlier established.

In a similar vein, the Hammer series does not flinch from the evocation and later overt illustration of the violence at the heart of the Frankenstein myth: the harvesting of body parts, and their reassembly and resuscitation compose vivid details of the narrative flow. Finally the Hammer series creates a momentary space for the expression of female erotic desire and power, with characters like Justine (*Curse of Frankenstein*), and, more problematically, Christina (*Frankenstein Created Woman*). However, women who occupy the space of the female Monster (Christina) or the feminine-as-monstrous (Justine) are eventually ruthlessly destroyed. Only women who remain safely within the borders of the domesticated feminine shadow (Elizabeth in *Curse of Frankenstein*, Margaret in *Revenge of Frankenstein*, Sarah in *Frankenstein Must be Destroyed*) are "saved." The Hammer series continues the Universal series' separation of the spheres of erotic and reproductive power, which are linked in Baubo's *ana-suromai*. Even though the creation of separate spheres serves, momentarily, to enable the expression of female erotic desire and desirability, it ultimately harshly reestablishes the parthenogenetic boundary lines. The safe space for women and "the feminine" lies in the realm of the Virgin-Madonna, which is the repressed feminine counterpoint to the myth of Baubo.

NOTES

1. David Pirie, *A Heritage of Horror; The English Gothic Cinema 1946–1972* (London: Gordon Fraser, 1973), 40.

2. Peter Hutchings, *Hammer and Beyond: The British Horror Film* (Manchester and New York: Manchester University Press, 1993), 6.

3. Donald Glut, *The Frankenstein Legend: A Tribute to Mary Shelley and Boris Karloff* (Metuchen, N.J.: Scarecrow Press, 1973), 189.

4. Alan Frank, *The Movie Treasury; Horror Movies, Tales of Terror in the Cinema* (London: Octopus Books, 1974), 24.

5. Paul M. Jensen, *The Men Who Made the Monsters* (New York: Twayne, 1996), 155–156.

6. Howard Maxford, *Hammer, House of Horror; Behind the Screams* (Woodstock and New York: The Overlook Press, 1996), 32. A copy from the University

of Southern California's Warner Brothers Film Archive titles the script *Franken-stein*; Maxford details it as *Frankenstein and the Monster*.

7. Ibid., 11.

8. R.D. Stock, *The Flutes of Dionysus; Daemonic Enthrallment in Literature* (Lincoln: University of Nebraska Press, 1989), 8.

9. John McCarty, *Splatter Movies; Breaking the Last Taboo of the Screen* (New York: St. Martin's Press, 1984), 29.

10. Jensen echoes this position. See Jensen, 178.

11. Ibid.

12. " 'Monster' Revived on Screens," *Los Angeles Times*, July 18, 1957.

13. Archer Winsten, " 'Curse of Frankenstein' at Paramount," *New York Post*, August 7, 1957.

14. Randy Palmer, "Reluctant Monster Maker," *Fangoria* 50 (1986): 48.

15. "Ask Roy Ashton," *Little Shoppe of Horrors* (July 1981): 36.

16. Robert Marrero, *Horrors of Hammer* (Key West, Fl.: RGM, 1984), 13.

17. Pirie, 69.

18. Glut, 191.

19. John McCarty, *The Modern Horror Film* (New York: Citadel, 1990), 19.

20. Christopher Lee, *Tall, Dark and Gruesome* (London: W.H. Allen, 1977), 197.

21. John McCarty, 19.

22. Ibid., 93.

23. Frank, 32.

24. Maxford, 44.

25. Jensen, 185.

26. McCarty, 30. See also Ken Hanke, *A Critical Guide to Horror Film Series* (New York. Garland Publishing, 1991), 186.

27. Stephen Jones, *The Frankenstein Scrapbook; The Complete Movie Guide to the World's Most Famous Monster* (New York: Citadel Press/Carol Publishing Group, 1995), 65.

28. Leslie Halliwell, *The Dead that Walk: Dracula, Frankenstein, the Mummy and Other Famous Monsters* (New York: Continuum, 1988), 169.

29. Maxford, 70.

30. "The Evil of Frankenstein," in *The Encyclopedia of Horror Movies* ed. Phil Hardy, Tom Milne, and Paul Willemen (New York: Harper and Row, 1986), 161.

31. Pirie, 75.

32. Jensen, 235.

33. Ibid., 250.

34. Glut, 196.

35. Ibid.

36. Jensen, 236.

37. Tom Johnson and Deborah Del Vecchio, *Hammer Films; An Exhaustive Filmography* (Jefferson, N.C.: McFarland & Company, 1996), 282.

38. "Durrant's Press Cuttings," *Daily Mirror*, September 29, 1966.

39. "Durrant's Press Cuttings," *Evening Standard*, September 28, 1966.

40. "Durrant's Press Cuttings," *Daily Sketch*, September 29, 1966.

41. Marrero, 55.

42. Maxford, 89.

43. Hanke, 190.

44. Gregory William Mank, *It's Alive! The Classic Cinema Saga of Frankenstein.* (San Diego and New York: Barnes, 1981), 198.

45. Pirie, 78.

46. Hanke, 191.

47. Hutchings, 109.

48. Cushing also played the part of Sherlock Holmes in *The Hound of the Baskervilles* (1959). Perhaps it is hardly surprising that these personae, alongside that of Dr. Van Helsing, the relentless scourge of Dracula, also played by Cushing, merge into each other. As John McCarty notes, "Peter Cushing even brought elements of his Frankenstein and Van Helsing personae to the character of Sherlock Holmes in *The Hound of the Baskervilles*. . . . Cushing's Holmes is not simply cerebral and dispassionate . . . but, like Frankenstein and Van Helsing, obsessive and, at times, even fanatical in his quest to attain the powers only God may possess." John McCarty, 30.

49. Jensen, 218.

50. John Elder, *Frankenstein Created Woman* (London: Hammer Film Productions, 1966).

51. Mank, 198.

52. Pirie, 77.

53. Hutchings, 111.

54. Hanke, 191.

55. Hutchings, 111.

56. Johnson and Del Vecchio, 310–311.

57. Hanke, 192.

58. Jensen, 227.

59. Ibid.

60. Hutchings, 113.

61. Pirie, 79.

62. Johnson and Del Vecchio, 309.

63. Hutchings, 112.

64. Johnson and Del Vecchio, 364–365.

65. Hanke, 192.

66. Hardy, Milne, and Willemen, 275.

67. Jensen, 230.

68. Maxford, 127.

69. Johnson and Del Vecchio, 364.

70. Jensen, 229.

—⚘—

CHAPTER 4

Beyond the Universal and Hammer Series

Since the whole episode of the monster's spying on the De Laceys is narrated in the novel by the monster himself, the text never describes the sight of his peering face. So we might construe this shot as an example of the way film reveals what the novel hides or suppresses.
—James A.W. Heffernan, "Looking at the Monster: Frankenstein and Film"

CINEMATIC DIASPORA

After Universal had ceased *Frankenstein* productions, and even before Hammer had begun casting its own versions of the monster tale, other motion picture companies had begun to realize the moneymaking potential of the narrative. The Frankenstein saga conquered international and genre boundaries, producing a broad array of narratives. Among these were the French parody, *Torticola contre Frankensberg* (translated as *Twisted Neck versus Frankensberg*) in 1952; the Spanish production of *El Testamento del Frankenstein* (*The Testament of Frankenstein*) in 1964; the Japanese Toho offerings (in collaboration with American producer Henry G. Saperstein) of *Furankenshutain tai baragon* (translated as *Frankenstein versus Baragon*, yet released in the United States as *Frankenstein Conquers the World*) in 1965, and its sequel *Furankenshutain no Kaiji—Sanda tai Gailah* (initially translated as *Frankenstein Monsters—Sanda versus Gailah*, but eventually retitled for U.S. audiences as *The War of the Gargantuas*) in 1967; and the "R"-rated *La Figlia di Frankenstein* (initially translated as *The Daughter of Frankenstein* and eventually released in the United States as *Lady Frankenstein* by New World Pictures). Frankenstein offerings that

Still from *Mary Shelley's Frankenstein* appears courtesy of the Academy of Motion Picture Arts and Sciences. TriStar, 1994.

were concurrent with, as well as succeeded, the Universal and Hammer sagas are legion and difficult to classify. Thus, for the purposes of *simplicity*, I am choosing two films as symptomatic of more contemporary evolutions of the Frankenstein myth. These are *Frankenstein 1970* (1958), which is arresting in its use of a filmic frame tale that destabilizes/problematizes the process of filming the evolving Frankenstein myth against a historical backdrop of Nazi violence, and the most recent attempt to visualize what resists visualization in the original novel—*Mary Shelley's Frankenstein* (1994). The reasons why I choose these two are partially spurred by pragmatic considerations such as the availability of not only the films but also the extensive production material housed at the University of Southern California and University of California–Los Angeles Archives and the Academy of Motion Pictures Arts and Sciences. However, more importantly, both productions, as bookends of postseries productions of the Frankenstein saga, have a certain sophistication in the way they treat the process of filmic narrativizing as visual retelling and thus are interesting to dissect in the way they render present the three shadows that hover in between appearance and disappearance. As such these films are thought-provoking lenses that magnify questions similar to those James Heffernan eloquently raises. "By forcing us to face the monster's physical repulsiveness, which he can never deny or escape and which aborts his every hope of gaining sympathy, film versions of *Frankenstein* . . . prompt us to rethink his monstrosity in terms of visualization: how do we see the monster, what does he see, and how does he want to be seen?"[1] Ultimately these films not only enable a glimpse into both the evolving thematics of the monstrous in relation to gender and technology, but also strikingly illustrate the changing format/mode of visualization in relation to the narration of the Frankensteinian myth.

FUTURISTIC VISIONS: *FRANKENSTEIN 1970*

Reviews of Howard Koch's *Frankenstein 1970* (1958) are generally bland rather than enthusiastic. Leslie Halliwell remarks, "*Frankenstein 1970* lingers as a dull and vaguely unpleasant film, but it is *Gone with the Wind* compared with *Frankenstein's Daughter*, released in the same year."[2] Nevertheless there seems to be consensus that the film's beginning scenes set a peak difficult to match or sustain. Donald Glut remarks, "These opening scenes were extremely atmospheric with their barren trees and steaming waters. Unfortunately the rest of the film did not compare with the beginning."[3]

Allied Artists' *Frankenstein 1970* begins with scenes of a blond woman crying out as she is chased by a creature whose only features the camera reveals are its limping, shuffling feet, and quivering, clawlike hands. The young woman trips, then wades into a lake as the creature follows her, and eventually strangles her as he submerges her struggling form. The scene is suddenly interrupted by a sharp male voice that commands a cut. It turns out to be a Frankensteinian film about making Frankensteinian films, and rather mischievously plays into the caricatures associated with the filmic saga of the Frankensteinian narrative at both the internal and metanarrative levels: the lonely and obsessed mad scientist; the obedient servant-slave; the self-absorbed director; the beautiful actress who uses the façade of weakness to manipulate men.

The film is rife with references to the filmic infusion of Germanic elements into the twentieth century rewriting of the Frankensteinian narrative. The actor (Mike Lane) who plays the part of the thespian who acts the part of the creature in the beginning sequence is marked as German and given the eponymous first name, "Hans," and the ominous last name, "Himmler." This actor playing an actor is unable to speak English, the language of the empowered American director and cast, and needs a rapidly speaking translator who speaks with a heavily Germanic accent to communicate his needs and difficulties. This mediator turns out to be Schuter (Norbert Schiller), Baron Victor Frankenstein's (Boris Karloff) obedient and self-effacing servant, whose brain and organs are eventually transplanted into the dormant monster's preserved body—a sign that even the innocuous-seeming German may be dangerous by virtue of his blind loyalty. Most significantly, Baron Frankenstein's hideous physical disfiguring is attributed to torture under the Nazis. Yet far from achieving freedom from Nazi dogmatism and cruelty through his unrelenting resistance to them, the baron is a reincarnation of that militant ruthlessness—precisely *because* he did not give in to them. The linkage between the monstrous and German fascism is a specter that haunts and orients the film, but the rampant film industry commercialism that exploits the Frankensteinian myth is also the butt of ironic humor, and does not escape censure.

For example, when Douglas Roe (Tom Duggan), the American director, asks his colleague, Morgan (Irwin Berke), how the chase-and-murder scene went, the latter replies, "Like a Rembrandt." The comparison is absurd, but the film emphasizes the diegetic lack of irony. For these characters the film they (re)create is the equivalent of a Rembrandt painting, which underlines the aesthetic decadence that characterizes the commercial plundering of the Frankensteinian narrative. Caroline (Jana Lund), the blond actress who is finally rescued from the German actor rather too vigorously acting out drowning her, remarks with a mocking irony that the film itself echoes at a metanarrative level: "How I suffer for Douglas Roe, Madison Avenue, and all those lovely sponsors: scalped by Indians one show to create a covered wagon massacre, boiled and eaten the show before, on the Donner party expedition, and now, nearly drowned to celebrate the 200th anniversary of Frankenstein. . . . Oh well, *achtung* and *heil* residuals."

Caroline's flippancy reveals how her "sacrifices," in her view, are not genuine sacrifices. Yet the film implies very early what her eventual fate may be, given the route fallen into by actress ingenues, whose youth and beauty are currencies all too readily spent in pursuit of momentary stardom. Roe, the director, is arguing with his fourth ex-wife, Judy (Charlotte Austin), who suspects he has romantic designs on Caroline, and the conversation reveals that the dark-haired Judy, not long ago, was an ingenue Roe directed.

The scene shifts to reveal the interior of a castle where Baron Frankenstein, and his friend, Wilhelm Gotfried (Rudolph Anders), discuss the inconvenience of having the American film crew overrunning the baron's castle and private grounds as the price Frankenstein has had to pay to acquire an atomic reactor. The conversation between Wilhelm and Victor is revealing because it highlights a disagreement concerning Frankenstein's character. Gotfried paints Frankenstein's portrait with strokes of heroic resistance, insisting that the Nazis could never own Frankenstein because they could never overpower his mind. Frankenstein mockingly speaks of his "victory" in terms of the only part of his body that remains unblemished: his hands, which the Nazis kept intact in the hope of using him to perform surgical operations for their purposes. Gotfried speaks with awe of Frankenstein's unbroken mind and spirit, as separate from Victor's broken body, but the baron knows that the mind-body split—a characteristic feature that ennobles the novelistic sketch of the Frankensteinian monster— is impossible to uphold within the realm of film. "My mind, ha. Would anyone ever believe that you and I are the same age? Or that I'm even still a man?" Frankenstein's scarred and grotesquely asymmetrical face, his shambling movements, his bitterness over his physical ugliness, and his obvious longing for female companionship mark him as the creature, and rip off the genteel and aristocratic masks with which the Universal and Hammer series camouflage (save with a few fleeting glimpses, as in Hammer's *Frankenstein Must Be Destroyed*) Frankenstein's character. Deformity is bred by deformity, and if Frankenstein was once handsome and morally upright, his rebirth as a product of Nazi brutality renders him an extension of, rather than departure from, their will to power. He recognizes his kinship to them with the words: "They believed in one thing; I believed in another. But they were running the country. That was my misfortune." (Karloff's earlier success as the monster in Whale's 1931 *Frankenstein* rendered his performance as the monstrous creator even more serendipitously effective, from the perspective of typecasting.) Gotfried ignores all these and instead turns the subject to Frankenstein's mysterious scientific activities, which have depleted his family's wealth; it is as if Gotfried intends to awaken Frankenstein's conscience, and to save his tortured friend from himself, as well as to shore up his precious image of Frankenstein as a war hero.

At the family crypt, the baron reads his great-great grandfather's written words concerning the humane intentions that led him to create a monster. The camera moves strategically, framing the baron alongside the small statue of a knight, then a cross, as he reflects upon the failure of his ancestor's experiment, and moves toward a large form hidden by a white sheet. As he raises a knife, a female voice shrieks, and Hans Himmler, the giant actor who had played the part of the creature in the earlier scenes, sits up, looking petrified. We again find out that the past scene has been staged for the sake of Roe's camera; Caroline, who had lost her composure because of the realism of the baron's speech, apologizes. Judy cynically remarks that "Uncle Douglas" (Roe, her ex-husband) would be certain to indulge in his favorite indoor occupation: comforting Caroline. Judy is the most cruelly circumscribed by this iteration of the Frankensteinian narrative, and occupies the position of the female-as-monstrous, the shadow formed from the conjunction of the feminine and the monstrous. As ex-wife, ex-ingenue, and ex-star—from very early on, she is marginalized and marked as one of the Monster's justified victims. Her acid tongue and seething jealousy justify her eventual death, which, in the grand scheme of the narrative, is meaningless: she is murdered accidentally, and her eyes, which are far from perfect (as evidenced by the fact that she wears glasses) are not usable for the Monster.

On the other hand, Roe, the director, mirrors the baron in many ways even if he is diametrically opposed to Frankenstein physically. He is manipulative, domineering, and thoroughly obsessed with anything that will enable him to maximize the economic and prestige-related benefits of creating a television production. Like Frankenstein, he is a ruthless creator, and intent on birthing a creature that is in between the realms of life and death, reality and make-believe, as evidenced by a crew member's acquiescence to Roe's directorial preferences with respect to lighting with the words: "Okay, it's your baby." Given how their profiles mirror each other, it is hardly surprising that they share the same lust for Caroline, the woman who "sacrifices" herself upon the high altar of commercialism and celluloid fantasy.

Left alone, the baron lurches about as he shuts the lights. As he bears a candle (another allusion to the decadent Promethean image at the heart of Shelley's novel), he descends into the vault. It turns out that the baron has been engaged in restoring the body of the creature: drying the skull so as to be able to reshape its features and grafting real and artificial skin together in anticipation of transplanting fresh organs and using the atomic reactor (in an unspecified way) to "reproduce a rebirth." The camera alternates between scenes of Schuter working around the castle, snuffing candles, and of the baron recording his results, foreshadowing an eventual confrontation between the two men. Schuter accidentally notices the cherubim's turned head and twists it, opening the sarcophagus. The baron is unrelenting as he hypnotizes his protesting servant and promises the rebirth of his brain and organs in the creature.

The next morning the women wonder aloud concerning the old retainer's absence. In a metanarrative flash of humor, the baron then reintroduces Hans as Schuter's replacement—implying the kinship between monstrosity and servitude that characterizes both men. The women flee quickly from the tall actor who had played the stalking creature earlier in the film, and who now wordlessly takes over cooking breakfast, his eyes shifting nervously about. That Mike Lane is both the actor who plays an actor playing out the part of the creature, and also fulfills the role of being the Schuter-creature Frankenstein assembles, is another clever typecasting device that blurs the lines separating the embedded tale from the outer narrative, and problematizes the relation between the real and the contrived.

Frankenstein intends to transplant his servant's eyes into the monster. However, he accidentally drops the glass container, rendering the harvested eyes unusable, thus making it necessary to harvest a new pair of eyes from someone else. He sends the new Schuter to murder Mike, but it ends up killing Judy instead. It is significant that Judy's murder occurs just as she is revealed to be equally as attractive and sexually alluring as Caroline. With her dark hair spilling over her shoulders and wearing a low-cut dark nightgown, Judy occupies the metaphorical space occupied by the woman in Fuseli's *Nightmare*: her stance is ambiguously both sexually accepting and rejecting; she is both jealous rival and maternal figure to Caroline—a destabilizing force that threatens the division between chaste and useful woman and ornamental, erotic object. The casualness with which the narrative dispatches her hides the degree of tension her character generates.

Meanwhile, Morgan, the photographer, lingers with Caroline in the vaults, lining up some new shots. The camera shares Morgan's gaze as he aims his lens at Caroline's leg. He calls the woman "doll" and requests her to lift her skirt higher, and murmurs, "Yeah, that's okay" in approval. Caroline boisterously counters, "Okay? According to my Hooper rating, it's perfect." The photographer then directs the actress to retreat into the shadows and to walk out, swinging her hips seductively. The young woman performs the motion twice, unaware that the creature lurks in the darkness, and twice, extends his arms forward, as if to embrace her. Surprisingly, she escapes, unscathed, and it is the photographer whom the creature attacks when Caroline, unsuspecting, has left. Yet even the photographer's murder is a wasted act because Frankenstein finds out he is of the blood type A-: a rare condition that renders his eyes incompatible with Schuter's blood type. Morgan, who seems jaded by his complicity in the conscious creation of simulacra, and is least appreciative of Caroline's assets, is a character the narrative disposes of just as ruthlessly as Judy. His murder is required in order to maintain the gloss of Caroline's semidivine status, and is justified as a natural consequence of his occupation as a photographer, whose prying curiousity and voyeuristic exploitativeness mark him as a victim deserving of punishment, even if he is only a pawn in a more complex gambit of power between Frankenstein and Roe. Ultimately even Gotfried is sacrificed, becoming the ultimate donor of eyes to the creature.

Roe finds a viewfinder in the vault, charges Mike with the responsibility of looking after Caroline, and rushes off to alert the inspector of foul play. The baron casts a hypnotic spell over Mike, efficiently extracts the information concerning Roe's whereabouts, and commands Mike to (mis)inform Caroline of Roe's return at an appointed time. Meanwhile Roe has managed to attract the attention of the reluctant police inspector, whom he draws with a clawlike grip reminiscent of the baron's hold upon Gotfried. Roe and the inspector arrive just as Caroline regains consciousness in the creature's arms. An extended sequence occurs as Roe desperately attempts to track down Caroline's whereabouts; Caroline struggles with the creature, addresses him as "Schuter," and orders him to bring her upstairs; and the baron urgently repeats his orders that Caroline be brought down into the secret laboratory. When Frankenstein realizes that the police have arrived and that Caroline has probably slipped from the creature's grasp, the baron begins flicking switches, intending to blow himself up with the atomic reactor. Strangely, he attempts to save his creation when it comes charging toward him, its arms extended vengefully. Fumes from the atomic generator sweep over the creature's body and flood the laboratory.

When visibility has returned, the camera lingers over a protective suit that covers a man checking for radiation levels. It is a suit that is remarkably similar to the bandages that swathe the creature. At his feet, Schuter-Gotfried lies, its bandages seared from the heat. The startling mimicry connecting the radiation suit and the creature's bandages leaves open the disturbing possibility that though the creature lies burnt and inert, his presence lingers and lives on, even in the very measures *we* take to protect ourselves against him, awaiting the possibility of a resurrection. The man in the suit opens the door and lets in the inspector, Roe, and Mike, reassuring them that radiation levels are safe. Significantly, Caroline is nowhere to be seen; her role as object of desire has been played out and her presence is no longer required. Roe tears open the bandages surrounding the creature's face to reveal the baron's visage (prior to his torture by the Nazis). Roe then experiments with some switches and comes across a tape of the baron's final recording: "I made you in my image so that the name of Frankenstein could survive. I gave you eyes, ears, a heart, a brain." Donald Glut remarks that Frankenstein "had modeled the Monster's face in his own image, apparently to one day [*sic*] have his own brain exchanged with that of Schuter, making creator and creature one."[4] The baron's characterization has come full circle—even in his surgically modified body, he would still be monstrous creator and creature combined: a self-enclosed system that cannibalizes all that is Other in order to sustain itself.

The ending is disquieting because, although Frankenstein and his creature are dead, the primary recipient of this legacy is Roe, who mirrors Frankenstein. Roe shares Frankenstein's Pygmalion complex: re-creating the young actresses with whom he works in his ideal image of the ingenue and discarding them once they have outgrown the ideal. Although Caroline has escaped from her encounter with Schuter-Gotfried, there is no guarantee she will escape her potential fate in Roe's hands. On the contrary, her absence in the final scene of reckoning, and her earlier attempts to run to Roe for safety, seem to reinforce her entrapment. The other man who survives the ordeal is Mike. But the film has repeatedly undercut his virility and authority, rendering him a pathetic second fiddle to Roe, and even an unwitting accomplice to Frankenstein. For the police inspector, the bizarre events have the ambience of a scene out of a horror movie; he cannot be relied upon to vouch for and transmit the dark undertones of the baron's failed parthenogenetic attempt. The film ends uncertainly with the borders separating a Frankenstein film, and a Frankenstein film about a Frankenstein film, remaining porous and fragile. The dark underside of the parthenogenetic myth, with its appropriation of the female power of birthing and attempts to circumscribe the monstrous, feminine, and female-as-monstrous shadows, unveils itself. But it is a problematic unveiling precisely because its presentation as filmic unveiling posing as filmic unveiling undercuts its representational authority. The film unmasks itself as a mask—a representation of a representation, which shores up, rather than confronts, the tensions regarding technology and gender embedded in the Frankensteinian narrative. Similar to Whale's *Frankenstein* and *Bride of Frankenstein*, Koch's *Frankenstein 1970* ends on a triumphant note, and yet does so with considerable narrative strain. Its use of an overt frame tale structure enables it to share the original novel's problematization of authorial perspective, and to show how subtle fluctuations of power and gender are in relation to visibility and narrativity.

THE LATEST IN THE SAGA: *MARY SHELLEY'S FRANKENSTEIN*

The germ for TriStar Pictures' *Mary Shelley's Frankenstein* (1994) congealed when James V. Hart, who had just scripted *Bram Stoker's Dracula*, grew interested in Steph Lady's draft *Frankenstein* screenplay, and brought it to the attention of Francis Ford Coppola and Fred Fuchs at American Zoetrope, who were then in the thick of making *Dracula*.[5] Coppola immediately recognized the cinematic potential of the original story, but declined another weighty directorial assignment. Kenneth Branagh was just concluding his postproduction work on *Much Ado about Nothing* when Coppola contacted him about the possibility of directing *Mary Shelley's Frankenstein*. Apparently part of what drew Coppola to Branagh was the young director's ability to "infuse classic literature with a contemporary sensibility."[6] Branagh eventually chose not only to direct, but also to play the role of Victor Frankenstein.

The other major task of the production involved convincing Robert De Niro to take on the role of the Creature. Part of the attraction for De Niro lay in depicting the Creature, not as a wordless and clumsy muscle machine, but as "an infinitely complex thing: gruesome but sensitive, murderous but childlike, chilling but also sympathetic."[7] Helena Bonham Carter was signed on as a much more fiercely independent and fierily passionate Elizabeth than her predecessors; Tom Hulce, one of only two American actors in the cast, was recruited to play a more comedic version of Henry Clerval.

Branagh conceived the project as a more faithful interpretation to the original novel, veering away from established cinematic traditions, such as the presence of the perennial hunchbacked assistant, named a ubiquitous German name, like "Hans." Although this version is powerfully condensed (to the point of bombastic and high-octane sharp cuts), the Branagh reenvisaging of the beginning of the narrative is more or less faithful to the original's spirit, with its unveiling of the obsessive kinship that binds Walton (Aidan Quinn) and Frankenstein, both of whom are decadent Prometheus figures, bringing death and destruction rather than life and hope. Frankenstein and Walton face each other with their disheveled long hair and matted beards, their thick shaggy coats, their grimey faces. Their physical similarities complement their emotional proclivities and ambitions, rendering them mirror images.

The screenplay details Victor's voiceover instructing Walton to listen to his story as a cautionary tale, but the film wisely deletes this, and simply flashes the caption: "Geneva, 1773," again, preserving the complex moral ambivalences the original had presented. The setting is a vast and airy ballroom, awash in blue, in the sun-drenched Frankenstein mansion. Tim Harvey, who designed the sets for the film, explains the concept for the Frankenstein home: "The bright color was a very deliberate choice. . . . We did not want a pallid, safe color range."[8] The ballroom is dominated by a magnificent staircase that towers and gracefully curves at one end: the stage for several dramatic scenes, heralding birth and death, and parthenogenetic rebirth. Harvey adds, "If you really think about it . . . there are no such rooms in real life, yet its effect on screen is realistic rather than stylistic."[9] Built in oversize dimensions (128 feet long and 64 feet wide), the ballroom is an illusion that sublates into apparent reality, as the site of Victor's golden childhood, depicted as a nostalgically reconstructed fiction, rather than a historical fact.

The seven-year-old Victor (Rory Jennings Linane) joyfully waltzes with his energetic and adoring/adored mother (Cherie Lunghi) as Mrs. Moritz sits at the harpsichord, playing music. Justine (Christine Cuttall), Mrs. Moritz's four-year-old daughter, seems entranced by Victor. His mother piles compliment upon compliment upon her delighted son, despite Mrs. Moritz's warning that she will spoil the boy. Laughing, mother and son collapse to the ground when Victor's father (Ian Holm) enters, bringing with him six-year-old Elizabeth (Hannah Taylor-Gordon). In the screenplay Victor's father orders Mrs. Moritz to leave them alone, and Victor's mother chimes in, adding the imperative that she take her daughter Justine with her. The released film, however, modifies that and has Dr. Frankenstein quietly requesting Mrs. Moritz and her daughter for a private moment with his wife and son. The change is slight, but it underlines how the film attempts to sketch less overtly patriarchal structures, with Mrs. Moritz and Justine being treated less as servants than as members of a large, extended family. The dynamics that result from that revision, however, render the narrative even more complex. Justine in effect becomes Victor and Elizabeth's sister, as well as maid and surrogate mother to William. She shares this role of surrogate mother with Elizabeth, her rival for Victor's love.

Ten years later, Mrs. Frankenstein, who is visibly in the final stages of pregnancy, enters the *attic functioning* as Victor's laboratory. With an impish smile she steals the paper upon which her son had been scribbling and runs off with it, with Victor running after her, laughing as well. The film renders visible the invisible mother whose traces in the original narrative form the justification for Frankenstein's driving desire to "pierce through" the secrets of nature—a sexually charged image not devoid of necrophiliac and incestuous tinges. Yet this is a mother who is also a child, a child bearing a child, whose irrepressible humor and love of life also render her a playmate, rather than simply a mother to Victor. In the *original* novel Elizabeth is made in the image and likeness of Caroline, Victor's dead mother, as evidenced in the fact that Caroline's mannerisms live on in Elizabeth. In the film Caroline is remade in the image and likeness of Elizabeth, with her dark, exotic beauty, impish girlishness, and full-blooded passion. For as long as Victor's mother's role as playmate eclipses her reproductive potential as mother, she lives and flourishes; as soon as she is recognizably a mother, she becomes a victim marked for death in a subtle twist of the parthenogenetic myth.

Victor is shown doing a brisk polka with his mother; his father is dancing with Elizabeth, now an arrestingly dark beauty. As before, Mrs. Moritz and Justine (Trevyn McDowell) are spectators, rather than full participants in the gaiety. Justine and Mrs. Moritz are characters that have been effaced in many of the film versions of the Frankenstein story; this film depicts their love-hate relationship, set in contrast with the relationship between Victor and his mother. In this version Mrs. Moritz seems an incongruous mixture of obedient and even obsequious servant and sadistically tyrannical mother, who severely punishes her daughter for the slightest infraction. Unlike Caroline, who fluctuates across the realms of mother and playmate, Mrs. Moritz stays rigidly within the realm of the maternal, which casts her in an unflattering light. Rather than being a nurturer and life-restorer, Mrs. Moritz's motherhood is associated with joyless, nunlike severity and a shrewish tongue stereotypically associated with barren old maids. Mrs. Moritz's motherhood is a far cry from Baubo's life-giving and scandalous vitality; it is hardly surprising that she survives, but Caroline does not.

The scene shifts swiftly to reveal Mrs. Frankenstein on a birthing stool, her dark hair disheveled, and her attractive features disfigured by pain. Victor's father looks agonized, unable to make a decision, when his wife urges him to "cut her" to save the baby. In the script Dr. Frankenstein is first urged to make a decision by Mrs. Moritz, the figure of the severe mother, and only seconded, though vigorously and passionately so, by Caroline. The film modifications associate motherhood that survives, within the Frankensteinian filmic narrative, predominantly with death and severity rather than life and nurturance.

In one of the few departures from the screenplay, the film moves one of the later sequences in the screenplay earlier. Three years later Frankenstein swears that he will bring an end to unnecessary deaths. In contrast the original screenplay depicts an extended conversation between the grieving Victor and Justine, to whom he confesses his determination to fight death itself, rather than simply heal sickness and preserve life. Justine is frightened, and recoils from the intensity Victor's own mother feared. The omission is striking as it is not Elizabeth, but Justine, to whom Victor makes this revelation, rendering their relationship with a vitality of its own, rather than a pale mimicry of his relationship with Elizabeth. Nevertheless, unlike the Elizabeth in this version, who would have argued more vociferously against Victor (like the hunchbacked Nina in *House of Frankenstein*), Justine falls silent too quickly, rendering her the apt vessel for Victor's confession, because she possesses neither the intellectual acumen nor fiery persistence to argue Victor down. The momentary mythic liberation of Elizabeth from the realm of the feminine shadow requires a scapegoat, and that must be Justine, in whom the figures of servant and surrogate mother converge.

Another sharp cut returns the scene to the castle ballroom, where Victor and Elizabeth make a strikingly attractive couple as they gracefully navigate their way through the sea of dancers. The Elizabeth in this version is depicted as strong-willed and passionate but is far from a nagging and domineering wife—at least at this point. Later on she dangerously skirts that border and is punished by the narrative for it. Nevertheless one of the clear revisions this iteration sought to achieve (and was crucial in convincing Bonham Carter to accept the role) was a more equal relationship between Victor and Elizabeth, with their love being more than a trifling romantic subplot. As Branagh writes, "We couldn't be strictly authentic to the period, because I wanted to say at every stage: These two people are equal. This woman is possessed of as large an intelligence, as large a capacity for compassion and understanding as he is."[10] Of their parting, Branagh explains, "She *allows* him to go off, because that is what he *needs* to do. It's not what she needs—she *wants* to stay at home. Every decision she makes is *not a reactive decision but a decision made by someone who has her own mind*" [italics mine].[11] Branagh's reinterpretation of the Frankensteinian narrative therefore explores the possibility of re-creating Elizabeth in the role Henry Clerval plays in the original novel, as Victor's genuine intellectual and spiritual complement, who nurses him back to health when he is on the verge of madness and death. In so doing it creates a stronger female character, and thus enables a shadow of Baubo's repressed myth of female erotic and reproductive power to emerge. However, the new version also purges the original narrative's homoerotic undercurrents, and makes Henry a character of comedic relief, a lovable buffoon whose repeated failures at anatomy serve to underline Victor's unassailable virility. Yet despite its re-creation of Elizabeth as a stronger character, its conclusions regarding the possibilities of sustaining that remain severely circumscribed by the Frankensteinian parthenogenetic myth; she, like Denberg's beautiful and tormented androgynously female creature in *Frankenstein Created Woman*, is eventually doomed to embrace her second death—the only remaining exercise of choice that the narrative ultimately leaves open for her.

The scene shifts to Ingolstadt, 1793; Victor rides into the city square alongside townsfolk who are heading for the marketplace, which is bustling with activity. The overall look of Ingolstadt is gray, dreary, and dirty, in stark contrast to Victor's home in Geneva. Ingolstadt is a city of decadence and disease, as opposed to Victor's home, which is a place of nurturance and health. This massive set, which utilized the entire Shepperton back lot, was the largest ever created by a British studio (70,000 square feet, with over 57 miles of scaffolding)—even larger than *Batman*'s Gotham City. The central feature of this set was a sweeping cobbled marketplace (which was laid with 2,630 square meters of cobbles, imported from Portugal) with 50-foot city walls, around which the high walls of the university, Victor's boardinghouse, and various streets, alleys, and buildings characteristic of a German-Swiss town of that period proliferated. Tim Harvey explains, "It was true to Middle European walled cities but much exaggerated. The increased height gives a much more dramatic relationship of the people to the architecture. . . . And the set decoration was meant to convey a strong sense of smell, perhaps of decay."[12]

After Victor's heated debate with Professor Krempe concerning the possibility of reanimating dead matter, Henry approaches the furious Victor, who, being in no mood to be further humiliated, swings around, shouting, "I am not mad!" (The screenplay simply has him stopping and declaring that statement matter of factly, but Branagh's reinterpretation of Victor's character renders him more hot-blooded.) Undaunted, Henry wins Victor over with his voluble stream of shallow witticisms. As Waldman's (John

Cleese) carriage passes them on the street, Victor and the mysterious professor exchange looks; when the carriage has passed out of sight, Victor and Henry return to a lighthearted conversation. The interaction reveals an interesting dynamic, with Henry being drawn to Victor, who in turn, is drawn to Waldman. The conversation between Henry and Victor is outwardly stripped of homoerotic tinges, with Henry talking about his aspiration to leading a "life of sacrifice" in the service of rich and beautiful young women; but the interaction with Waldman retains some of that ambiguity, with its pregnant silences. Though Julie Burchill writes in a tongue-in-cheek fashion, she observes similarly:

Sexiest of all is Frankenstein's relationship with his teacher, the disgraced Dr. Waldman. From the moment the young Victor sees him pass by in his carriage, and their eyes lock . . . you know that here is the love story. When Victor finally gets up his courage to ask Waldman to initiate him . . . the older man talks to him like a lover: "Lock the door. You shall, of course, tell no one."[13]

Elizabeth sits, writing a letter to Victor, informing him of Mrs. Moritz's loving torment of Justine, and his father's pride in him. She begs him to write, and the scene shifts abruptly. Unlike the earlier scene, shot sedately and almost as a still, this scene is shot at a fast pace, revolving around close-ups of Victor, Henry, and Waldman sharing a meal. The contrast between the two scenes, which immediately follow each other, serves to convey the difference between the sedate domestic pace in which very little changes, and the feverish excitement in which Victor is caught. However egalitarian in conception the film may have been, it begins to underline Elizabeth's role as both maternal and passive, nurturing the home that awaits Victor's return.

Even in the exhilaration of discovery, Branagh's rendition of Victor depicts him, not as a madman in the typical filmic tradition, but as an intensely sane, enviably intelligent, and extremely idealistic man. He is more a visionary, a potential Renaissance man who, somewhere along the way, pays the price for letting his vision take precedence over his love for Elizabeth. Branagh adds further dimension with the following remarks: "Victor is also tremendously romantic. He feels that the natural balance—we all arrive and know we are going to die—is not necessarily a perfect one. The romantic idea of souls being together—and in the wake of this scientific knowledge, *literally* together forever—is something that appeals strongly to his visionary instincts."[14]

Victor leaps for the professor's old notes and begs to be allowed to read them, but the professor again firmly replies that his work now deals purely with the preservation of life; his other work had resulted in "abomination." Both these modifications once again strengthen the parthenogenetic myth, as well as create a curious inversion-continuity: Branagh's idealistic and tormented Victor becomes the center of the narrative, rather than the lonely and ambivalently charismatic creature. Ultimately Branagh's Frankenstein seeks to rebirth his intellectual father-beloved, Waldman, with whom he closely identifies, by using his brain for the creature. Elizabeth Pincus, with a movie critic's more scathing tone, states the following: "In James Whale's *Frankenstein*, it's Karloff's fiend . . . who bears the story's emotional cross. In the paws of Branagh, however, the scales are tipped the other way. Frankenstein is a hunky, tragic hero; his offspring a wretch."[15]

When Waldman is fatally stabbed by a one-legged man, the camera moves from close-ups to a ceiling shot, hovering above as Victor screams in protest, echoing his statements concerning his mother's death: "It shouldn't happen, Henry. . . . It needn't happen." Yet it is clear that the search for the dead mother is going to be overlaid by the desire to be one with the dead father.

At the town square, a crowd gathers to watch the execution of the one-legged man. The man's final words are a curse prophesying divine wrath (another obvious ironic foreshadowing device); he is pushed from the gallows, and we hear the snap of a broken neck above the din of the cheering mob. Like Karloff's Monster, De Niro's creature is made from inferior and criminal clay from the start, even before he becomes the patchwork man. De Niro's one-legged man (from whom most of the creature is made) is characterized as a man who is blind in one eye and has a wooden stump for a leg; he is set up as drunk and ignorant from the very start. Even in this most contemporary version, the demonization and criminalization of the Monstrous shadow persists.

Another quick shift reveals Elizabeth angrily tearing sheets of paper and letting them flutter way. Justine follows quickly, puzzled at why Elizabeth is tearing up Victor's letters, which she had lovingly read to everyone. Elizabeth's dark hair is tousled, though an attractive brown ribbon sets it off, along with the brown dress she wears with careless grace. In contrast Justine's blond curls are braided tightly against her head, and she wears a modest blue dress, which marks her as the more levelheaded and maternal of the two. Elizabeth finally admits she authored those letters, and that she hasn't heard from Victor in months. Elizabeth says tearfully that Victor has already probably found someone else, but Justine, in perhaps her only show of genuine strength, convinces the distraught woman to go to him. The script has Elizabeth suddenly realizing and sympathetically acknowledging the depth of Justine's feelings for Victor, but the film simply cuts that conversation short. The bond of sympathy and friendship that binds Elizabeth to Justine in the original novel—a bond that causes her protest, even more strongly than Victor, against Justine's execution, and her subsequent loss of optimism in human nature in the aftermath of Justine's death—is watered down in favor of strengthening the romantic subplot. Elizabeth may have become more Victor's equal in this version, but she displays the same self-centeredness he does in relation to the suffering Justine.

The task of (re)creating the Monster fell on U.K. prosthetics and make-up designer Daniel Parker. The only instruction that he had been given by Branagh was to "construct a man made from other parts of men." He had wanted a being marked by being birthed in great haste during a plague epidemic, with an assortment of mismatched body parts in varying degrees of life and senescence. In addition the screenplay describes the creature's body incongruously as lying "on a pile of crates, draped like Christ in Michelangelo's *Pieta*."[16] The visual allusion harkens back to Whale's depictions of the creature as a parodic Christ—a second Adam whose destiny is to bring death and destruction, rather than salvation and new health. Finally, Parker was also concerned that the creature should look like De Niro, and that its appearance should be in keeping with medical knowledge at the beginning of the nineteenth century. For that end "an extremely complex set of prosthetics was developed, not just for the face, but for the full body, with skin flexible enough not to impair De Niro's performance."[17] The result is a creature who is "more 'human' and sensitive than in previous incarnations, but is nonetheless gruesome, murderous and chilling."[18] Ironically, precisely by rendering the creature less of a demonic technological shadow, the narrative shifts its center, rather than effecting a rapprochement between Ego and shadow. David Hunter notes how the visual humanization of the creature somehow renders it mythically less compelling:

One is invited to stare for long stretches at the Creature's puffy, scarred face, a technique that, while surely humanizing the tortured figure, also swiftly undermines the character's mystique. This Creature talks, but his fearsome physical attributes . . . and his violent nature are not adequately established. Too much of the killing, quite frankly, takes place offstage.[19]

Elizabeth forces a choice between Victor's commitment to her and his work. Branagh's version of the confrontation between Elizabeth and Victor is well staged, and renders both more credible characters. Unlike the novel, where Victor's relationship with Elizabeth seems pallid and lifeless, this version renders their passion with vivid strokes. Victor's love for Elizabeth painfully rivals his commitment to his work, and he realizes the price that obsession requires as he seals his Faustian bargain, still convinced that the promise of being a Prometheus outweighs his personal sacrifice. However, whereas Victor's actions still lend him a semblance of power and control (it is still he who sets the tone of the conversation and draws it to its inevitable conclusion), Elizabeth's final actions cast her in the role of scorned lover. Like Ophelia, she rushes headlong into the stream of filthy bodies, plunging deeper into the heart of the cholera-ravaged city, rather than seeking to save herself. Slowly but inexorably Elizabeth's early equality with Victor is chipped at by the evolving narrative.

The scene is set for staging the parthenogenetic birth, and we finally see Victor's laboratory unveiled, in its mechanical glory. The centerpiece of the laboratory is the "birthing" apparatus, comprised of a "womb"—the large copper sarcophagus, which is heated by a coal-fired furnace. Hanging from the ceiling is a gigantic sack, jokingly referred to in production history accounts as the "bollock" or scrotum,[20] from which Frankenstein releases his electric eels to provide the final jolt of electricity. This is an amendment that allows not only for the visual appropriation of the nurturing power of the womb, but also the exaggeration of the power of the scrotum, with the eels functioning essentially as sperm that impregnate the patchwork homunculus warmed by the artificial womb. In effect the staging of the birthing sequence ironically capitulates to the ancient belief, articulated by Aristotle, among others, that the woman is simply a warm vessel that provides nutrients, rather than contributes to, the generation of the child. Again the rebirth of the parthenogenetic myth necessitates the murder and covering over of its feminine mythic counterpart—the scandal of Baubo's *ana-suromai*—and emphasizes the patriarchal elements of the parthenogenetic birth.

Wearing an elaborate red-orange cape that swirls out dramatically after him, Victor strides into his workshop like "Merlin the Magician."[21] He gets a steam engine moving by manually turning wheels as he passes; he discards his cape in order to remain unencumbered as he raises the grill upon which his creature lies, covered, its arms spread out in the image of a crucified figure. He conveys the wildly thrashing eels from the squirming, scrotal-shaped container through a glass tube that fits into the sarcophagus. "Live, live, live!" he cries as he looks through the porthole. The scene is loaded with erotic overtones, which one does not have to share Freudian sympathies to recognize. As Branagh writes, "There is a tremendously thrilling, sexual, musical sequence leading up to the moment that is without music—you hear just the shlurping of the fluid and the Thing, grunting and groaning."[22]

It initially appears Victor's sacrifices have been in vain, and he staggers away, his head held in his hands, in between shouting and sobbing as he protests. Suddenly the camera veers back to the creature's hand, which opens. The sarcophagus suddenly begins to convulse, and Victor utters the all too famous line: "It's alive. It's alive," as he races back to undo the lid of the sarcophagus. Before he can get there, the lead bolts suddenly snap, and he is knocked off his feet and deluged by a flood of amniotic fluid that spurts out of the artificial womb—an act that simulates a pregnant woman's loss of amniotic fluid that initiates labor. Victor slowly walks over to the still sarcophagus. Suddenly the creature flings itself up and grabs on to him and the sarcophagus tips, spilling more of the amniotic liquid on the floor. In the screenplay, Victor exults to himself, and then talks to the creature, pleading with it to stand up, and trying to communicate with it. In contrast, the film removes any dialogue. In a riveting revision, the film has Victor pushing fluid out of the creature's lungs by pushing against its chest—a procedure done to newly born babies by holding them upside down to drain any liquid remaining in the lungs. What ensues next is a striking, wordless scene, in which Victor repeatedly attempts to hold his creature up, but they both keep slipping into the slimelike amniotic fluid. The entire sequence, though hauntingly filmed, seems shot from a masculine point of view, with its envy of, and disgust with, the miraculous filth/ feat of birthing. As Branagh writes,

It's been said that, in part, the story of Frankenstein is an expression of the frustration men feel at being unable to have children on their own, and alongside that goes the revulsion at the birthing process. For example, after the operatic fervor of the creation process, as this film depicts it . . . the sarcophagus is suddenly thrown open and reveals this little stained burping thing which Victor is revolted by.[23]

The creature is certainly far from a "little" thing, but it is not a giant either—it is simply larger than normal, and is incapable of standing on its own. Victor strikes upon the idea of using chains to help prop up the creature. Unfortunately he loses his balance and grabs a rope, which releases a counterweight, lifting the chained creature, moaning and twitching, to the ceiling. In the film a block of wood falls upon the creature's head, and it goes limp. Its naked form, suspended from the ceiling, is a grotesque mimicry of the crucified Christ, which is a theme glimpsed as early as Whale's 1931 *Frankenstein*. In the screenplay the creature continues struggling until it begins to convulse in what seem to be its death throes.

Awakened from his exhaustion-induced sleep, Victor spies the creature standing before him. It resembles a macabre and pitiful mass of flesh arbitrarily and crudely stitched together, "as though someone has been hung up by barbed wire."[24] The creature seems to have some difficulty standing up because it has uneven legs and yet follows Victor with surprising speed. Yet, like a newborn, its strength is limited, and it collapses to the floor, in pain. Abandoned, the creature instinctively grabs Victor's coat and drags it over himself and escapes from a mob that attempts to kill him. David Denby describes the creature in the following manner: "De Niro's Monster is nearly bald, with a strong nose and blackened eye sockets (the eyes are different colors), and he moves rapidly but unsteadily on legs of different lengths, darting at times like a nervous animal."[25] This description brings out how this particular visualization of the Monster combines the oxymoronic attributes of being both newly birthed and of decaying flesh, of being both young and old, on being superhuman and bestial, and with these transgressions, being the perfect scapegoat.

The scene dissolves to a close-up of Victor opening his eyes; Henry has been nursing him from pneumonia. Later, as Victor lies back, he hears piano music. The camera follows his gaze, and at the far end of the now empty garrett, under a shaft of sunlight, he sees Elizabeth, dressed in white. Victor calls her name softly and dubiously at first, as if he were afraid this is a mirage; he is vulnerable, childlike, unsure of himself. When she turns around, however, he calls her name more urgently and passionately. They begin to run toward each other. The script details a physically weaker Victor, who is unable to match the speed with which Elizabeth runs to him, and who practically "collapses into her arms."[26] Yet the film depicts a more vigorous Victor, who runs energetically to Elizabeth, and even lifts her off her feet in ecstasy. Victor begs for her forgiveness, and she grants it wholeheartedly, seeking to bring him comfort. The camera whirls around them as they kiss passionately. In the screenplay, Elizabeth, through her tears, murmurs that Victor's work, which she knows nothing about, and does not want to know anything about, almost killed him. The film has her holding Victor by the shoulders and almost pummeling him with her fists; though she says the same thing, the sentence is uttered as a reproof rather than a sentimental statement. Victor reassures her (and himself) that his work is now dead. In the screenplay, they embrace tenderly, but in its characteristic full-blooded interpretation, the film has the lovers grab each other with a passion that is almost violent in its intensity. The modifications from script to film strengthen the characters of both Elizabeth and Victor, but it does maintain the separation between the domestic realm from the world of science. In both, Elizabeth is ignorant of, and chooses not to know more about, Victor's potentially deadly work. Later, when she does attempt to pierce through this division, and demands an explanation, Victor resists it, implying that in his view, her "choice" has been an inevitability.

The creature stumbles on to a small family: Felix and his wife, Marie; their children, Maggie and Thomas, ages six and eight; and the blind grandfather (Richard Briers), whose music had attracted the creature. The camera then zooms in on the creature's mismatched eyes, with one eye normal, and the other severely scarred with stitches, as it peers in, voyeuristically enjoying the delights of domesticity. For the first time, we become aware of what it is like to occupy the visual space of the creature, as both looking and looked upon. Its mismatched eyes remind us of how "normality" is constructed in terms of visuality, and how the creature's appearance bears the epistemological weight of its alienness. After the creature rescues grandfather from the blows of a sadistic landlord, the old man ushers in the reluctant creature. The old man speaks soothingly, and for the first time, the creature has a meaningful and extended conversation with a being that is like himself: lonely and physically infirm. The old man's face seems to mirror the creature's own, as he has one eye shut, and has cataracts in the other. Just as the creature is replying to the old man's question regarding

friends, Felix attacks, causing the sobbing creature to flee. When the creature returns, he finds the place deserted, with signs of a hurried getaway.
Recognition dawns: he reads Frankenstein's journal and claws open his
coat to look upon his chest, revealing the massive scars spanning his entire
body, matching the drawing. He screams in primal rage, his features distorted even more hideously—signaling the gravitation back to the demonization of the monstrous shadow despite this version's more sympathetic
initial treatment. A rapid cut shows the creature's misshapen hand holding
a torch; he sets fire to the cottage, turns to face the camera, and swears
revenge—an anti-Promethean act correspondent with Victor's failed Prometheanism. This time, in a revisioning of the Promethean myth, fire is
used to destroy, rather than nurture; fire becomes a curse, rather than a
gift.

Standing on top of a table, Elizabeth exuberantly flings a filmy shawl of
white into the air as Justine and Mrs. Moritz bustle about her, doing final
adjustments on the wedding gown. In the screenplay, Justine looks up at
Elizabeth and unthinkingly jabs her mother, who is holding the fabric. In
the film, Mrs. Moritz brutally reprimands her with the words: "Anyone
would think that you're the one who's getting married!" before she can jab
her with a needle. Elizabeth notices Justine's distress and asks her what is
wrong (a totally unnecessary question, given what she knows of Justine's
feelings for Victor, as well as Mrs. Moritz's constant harassment of her
daughter). Yet when Justine continues to try to help with the gown, her
mother rejects her with the words: "Just leave it. You've ruined it now"—
which leaves the poor woman with an unbearable burden of guilt over her
failures as a daughter, servant, and sister-friend to Elizabeth. The burden
of being the feminized shadow, or the feminized scapegoat, at least in the
earlier part of the film, lies predominantly upon Justine's, rather than Elizabeth's, shoulders.

William runs by a pond when he hears the sound of a wind instrument
being played, which we recognize as the same instrument and melody the
blind man had been playing earlier. The screenplay lists the music at this
point to be a simple version of the waltz/love theme, the leitmotiv of Victor
and Elizabeth's earlier dance. Yet the film modification is apt because the
monster's only love relationship so far has been with the blind old man.
William, drawn as if to the Pied Piper, hides in the bushes to get a glimpse
of the figure playing the music. Suddenly the creature whirls around to
return the boy's scrutiny. The boy flees, dropping Victor's engagement
locket and screaming wildly. Like Whale's version, this iteration depicts
William as an unambiguous innocent, whose life is uselessly sacrificed in
the conflict between parthenogenetic father and son. Unlike the original
novel, which depicts William as verbally attacking the creature, loading
epithets upon him because of his ugliness, this version has the creature as
the outright aggressor, cold-bloodedly wreaking revenge upon someone

whom he views as an extension of Victor. The splitting off of the technologized or overdeveloped shadow continues; this is a trend discernible as early as the Universal studios productions and continues even in this most recent version.

A quick shot reveals Justine, looking haggard, disheveled, and wet, tossing in disturbed sleep upon the barn floor. A shadow looms over her, and the creature is suddenly shown standing above her. The screenplay speaks of his desire to "caress the swell of her breasts at the neckline of her bodice,"[27] but the film simply has him gently touching her face as she shakes her head, as if she were semiconscious of his presence. The original novel has the creature uttering a speech that aligns its self-conceived entity with Milton's Adam, rewriting Justine's identity as its Eve, before it lays the locket gently upon her bodice and slips silently away. The film skips over this allusion, choosing to replace a textual allusion with a visual one: Justine's contorted body, as she lies in a less than restful repose, is in the same stance of ambivalent rejection and acceptance of the creature, who casts an ominous shadow over her. This pose is reminiscent, once again, of the sleeper in Fuseli's *Nightmare*; it marks Justine's body as a site of the creature's frustrated sexual desire, and foreshadows her eventual destiny as his intended Eve.

Mrs. Moritz tearfully requests for Victor's help in finding the now missing Justine. A quick close-up reveals Elizabeth's silent face. Perhaps her grief over William's death renders her as mute and immobile as Victor's father, but there has already been earlier evidence of her inability to respond in a manner that addresses the complexities of the love triangle that binds her to Victor and Justine. Victor promises to organize another search party, but before they can act on it, a messenger arrives, announcing the apprehension of the alleged murderer: Justine. Justine addresses her final words to Victor, in which she acknowledges her fatal error as a failed mother: "He's so tiny . . . I'm sorry." In a frame that parallels the sharp featured man's execution, Justine's body is flung over the wall, and bobs up and down, as the sound of a neck snapping is heard above the mob's crazed cries of blood lust. Mrs. Moritz runs to her dead daughter's body, and repeatedly jumps up fruitlessly in the attempt to touch the corpse's dangling feet. Ironically it is now Justine's turn to prove elusive to her characteristically aloof mother, and her bobbing body remains out of reach to the sobbing woman. Elizabeth, who plays a greater role in the novel and actively grieves over Justine, here takes a merely secondary role. The narrative consistently sunders or considerably weakens women's relationships as it strives to give the relationship between Victor and Elizabeth center stage, once again burying the myth of Baubo and her comradeship with the eternal mother-daughter dyad, Demeter-Persephone.

Victor is shown marching across the lawn, heavily armed, his face set. Elizabeth reveals exasperation and says that she, too, no longer understands

Victor, and he coolly says that she should simply accept that. The equality she shares with Victor is slowly but inexorably being taken away from her. Justine's death has not freed her from her rival—it has opened a lacuna that places her squarely in Justine's place as frustrated lover and barren surrogate mother.

From a high overhead shot, Victor is shown arduously climbing a perilous mountain, which glistens with ice. The camera dwells on the creature's powerful and graceful leap through the air through a slow motion shot, and then suddenly resumes a high-octane pace. The creature knocks Victor off his feet and sends him flying into a tunnel to land in a misty pool in an underground cave. The screenplay creature invites the awakening Victor to warm himself by the fire if he wants to, but the film monster roughly tells him to get up twice. In the screenplay Victor inquires if the creature means to kill him, but the film has Victor categorically stating that, as if it were an obvious fact; the creature replies negatively. Victor then frames his suspicions concerning his brother's murder in a provocative sentence that reveals itself to be yet another statement rather than a question: "You murdered my brother, didn't you?" The creature's reply in the screenplay differs radically from the film. The screenplay paints a more sympathetic portrait, with the creature asking (also rhetorically) whether Victor thinks it is evil, and in the same vein, inquires whether Victor thought that "the dying cries of [his] brother were music in [its] ears." The film creature skips over these lines and moves straight into the succeeding lines. Thus the film creature casts a more sinister shadow and seems to exult in a dark, sadistic pleasure in recounting his murder-revenge as he raises his bony fingers, as if crushing an imaginary throat: "I took him by the throat, with one hand, lifted him off the ground, slowly crushed his neck, and as I killed him, I saw your face." He then turns accusingly to Victor, claiming that because Victor had given him emotions, but had never instructed him on how to use them, they were both responsible for William's and Justine's deaths. This film creature is both intelligent and eloquent, closely resembling the novel's original monster. He not only succeeds in piercing through Victor's self-centeredness, but also engages in an intense interrogation concerning how he was made and his resulting capacities. Victor finally slowly asks what he can do, and the creature makes his request-threat for a mate like himself.

In a quick intervening scene, the creature harvests Justine's body. It is a simple scene, but the way in which it is framed is provocative. The point of view of the camera is from within the grave, as if from the dead Justine's perspective. The creature leans down, close to the camera, "almost close enough to kiss."[28] The image of a reanimated patchwork of flesh coming to rouse its temporarily sleeping beloved visualizes the necrophiliac and erotic undertones at the heart of the novel. Interestingly the task of "piercing through the hallowed damps" of graves and nature is reserved in this version for the creature, rather than Victor, who had earlier gone about his business through the more "civilized" media of charnel houses and mortuaries. Again the demonization and hyperbolization of the technologized shadow occurs, saving Victor from the direct encounter with the filth of graves and of bodies decomposing directly in nature.

In another abrupt cut, we are shown Justine's mottled corpse, and we share Victor's horrified gaze. Victor haltingly asks, "Why her?" and the creature replies, with a touch of gallows humor, that he was simply choosing "Materials, remember? Nothing more. Your words." It is at this point in the film that Victor chooses to defy the creature. As he starts to walk away, the creature pins him down by Justine's corpse and demands that he keep his promise. Victor swears that he will not, and goads the creature into killing him. The creature swears that such a punishment would be mild compared to what is to come, and promises to be with him on his wedding night. The film (and screenplay, from which it does not differ) is fairly faithful to the original novel, although once again, Victor's motivation, less for resisting the male creature, than destroying the creature's intended bride, is covered over. The fear of an aggressive and powerful female—a manifestation of the buried figure of Baubo, as linked with the figure of the feminine archetype; a monstrous female with an independent will with which to enforce her sexual choice, as well as to breed—terrifies Victor in the novel, and that is the reason why he eventually breaks his promise with the creature. In this film (as in all the earlier films), this fear of the monstrous female is once again covered over; it makes it appear as though the creature's choice of Justine—his frustrated lover-sister who dies because of him—as "material," is what renders the project unbearably unpalatable.

Victor pursues Elizabeth, who is heading for the outer door of the chapel, intent on leaving. In an unprecedented twist, she finds a solution to the quandary that traps him: she simply asks him to marry her this very day, and then to tell her the whole truth the day after. The music rises to a romantic lilt as she swears her love for him and sounds confident that their love will survive any crime he has committed. This, more than any other gesture in the film, characterizes Elizabeth, not merely as Victor's equal, but even as his emotional superior. But it is equally clear that what pulls Elizabeth back to Victor is his childlike vulnerability. It is as if her role as lover/beloved is rooted in her maternalism, and it is eventually as Caroline's surrogate that she transcends Victor in strength. For a moment, the Frankensteinian narrative appears to acknowledge the strain it takes to repress traces of the myth of Baubo, but this does not last very long.

On the eve of the wedding, the film then shows what never transpires in the novel—an erotic not-quite consummation, which the camera visualizes by drifting around the lovers in slow circles, then rapidly cutting to tight close-ups as the two kiss, caress, and arouse each other in mutual seduction.

The screenplay details the build-up of erotic tension: "And now onto the magnificent canopied bed. Kneeling together. Bodies touching, hands seeking, mouths joining . . . Elizabeth lying back. Victor sinking down, running his hands up her thighs, making her shudder with desire . . . and he kneels up to pull the strings of her bodice while Elizabeth starts to undo the buttons on his breeches."[29]

The scene is completely in keeping with the film's rewriting of the relationship between Victor and Elizabeth, yet it again obscures the murderous urges that seem to lurk in the original novel's Frankenstein. The film also cuts out the nightmare Victor sinks deliriously into, after he has birthed the creature: it is the dream in which Elizabeth, in the glow of youth and health, walks into his arms and is suddenly transformed into a worm-ridden corpse—a transmogrification that aligns her with his desire for and repulsion with the rotting body of his dead mother. Thus, once again, the narrative falls back upon domesticating and sanitizing the necrophiliac and violent dimensions of the parthenogenetic myth—a filmic strategy that remains little changed from Whale's *Frankenstein* onward.

Suddenly the mournful tones of a recorder reach them. Elizabeth smiles, but Victor jumps off and tersely orders her to lock the door as he picks up his guns and shirt and dashes out. The camera reveals, in a flash of lightning, the silhouette of the creature hanging like a gigantic black spider atop the bed canopy. The creature tears open the canvas, lands on top of Elizabeth, and covers her mouth—an erotically and violently charged scene that once again mimes Fuseli's *Nightmare* and visualizes yet another unseen episode in the original novel. The creature, like a rapist, tells her not to bother to scream, and she nods obediently. He releases her mouth and leans closer to her, so close that their lips almost touch—a grotesque parody of the passionate love scene that had transpired earlier. "You're more lovely than I could have imagined," he murmurs admiringly as she gazes at him, trying to understand. But this moment of possible sympathy, as well, cannot be sustained. Victor and his men burst through the door as the creature thrusts its hand into her chest and pulls out her still beating heart. "I keep my promises," the creature crows scornfully, miming Elizabeth's earlier statement concerning Victor and his eternally broken promises and flees.

Another swift cut reveals the second strange pieta (with the first being Elizabeth bearing Will's body). Victor strides grimly back into the Frankenstein mansion, carrying Elizabeth's limp body, which is wrapped in a long red cloak. Victor carries Elizabeth's body up that dramatic flight of steps, with her red blood cloak trailing after them. The scene is framed as a reversal of his father's earlier descent, with his hands bloodstained, announcing his mother's death, and as a replication and enhancement of the earlier birthing scene, in which Victor wears a dramatic cape that trails behind him as he sets the equipment in motion. Again lightning flashes as he bears Elizabeth into the darkened attic room, where his equipment is set up. He then lays Elizabeth's body close to Justine's. The camera shows a montage of shots that mirror the earlier parthenogenetic scenes: Victor shaving off Elizabeth's hair; stitching up her burnt and wounded face; Victor rapidly attaching Justine's torso to Elizabeth's head; Victor chopping off Justine's hands to replace them with Elizabeth's. The logic of the operation is clear—Justine's body is simply a source of organs, used to replace whatever part is lacking in Elizabeth, save her face, which is stitched together to retain its features. Because Elizabeth's torso has been punctured, Justine's body is substituted; however, because Victor intends to have the new Elizabeth still wear her wedding ring, he chops off Justine's hands and reattaches Elizabeth's hands to Justine's body. Even in death, Justine's status as servant never changes. Yet now Elizabeth is artificially conjoined with Justine's body and joins her in the realm of the feminized and monstrous shadow.

Again Victor raises the composite body to the ceiling, and lowers it into the sarcophagus. He inserts the giant acupuncture needles and locks in the coffin. The earlier parthenogenetic sequence is replicated, with one exception: the surging of the eels from the bollock into the artificial womb—a powerful visual cue kept harnessed within the realm of the birthing of the male creature. Victor lifts the lid of the sarcophagus and pulls out his monstrous Eve, and bangs her gently on the back to free her lungs of liquid. He strokes her head and softly whispers the imperative, "Live!" She coughs, expelling a red-stained liquid; he then clothes her in the wedding dress and places Elizabeth's wedding ring upon her finger. Once again everything about the female creature is passive; unlike the male creature who had the strength to break open the sarcophagus, she lies limply, and he has to save her from drowning. Unlike the male creature, which is depicted in action as soon as it is animated, her head droops, and she seems oblivious to her surroundings. This is a characterization we have seen as early as Whale's 1935 *Bride of Frankenstein*.

Victor stands before/over the composite female creature and, in the film, urgently begs her to say his name. (In the screenplay, he uses an imperative, rather than an urgent plea.) Nevertheless the request/command to utter his name functions as his way of exacting from the new Elizabeth-Justine the combined status of father and lover. When she does not respond, he kneels and piteously begs her to remember his name as he calls her "Elizabeth." The name "Elizabeth" seems to have triggered a memory (and if one were to be narratively coherent, his piteous, pleading, childlike manner), and the female creature looks up. Like the patchwork man initially, Elizabeth-Justine slowly and awkwardly raises one white arm and gazes upon it with a vague recognition, but continues to raise the hand with the wedding ring until it rests upon Victor's shoulder. Slowly and falteringly, Victor and the female creature begin to dance as tears glisten in Victor's eyes. A dissonant version of the "Waltz/Love" theme swells to a dizzying pitch as Victor sweeps Elizabeth-Justine off her feet, carrying, rather than dancing with, this hideous semblance of his beloved.[30] Intercut with this piteous revision, shot from overhead, are close-up flashes of the originals, in which Elizabeth and Victor happily and energetically waltz to music. At the pitch of its cacophonic dementia, the music suddenly stops as Victor notices the male creature standing by the sarcophagus.

A rivalry between the creator and his fallen Adam for the hideously deformed Eve takes place.[31] Victor lays claim to her because she remembers his name, but the creature stakes his ownership based on their physiological similarities and the manner of their birth. What results is an extended sequence that resembles and yet reenvisages Whale's *Bride of Frankenstein*. Again the "bride" is dressed in a wedding dress that resembles a shroud, particularly as it is soiled. Again the female creature is trapped in the attempts of two men to control it. This time, however, the female creature is genuinely hideous, rather than a complex blend of the beautiful and the grotesque. And this time, Elizabeth-Justine's choice is ambiguous, as she hesitates between Victor, whose knowledge of Elizabeth's name bears a ring of authority, and the male creature, whose visage fascinates her. The female creature responds to the male creature's call, and traces his scarred features with a finger. The male creature seems genuinely enraptured with his intended bride, several times calls her "beautiful," and even gently kisses her fingers.

Elizabeth-Justine suddenly begins to examine the scars on her hands; she touches her face, and tears come to her eyes as she realizes what Victor has done. Yet her moment of enlightenment only leads to the embrace of her self-destruction, which the narrative ritualistically demands. She grabs a kerosene lamp, holds it over her head with a look of sheer anger and loathing on her face, and sets herself aflame before either can stop her. She flees—a bright ball setting fire to every part of the house with which she comes in contact. In the screenplay she attempts to claw away bits of herself, but the film simply shows her running away until she hurls herself to the floor below.

Admittedly this version endows the shadow of the female creature with the greatest amount of freedom and sympathy. Yet ultimately it still relegates the monstrous female to the sphere of the inarticulate and essentially powerless. It is striking that its exercise of free will can only result in its suicide, and in a murderous self-loathing that is more evident in the screenplay than it is in the film. Interestingly enough, as in Hammer films, Elizabeth-Justine's potential reproductive power is never a focus in the film; what does take center stage is her status as an object of erotic desire, as shorn away from her reproductive potential. Again the potency of the parthenogenetic myth of birthing covers over the murder of Baubo's *anasuromai*, with its provocative unveiling of both female sexual and reproductive power.

To close, the film returns to the outer narrative frame, where Walton finds the creature sitting by Victor's corpse, hunched in grief. The scene is close to the original novel's account, but it sunders the male creature's intertextual connection to the dead Elizabeth, with the novel's allusory binding of the shadows partially obscuring the creature's face with the description of the dead Elizabeth's hair cascading over her face. The film creature is unambiguously male, unlike the novel's ambiguously gendered entity, which fluctuates across the hypermasculine in its physical aggressiveness and combative eloquence, and the hyperfeminine, with its emotional extremes and sensitivity. Part of the monstrosity of the novel's creature is that it is never allowed to integrate its hideously fragmented and exaggerated gender identity, whereas the film creature, despite the torments it undergoes, is saved that burden by being unambiguously gendered as masculine, with his desire for a bride directly aligned with erotic desires, rather than the longing for sympathetic companionship the novel emphasizes.

The final scenes depict Walton's gaze as the camera cuts through the mist to reveal the creature relentlessly swimming, with visible difficulty, toward Victor's funeral pyre. He hauls himself up from the icy water, and cradles his dead father in his arms, forming yet another strange pieta. Yet it is the creature, rather than its parthenogenetic father, who occupies both the positions of decadent Christlike sacrificial victim and grieving father-killer/nurturer, in this strange tableaux. Like Elizabeth-Justine and all female monsters given a "choice," the patchwork man's only real option in breaking the cycle of violence is the self-infliction of violence. Suicide becomes his only genuine exercise of power, and the way through which he ironically regains some of his humanity and the sympathy he had spent his tragic lifetime seeking. This is the only point at which the male monster becomes more than a technologized shadow. Vulnerable, tortured, and sympathetic, he veers closely to the realm of the feminine shadow, reveals the kinship of the two shadows, and hints at how they are generated. But it is a moment that cannot be sustained for very long within the traditional horror Frankenstein narrative. The creature rams the torch into the pyre, a reification of Frankenstein's failed Prometheanism, and the crew gazes on, in wonder and horror, as the hideous son cradles the ashen-faced corpse of his father in his arms. His features are resolute and peaceful, even as the flames rise around him, voraciously licking at wood and flesh. The flames of the pyre begin to simmer as Grigori turns to Walton, repeating the question concerning their next destination. "Home," the captain answers softly, and the *Nevsky* moves off, intercut with misty images of the burning pyre.

As a final word, one relevant bit of trivia is that three ships were built as sets for the scenes on the *Alexander Nevsky*: (1) a full-sized vessel that was 100 feet long and 23 feet wide, weighing 60 tons; (2) a quarter-sized replica; and (3) a 5-foot-long model. The largest set, in particular, was designed with utmost care, and it bore on its prow a figurehead cast in the likeness of Mary Shelley and her baby—"an image suggesting the spirit of hope and endeavor in which the voyage and film were made."[32] Although the novel and the film have essentially the same endings, down to the visual replication of the narrative device of the frame tale, they each possess a very different atmosphere. The film ends on a redemptive note (in keeping with the ship's image), whereas the novel ends ambiguously, with the creature simply disappearing into the white mists of snow, perhaps one day to reemerge as an unpredictable threat. The outermost frame of the novel is the perspective of a mysterious woman, Margaret Walton Saville, whose initials are the same as Mary Wollestonecraft Shelley, and whose judgment of the tale of Frankenstein remains open-ended. The film, on the other hand, arrogates that position of judgment for Captain Walton, whose moralistic read closes the narrative possibilities of the tale. Once again the ambivalent dynamic of being both author and invisible reader of, as well as maligned object of the narrative, is dissolved, and we are left with a simpler tale that maintains the dichotomies between the masculine and the feminine, the empowered and the disempowered, those who possess voices, and those who are silenced.

CONCLUDING REMARKS

These post-Hammer series films were chosen primarily because they highlight the tensions of narrativity and visualization in the evolving depiction of the *Frankenstein* cinematic saga. With the iconic association of Boris Karloff with the Monster, and of Peter Cushing with the Baron, contemporary depictions of what "monstrosity" is wrestle with the shadow of these virtual monuments. Furthermore both *Frankenstein 1970* and *Mary Shelley's Frankenstein* bring to the surface the strain of bringing a fresh new perspective to a tale countlessly reenvisaged. To varying extents, both succeed in unveiling what is covered over in the novel, and in contemporizing the face of the Monstrous in relation to power fluctuations relative to depictions of gender and technology. Thus *Frankenstein 1970* associates monstrosity with fascism, and *Mary Shelley's Frankenstein* attempts to equalize the relationship between Elizabeth and Victor, which is achieved through the total debasement and sacrifice of Justine. Both are powerful illustrations of the potential and limits of the Frankensteinian narrative. Although it is malleable enough to allow multiple rewritings and at times enables hints at the possibility of the Ego's reconciliation with its three shadows, even these contemporary Frankensteinian filmic narratives ultimately end up severely harnessing their borders. The narrative strain such a disciplining of borders necessitates only points out the degree to which the feminine, monstrous, and monstrous-feminine/female shadows threaten the borders' stability by strengthening the myth of male self-birthing while attempting to suppress its female counterpart. Although Kenneth Branagh's *Mary Shelley's Frankenstein* is separated from James Whale's *Frankenstein* by more than sixty years, and the two differ from each other in numerous ways, they ultimately end up with strikingly similar mythic narratives.

NOTES

1. James A.W. Heffernan, "Looking at the Monster: Frankenstein and Film," *Critical Inquiry* 24 (1997): 136.

2. Leslie Halliwell, *The Dead That Walk: Dracula, Frankenstein, the Mummy and Other Favorite Monsters* (New York: Continuum, 1988), 176.

3. Donald Glut, *The Frankenstein Legend: A Tribute to Mary Shelley and Boris Karloff* (Metuchen, N.J.: Scarecrow Press, 1973), 206.

4. Ibid., 209.

5. Kenneth Branagh, "The Filmmakers and Their Creations," *Mary Shelley's Frankenstein*, with the screenplay by Steph Lady and Frank Darabont (New York: Newmarket Press, 1994), 144.

6. Ibid., 145.

7. Ibid., 151.

8. Ibid., 163.

9. Ibid.

10. Kenneth Branagh, "A Tale for All Time," *Mary Shelley's Frankenstein*, 25.

11. Ibid., 26.

12. Branagh, "Filmmakers and Their Creations," 164.

13. Julie Burchill, "Mary Shelley's Frankenstein," *The Sunday Times* November 6, 1994: 6, 10.

14. Kenneth Branagh, "Frankenstein Reimagined," *Mary Shelley's Frankenstein*, 19.

15. Elizabeth Pincus, "Skin Flick: *Mary Shelley's Frankenstein* and the Hideous Beauty of the Beast," *Los Angeles Weekly*, November 4, 1994, 41.

16. Steph Lady and Frank Darabont, Screenplay, *Mary Shelley's Frankenstein* ed. Kenneth Branagh, 73.

17. Bob Jacques, "Frankenstein: Creature Feature," *Screen International* November 4, 1994, 34.

18. Ibid.

19. David Hunter, "Frankly Lousy Don't Shell Out the Bucks for Latest Shelley Adaptation," *L.A. Village View*, November 4–10, 1994.

20. Branagh, "Filmmakers and Their Creations," 167.

21. Lady and Darabont, 76.

22. Branagh, "Frankenstein Reimagined," 20.

23. Ibid., 19.

24. Lady and Darabont, 84.

25. David Denby, "What's Up, Docs?" *New York*, November 14, 1994.

26. Lady and Darabont, 90.

27. Ibid., 108.

28. Ibid., 119.

29. Ibid., 123.

30. Ibid., 131.

31. For a sustained analysis of the oedipal conflict that connects *Mary Shelley's Frankenstein* with the simultaneously Promethean and Satanic impulses in *Paradise Lost* (where Satan, in his battle with God over the right to create, parthenogenetically begets Sin, and then rapes her to sire Death, which also rapes its mother to produce the hellhounds that torment her), refer to Heffernan, 155.

32. Branagh, "Filmmakers and Their Creations," 166.

CHAPTER 5

—◦◦◦—

Mythic (Im)Mortality

> Storytelling in *Frankenstein* is far from an innocent act: narratives have designs on their narratees that must be unraveled. The issue posed by such a narrative relation relates to intersubjective relation, and the relation of relation.
> —Peter Brooks, "What Is a Monster? (According to *Frankenstein*)"

If nothing else, studying the *Frankenstein* narrative cast in film leads one to the conclusion that the production/evolution of a film is itself a Frankensteinian exercise.[1] It entails the serendipitous sewing together of numerous elements: bits of scripts, copyright and budgetary considerations, commercial packaging, the generation of new visual iterations of what the "monstrous" entails, directorial prerogatives, and actors' interpretations. The tense dialectic binding word and image, which is at the heart of the novel, becomes radically reworked, particularly as we now see the monster before we see him speak—the chaos of his physicality takes center stage, and he can no longer, as in the novel, deprive us of the sight of his mangled and mismatched body, in order to enable us to occupy the "visual" space of the blind de Lacey.

In my view the evolution of *Frankenstein* films is built from the undulating ground of competing meaning systems, which necessarily entails an ambivalent affirmation-negation of ideologically progressive and conservative forces. Hence the approach I have used does not mute these contradictions, and painstakingly draws from a broad variety of sources: principally scripts and released film versions, but also publicity campaigns, censorship files, and popular and scholarly reviews. In juxtaposing such

Still from *Frankenstein* appears courtesy of the Academy of Motion Picture Arts and Sciences. Universal, 1935.

diverse prisms, I have aimed to avoid a unidimensional summary of the films which reifies traditional critical hierarchies that privilege "classics" over "derivatives" or "A" films over "B" films. Rather my focus lies in tracing the evolving, contradictory relationships among social, institutional, economic, and creative discourses and contexts in the filmic evolution of the Frankenstein myth.

Even more significantly I have shown that the "monstrosity" of the creature's body lies not simply in that, as Judith Halberstam argues, it functions as a "machine that, in its Gothic mode, produces meaning and can represent any horrible trait that the reader feeds into the narrative."[2] Although there is a malleability that characterizes the depiction of monstrosity, there are also certain parameters within which that monstrosity can either be tamed and rendered sympathetic, or hyperbolized and demonized. As Rhona Berenstein has remarked, "The image of male monsters that do nothing more than victimize women and the conventional scenario of heroism can both be read as cultural wish-fulfillment. . . . Powerful fiends have to be vanquished by heroes, so patriarchy would have it, and, whether as monsters or saviors, power always rests in male hands in these . . . accounts of classic horror."[3]

What this book has sought to illustrate is that the parameters of the *Frankenstein* film saga/s are intrinsically tied up with anxieties about gender and technology that achieve mythic form through (re)framing, generating the three "shadows" (understood in Rushing and Frentz's Jungian characterization of "shadow" as a site of primordial ambivalence—exciting fascination and repulsion). The first type is the "feminized" or "inferior" shadow, often exemplified in the ruthlessly domesticated figures of Elizabeth and all absent mother figures excised from most of the filmic iterations of the Frankensteinian narrative. The second type is the "monstrous" or "overdeveloped" shadow, which is often embodied in the figure of the male creature, and is often reduced to a mute muscle machine in the films, as opposed to the novel.

The third type is a complex conjunction of the first two. It is the shadow of the female monster, or the female/feminine-as-monstrous. As Barbara Creed has remarked, "The horror film is populated by female monsters, many of which seem to have evolved from images that haunted the dreams, myths and artistic practices of our forebears many centuries ago. . . . Although a great deal has been written about the horror film, very little of that work has discussed the representation of woman-as-monster."[4]

This third type of shadow is exemplified in many forms, all of which are cruelly disciplined by the Frankensteinian narrative. One subtype of the third shadow is the female creature who oxymoronically combines in her very body the potential for life and death, beauty and the grotesque, the promise of biological immortality and the threat of untamed female sexuality. This character, as exemplified in films as diverse as Whale's *Bride of*

Frankenstein, Fisher's *Frankenstein Created Woman*, and Branagh's *Mary Shelley's Frankenstein*, inherits the semiotic status of the "?" that is usually appended to the male creature. Often her birthing provides the narrative with the opportunity to invest the male creature with more human traits, such as the power of speech and the ability to be readable, in terms of motives, thoughts, and feelings. In contrast the female creature spawned by the filmic versions is often cold, forbiddingly impenetrable, and mute. Within the Frankenstein filmic tradition, female monsters seldom live for very long; when they enjoy an extended screen existence, it is usually because they perform a function as indispensable servants to Frankenstein-esque characters. Examples include Nina, the hunchbacked nurse in *House of Frankenstein*, or Christina Kleve in *Frankenstein Created Woman*. These female monsters are infused with masculine spirits that are trapped in female bodies. Often their only genuine exercise of freedom is suicide. Christina-Hans jumps to her second death from a cliff into rapidly flowing waters in *Frankenstein Created Woman*; Elizabeth-Justine burns herself with a lamp before she jumps to her fiery death in *Mary Shelley's Frankenstein*. Even when they fiercely cling on to life, another male character chooses death for them. Elsa Lanchester's violent hiss at the end of *Bride of Frankenstein* is perhaps the only visible gesture of revolt against the Frankensteinian narrative's scapegoating of the female creature.

Another subtype of the third type of shadow is the vision of the female/feminine-as-monstrous. This may take the form of the unabashedly sexual or overly aggressive female, such as Ilonka in *House of Frankenstein* or Justine in *The Curse of Frankenstein* or the aging crone, who often cuts the ridiculous figure of being a meddling gossip, such as Minnie in *Bride of Frankenstein*. Nevertheless both types are just as cruelly murdered as the narrative unfolds, and their violent deaths are often depicted as self-instigated and deserved.

Despite these designations, it is important to note that a complex dialectic connects all the different types of shadows together as the Frankensteinian filmic saga/s evolve. The "feminized" or "inferior" shadow is simply the feminine-as-monstrous that has been safely domesticated or harnessed within the confines of the Frankensteinian narrative, as visually evidenced by the mirror-imaging clothes worn by both Elizabeth and Justine in *The Curse of Frankenstein*. This border, separating the "safe" from the "monstrous" female is a tenuous and arbitrary one, as the monomaniacal Frankenstein in *Frankenstein and the Monster from Hell* acknowledges when he nonchalantly reveals that he intends to mate the silent "Angel" of the asylum with the beast he has created. Similarly the "monstrous" or "overdeveloped" shadow is often "feminized"—that is, placed in the position of that which deviates from rational Ego-consciousness—as a vulnerable child, a physically incapacitated and uncoordinated buffoon, a mindless automaton. The male creature's position as the tortured male body renders him simultaneously dangerous and endangered—a position typically feminized and that Mary Russo designates as the role of "the female grotesque."[5] He is an object of the gaze who can never transcend his object-ness, despite his overdetermined masculine physicality in films. Similarly, part of the reason why the shadow of the monstrous female is the most viciously destroyed in the narrative is because she freely embodies all that has been successfully suppressed in the repressed feminized shadow, such as unabashed erotic and reproductive power, combined with the demonic physicality associated with the monstrous or overdeveloped shadow. The body of the female monster is potentially a body thrice monstrous—as female (and as such, already biologically aligned with the freak and the grotesque, as Marsha Meskimmon points out,[6] or at least in the tradition of Aristotle, the inferior or aberrant male); as unnaturally conceived (a testament to the failure of the male attempt to appropriate the womb's power); and as potentially pregnant. Lucy Fischer vividly excavates the mythic-filmic associations between the evil, the macabre, and pregnancy and parturition. "Rich speaks of female reproduction as conventionally assigned 'malign occult influences,' as being 'vulnerable to or emanating evil.' . . . Kitzinger talks of parturition as a 'ritual state' necessitating the intervention of shamans, priests and priestesses. . . . Both associate pregnancy with 'possession.' "[7]

Fischer's article references the filmic gynecological Gothic, Roman Polanski's *Rosemary's Baby* (1968). However, whereas this film depicts Rosemary precisely as a "feminized shadow"—one whose reproductive powers are harnessed, without her knowledge and against her will by her ambitious husband, the Frankenstein films envisage a monstrous mother, whose powers of reproduction and of sexual choice threaten masculine hegemony. The scandal of the female creature's body is that it is artificially engineered and should therefore promise total control, unlike the naturally generated female body. Ironically the monstrous female's corporeality presents nothing save the specter of the eruption of uncontrolled female reproductive and sexual power. Thus, this book shares Creed's observation that "the presence of the monstrous-feminine . . . speaks to us more about male fears than about female desire or feminine subjectivity."[8] As such I have sought to explore not a simplistic tale of male domination and female subjugation, but a tense dynamic between polysemic structures of masculinity and femininity, which branch out and intersect with each other in lacunae that momentarily congeal. The degree of strain required to uphold a patriarchal version of Dionysus's parthenogenetic birth alongside the repression of Baubo's *ana-suromai* ironically unveils what the Frankensteinian myth aims to hide: that masculinity and the Ego are not stable and pure essences.

Ultimately this book illustrates how the filmic evolution of the Frankensteinian myth parallels the competitive movement of an older set of classical myths: the myths of the parthenogenetic birth of Dionysus from the thigh of Zeus, and of Baubo's scandalous and humorous lifting of her skirt to reveal her womb and genitalia, a gesture Winifred Milius Lubell calls *ana-suromai*. Both are implicated in reproductive myths, and the Dionysian myths intersect with myths surrounding Baubo through the narrative of Persephone's rape by Hades. Dionysus, conceived by Semele, a mortal woman impregnated by Zeus, is the only half-mortal, half-divine god allowed to join the Olympian pantheon; as half-mortal he shades into the figure of Hades, the god of death and the underworld. More importantly Persephone is drawn to the valley of Nysa (the place Dionysus is raised by his surrogate mother, Gaia, after he has been birthed from his father's thigh), where she bends to pick up a flower associated with Dionysus, as Hades startles her by bursting from the underworld. Either way Dionysus is somehow complicitously implicated in Persephone's rape and Demeter's subsequent self-willed barrenness. Dionysus is a son born of a father, through the seduction-rape and fiery destruction of his mother by his father, who snatches his unborn son from her womb, to transplant him into his thigh. Like the Frankenstein myth, it is the story of the usurpation and coercive appropriation of the female power of birthing, and the attempt to graft that power on to a male body.

In contrast the myth of Baubo's *ana-suromai* is a story concerning the restorative transcendence of humor as aligned with the female body's irrepressible potential for erotic pleasure and reproductive power. Baubo combines the figures of a wise, compassionate, and healing nurse, as well as female jester who causes a goddess to laugh with her lewd jokes and gestures. It is she who reawakens Demeter's awareness of herself as goddess, mother, and sexual being, and seems to signal a resistance to, and break from, the patriarchal erotic of violence and death.

As Irigaray has argued, his-story has gradually allowed the triumph of patriarchal myths over matriarchal myths, leading to a covering over of the dynamic *agon* that enabled patriarchal and matriarchal myths to flourish alongside each other. The Frankensteinian filmic narratives examined in this book generally follow that same trend, and tend to hyperbolize the potency of the parthenogenetic birth while repressing its feminine counterparts, thus generating the feminized, monstrous, and monstrous feminine shadows. Yet precisely through showing the dark underside of the parthenogenetic myth, done via these films' unveiling of the narcissism and violence that link the feverish quest for power, beauty, and immortality which animates the Frankensteinian odyssey, Frankensteinian films ironically undercut the exaggeration of the parthenogenetic narrative. Precisely by so ruthlessly and unequivocally attempting to silence the feminized, monstrous, and monstrous feminine shadows, they allude to their potential power as disruptive forces that resist patriarchal control.

This is not, of course, to say that the films that make up this extremely diverse spectrum are homogenous and interchangeable. On the contrary, despite the inevitable intertextuality, there are distinct stylistic/methodolog-ical, as well as narrative features, which distinguish the Universal produc-tions from the Hammer films, which, in turn, are different from the individual offerings from other studios.

The Universal series, and, in particular, Whale's films, bear the stamp of German expressionism, with their atmospheric and symbolic settings. Em-ploying the aesthetic of black-and-white film, they utilize techniques of chi-aroscuro (such as a scene in Lee's *Son of Frankenstein*, in which the storm effects from the outside are projected on to the castle wall behind Wolf Frankenstein and his wife, reflecting their differing psychological states in relation to arriving at the castle) and subtly incorporate symbolic framing (such as Whale's framing of the body scavenging scene at the beginning of *Frankenstein* as a prelude to a parodic Resurrection, or his more overt tying in of the creature's suffering with Christ's through a close-up that shows the Monster's being strung up on a pole, its arms tied painfully above it in a pose resembling a crucifixion in *Bride of Frankenstein*).

In contrast the Hammer versions, particularly Fisher's films, on one level, are more concerned with realistic depiction rather than symbolic gesturing. Fisher's films are animated more by the complexity of human characters enmeshed in deadly situations, and his use of lavish background sets serve to ground and cement a realistic lens with which to view the characters. The only exception to this generalization concerning luxuriantly vivid back-ground sets is *Frankenstein and the Monster from Hell*, the last film Fisher directed, in which the use of subdued grays symbolically fuses with the air of decadent nihilism that characterizes that story. Nevertheless, in general Hammer's hallmark of using intense color tends to strengthen the view that these films indulge in gore and sexual violence. It is true that Hammer films lays bare the repressed sexuality of the Universal series (and the original novel), with its display of buxom breasts and less restrained detailing of both the scavenging of body parts, as well as the surgical construction of the creatures. Yet Fisher, again, with the exception of the final Hammer offerings, like *Frankenstein Must Be Destroyed*, and *Frankenstein and the Monster from Hell*, is remarkably restrained in his use of the camera. Under his direction surgical scenes are often shot with the camera slightly above the hand level, rendering invisible the manual procedure, yet provocatively evoking its workings through expressions upon the characters' faces (such as Krempe's look of disgust in contrast with Frankenstein's detached clin-icalism as he decapitates a corpse in *Curse of Frankenstein*) and the use of sounds, like the sound of a saw grating against bone.

It is difficult to generalize across the two poststudio series films I have chosen, though both reveal indications of technical and thematic allusions back to these earlier Frankenstein film offerings. Allied Artists' *Franken-stein 1970*, for example, employs similar techniques of symbolic framing (as in the baron's speech concerning his great-great grandfather's initially idealistic ambition to overcome death—against the figure of a knight, and then against a crucifix in the background) reminiscent of the Universal series. TriStar Pictures' *Mary Shelley's Frankenstein* also heightens the strategic use of the camera to frame characters and events symbolically. The camera in this picture constantly draws attention to itself by reflecting the diegetic pace and mood. It whirls around in slow circles, featuring close-ups of Victor, Henry, and Dr. Waldman, reflecting the feverish excitement of their intellectual debate; it zooms in so imperceptibly that when it reveals Elizabeth writing a letter to Victor, the shot is virtually a still, as if to mirror her mood of waiting and stillness, and the monotony of domestic events she writes about; it circles the lovers, visually caressing their intimate gestures, voyeuristically partaking in the beauty of their bodies touching in the heat of passion, sharing and heightening their mood of erotic arousal on their wedding night. This same motion is eventually repeated, though it is rendered a sick parody of earlier dancing scenes (which have the same animated tempo to them), when Victor finally dances with his rebirthed Elizabeth-Justine, through its use of a dissonant version of the waltz/love theme and its veering away from the dancing pair to a high overhead shot— the same camera angle used to depict Waldman's death, despite Victor's frenzied efforts to revive him.

Mary Shelley's Frankenstein continues the Hammer films' provocative use of color, their unabashed display of sexuality, and startling showcase of dismembered body parts, yet does so with a certain deftness that prevents these technical resonances from being mere clichés. Some of the most disturbing and memorable scenes from the movie that continue these elements include the *monster's* pulling out of Elizabeth's heart from her chest and the creature's vindictive display of the still beating organ to the horrified Victor, and Frankenstein's graphic hacking up, sewing together, and revivification of the new Elizabeth-Justine.

There are narrative differences alongside the stylistic ones. The Universal series begins with a mute creature that starts life as a vulnerable child, and eventually learns how to be vicious by virtue of his maltreatment by others. Although this creature does not speak, it is fairly easy to sympathize with him; his groans, smiles, and grunts—though they are subhuman—provide a bridge of understanding. *Bride of Frankenstein* further humanizes this creature by granting him the power of speech (though his awkward and fragmented use of language still contrasts strongly with the novelistic creature's eloquence) and enabling him to learn how to indulge in masculine rites of hedonistic and fraternal initiation such as smoking and drinking. In contrast both the female creature and the significant women in the narrative, such as Elizabeth and Minnie, are either undeveloped ciphers, sacrificial lambs awaiting slaughter, or potential Cassandras whose gossipy natures undermine them. Eventually the Universal series ends up transforming the creature into a mindless automaton—a standard horror prop that is momentarily resurrected, only to enact its ritualistic chase and destruction by an angry mob. By the end of the Universal series, the Frankenstein monster simply becomes one of a coterie of horrors, inclusive of Count Dracula and the Wolfman; worse, it becomes a sick and inferior monster not only physically but also mentally. For example, in *Frankenstein Meets the Wolfman*, the creature is characterized as not only in need of protection from the mob because of his initial blindness and enervation, but he is also power-hungry and lustful (as opposed to the Wolfman's sincere desire for freedom from his inhuman strength and bestial desires). The Universal series develops the tradition of having a German-named sidekick, who either becomes an extension of the Frankenstein character (Fritz as a monstrous son and servant of Henry in *Frankenstein*; Daniel the hunchback plays a similar role to Dr. Niemann in *House of Frankenstein*), or the more eloquent and sinister mouthpiece of the creature (such as the twice resurrected Ygor in *Son of Frankenstein* and *Ghost of Frankenstein*). Attractive, confident, and sexually aggressive women such as Ilonka in *House of Frankenstein* and Rita in *House of Dracula* or Elsa in *Ghost of Frankenstein* are radically disciplined through either a violent death or a potential brush with one. Female characters that combine monstrosity and beauty, through whom the myth of Baubo momentarily resurfaces, such as the nameless bride in *Bride of Frankenstein* or Nina in *House of Dracula*, are both lusted after and loathed, and eventually killed. Only the safely domesticated female characters in whom the spheres of the maternal and the erotic are not only kept apart, but also are kept harnessed within the chains of conventional civility, such as Elizabeth in *Frankenstein* and *Bride of Frankenstein*, or Elsa in *Frankenstein Meets the Wolfman*, or Miliza in *House of Dracula*, survive.

In contrast the focus of the Hammer series is the baron, rather than the creatures he spawns. The baron effortlessly moves across porous boundaries of the respectable bourgeoisie and disreputable social misfits, and effortlessly takes from each what he requires in order to support his only passion: giving birth to the perfect creature. From the rich, he exacts exorbitant medical fees, and condescends to play their games of civility; from the poor and/or insane, he extracts limbs—raw materials for his work—under the pretext of looking after their medical needs (as in *Revenge of Frankenstein* as well as *Frankenstein and the Monster from Hell*). Part of the baron's appeal, at least in the earlier offerings, is that he is both genuinely charming and dangerous, engaging and savage, a gentleman and a monomaniac. In *The Evil of Frankenstein*, he even develops a sense of humor about himself, and wonders aloud why someone like Hans remains loyal to him in spite of his many failures and frustrations. In *Frankenstein Created Woman* as well as *Frankenstein and the Monster from Hell*, his assumption of an air of authority verging on smugness is undercut by his burnt hands. This disability renders him dependent on others around him, such as the bumbling but humane Hertz, as well as the hotheaded but equally loyal Hans in the earlier film, and Sarah, the asylum's silent "Angel," as well as the worshipful protégé-student-son, Helder, in the latter film. All these characters function as extensions of Frankenstein's disfigured body. Yet Frankenstein's virility, as well as his monstrous inhumanity, are most strongly emphasized in *Frankenstein Must Be Destroyed*; here, the opening sequence, which strikingly features the bloody harvesting of a doctor's head by a grotesquely masked man—a man who eventually whips that mask off to reveal the now-readily recognizable face of Peter Cushing as the baron—immediately unmasks who the real monster is. With dark black hair and an unblemished body, this Frankenstein effortlessly blackmails, rapes, and murders.

In the Hammer series, there are only two instances in which Frankenstein is momentarily eclipsed by his creations. In *Frankenstein Created Woman*, Frankenstein is less the figure around whom the narrative gains momentum than a catalyst who unwittingly sets a tragic chain of events in motion. The Frankenstein who emerges in this film is less in control: The beginning sequence shows him being wheeled out, temporarily dead and frozen—the very object of experimentation. Despite his confidence in the eventual success of his experiments, it is clear that without Hertz, he would amount to very little. It is Hertz (with Hans's assistance) who brings him back to life; it is also Hertz who helps Frankenstein with a malfunctioning piece of equipment when the baron is unable to tend to it properly because of his burnt hands; and it is Hertz who does the surgical work on Christina's face and body. Although Hertz proves capable of these things only under strict supervision from Frankenstein, Hertz is indispensable, and even serves to temper Frankenstein's cool rationalism with sympathy in his dealings with the new Christina.

The fulcrum of *Frankenstein Created Woman* should have been the new Christina—the woman reborn, devoid of physical imperfections, and infused with the soul of her dead lover, Hans. However, partly because of Susan Denberg's evident inexperience in acting, and in the fact that the character was never really developed, a vacuum exists at the heart of this iteration. Christina-Hans again occupies the status of the "?": her motivations remain opaque, and other than following Hans's murderous commands, she appears to have no will of her own. She fluctuates across the realms of domestic angel and dangerous seductress, with little revealing her internal state, save her desire to please her new father figures, Frankenstein and Hertz, or to appease her dead lover, who inhabits her body. When, in the end, she finally makes the only "choice" open to her—suicide—this appears more an inevitability, rather than a tragic event evoking sympathy and indignation.

In marked contrast is the depiction of Brandt-Richter in *Frankenstein Must Be Destroyed*. This male creature is fashioned from the brain of a brilliant collaborator of Frankenstein, Brandt, and the body of another renowned, though conventional, surgeon, Richter. When Brandt discovers himself in another man's body, realizes what has happened, and begs for help from the terrified Anna, who stabs him, the effect is genuine pathos. The scenes in which he returns home to watch his wife sleeping as he weeps, and hides himself behind a screen to prevent her from seeing him, are powerful and touching. And when his wife rejects him in his new body, one easily ambivalently shares in his consuming desire for revenge against his opportunistic and narcissistic "benefactor," Frankenstein. Even the misfortunes of the blackmailed lovers, Anna and Karl, do not approach the tragic immensity of Brandt-Richter's creature because unlike him, they are, from the start, established as a couple capable of stealing (even if for altruistic purposes). This is the only film in the Hammer series that ends with the creature destroying himself, together with his violently protesting creator—a testament to Brandt-Richter's vitality as a character, over even Frankenstein. It also constitutes one instance in which the tensions of the parthenogenetic narrative, and its attempt to demonize the monstrous shadow, manifest themselves.

Similarly *Frankenstein 1970* continues Hammer's identification of the scientist, rather than the creatures he births, as the genuine monster. Set in the future (as it was released in 1958), the film is nevertheless haunted by memories of the two world wars, and the specter of German fascism. Nevertheless it does share a trait with later Frankenstein iterations—a self-consciousness of itself as an active appropriation, a tale telling of a story that has been told and reworked many times. Thus it re-creates motifs typical of the Frankensteinian myth, such as the scene of Caroline being chased by a monster by a lake, or the scene of the baron speaking about his great-great grandfather's parthenogenetic aspirations in his family crypt, and uses the technique of the frame tale. That is, it embeds the story of making a film about creating a monster within a film about (re)creating a monster. Furthermore, the casting of Boris Karloff as the baron (whose unblemished face, prior to his being tortured by the Nazis, constitutes the template from which the creature's face is designed) alludes to his earlier performances as the creature under Whale's direction, and brings together creator and creature as equally victimized and monstrous. In addition, the dual casting of Mike Lane, as both an actor playing the part of the monster in the beginning scenes, and the reanimated Schuter-monster in the film, playfully blurs the lines separating the different levels of the frame tale. The result is an apparently "happy" ending that hints at a dark underside: though the baron and his creature lie dead, Douglas Roe, the director who is instrumental to Frankenstein's suicide and his parthenogenetic son's inadvertent murder, is set up as a mirror-image of Frankenstein. Caroline, the woman whom both the baron and the director had desired, is invisible in the final stages of the film, and it is implied that she has found deliverance through Roe. Nevertheless, given Roe's record for consuming, exploiting, and discarding young ingenues, this "salvation" appears tenuous. Once again, though overtly, the traditional narrative polices its boundaries, and the strain of doing so is evident.

In continuity-contrast, TriStar Pictures' *Mary Shelley's Frankenstein* attempts to preserve the narrative structure of the frame tale and the strengthening of Elizabeth's character. The film manages to accomplish these, but with mixed results. Although the film conscientiously alludes to Mary Shelley's ambivalent exertion of narrative power, it loses the original narrative's flexibility: its ability to destabilize, problematize, and deauthorize the shifting authorial frames characteristic of the novel. The film becomes a more linear narrative, shot predominantly from the point of view of Victor, as opposed to the original novel, which fluctuates across the warring fictions of the creature's account, to Victor's narrative, to Walton's narrating the unknown stranger's (Frankenstein's) story, and finally to the ambiguous reception of the embedded tales by a woman reader whose initials are the same as the author's: M.W.S.

Justine, a character who is usually nonexistent in most of the Frankenstein films (with the exception of *The Curse of Frankenstein*, in which she becomes a seductive maid and aspiring social climber), is shown with greater vividness in *Mary Shelley's Frankenstein*. Here, she is, like Elizabeth in the original novel, a surrogate mother to William; yet the film makes her the third member of a love triangle, composed of Victor, Elizabeth, and herself. In place of the homoerotic elements that bind Victor to Henry is a more conventional heterosexual worship from a distance. The arrangement proves even more endangering to Justine: She becomes the proverbial sacrificial lamb upon whom both Victor's and Elizabeth's crimes of self-centeredness become dumped. Even in death her body becomes a mere source of body parts, which Victor mines in order to (re)produce the new Elizabeth.

At the beginning of the narrative, Elizabeth is depicted as Victor's equal, and perhaps even his emotional superior. She chooses not to marry him and to follow him to Ingolstadt, but to stay at the Frankenstein home, in order to reinfuse it with life after Caroline's death. Likewise, when Victor impulsively offers to stay and give up his medical studies, she refuses, knowing that his fascination with science would lead him eventually to regret that decision. This is an Elizabeth who combines the aspects of nurturing mother and passionate, erotic equal; nevertheless her femininity remains carefully circumscribed, devoid of the potentially combative and disruptive elements of Baubo's *ana-suromai*. Her "choices" are ultimately extremely conventional. When she crosses these gendered borders defiantly, as when she hotly demands an explanation for Victor's strange behavior after Justine's and William's deaths, Victor coldly shuts her out. Justine's death does not free Elizabeth from the tyranny of a love triangle. Instead it moves her into Justine's place, and brings into prominence an earlier love triangle that coexisted subtly alongside the Justine-Victor-Elizabeth one: the complex relation that binds Victor to herself and the creature. Yet the film gives the novel a different twist. As resurrected monstrous female, Elizabeth-Justine now becomes the object of desire fought over by Victor and his parthenogenetic son. As Victor's rebirthed daughter, sister, and wife, she embodies the image of the mangled body of the mother, lusted after and loathed, bringing to the surface one of the novel's animating undercurrents of incest, violence, and necrophilia. And her final choice is her inescapable fate: suicide by self-burning—an image that symbolically underlines her refusal to partake in Victor's decadent Prometheanism, and the only choice that the parthenogenetic narrative leaves her.

The modifications surrounding Elizabeth and Justine impinge upon Victor's and Henry's characterizations. Both are now unambiguously masculine. Unlike the novel in which the relationship of equality exists between Victor and Henry, and not between Victor and Elizabeth, Henry is now Victor's inferior: He consistently fails anatomy, and often uses his wit, at least in the earlier part of the movie, for amusing prattle. Victor becomes a genuine Renaissance man—one who has the potential to succeed at whatever he puts his mind to, and who is not a phlegmatic and pale intellectual, but a vigorous, extremely physical, and passionate explorer. This film gives the parthenogenetic myth an idealistic motive: the desire to enable love to endure forever through immortal physical union. Nevertheless it does not successfully purge the Frankensteinian narrative's murderous propensities. Ultimately the parthenogenetic and masculinized elements are strengthened and clarified at the expense of the evocative ambiguity of the elements reminiscent of Baubo's *ana-suromai*. The appropriation of the disruptive power of laughter unto a masculine character (Henry), in whose hands it becomes a mere source of entertaining blather, is in line with the narrative's attempt to iron out all homoerotic tinges and to replace them with more conventional heterosexual dynamics. *Mary Shelley's Frankenstein* proves a thought-provoking experiment in examining the conditions of possibility within which the three shadows may be reintegrated with the Ego; though it succeeds temporarily in liberating Elizabeth from her iconic status as narrative scapegoat, it exacts a high price. In relation to Justine, Elizabeth, too, possesses Victor's self-centeredness, and is eventually moved into Justine's position with a vengeance. With this film's attempt to stabilize gender relations and to press them into conventional molds, this most recent version ironically continues, rather than breaks away from, the filmic evolution of the Frankensteinian narrative, with its ambivalent exaggeration of its parthenogenetic elements and its strained attempts to repress its feminized counterpart.

As a closing caveat, it is important to note that the limits I have outlined in the genealogy of selected *Frankenstein* films are, to some extent, preset by the structure of traditional *Frankenstein* interpretations of the narrative. In other genres, such as comedic or parodic versions (Charles Lamont's *Abbott and Costello Meet Frankenstein* [1948]; Mel Brooks's *Young Frankenstein* [1974]; Jim Sharman's *The Rocky Horror Picture Show* [1975]), the strained triumphant note of the hyperbolized parthenogenetic myth is even more evident because of the further destabilization of demarcations characterizing implicit hierarchies of sexuality, gender, and humanity. The Invisible Man's dark laughter that closes *Abbott and Costello Meet Frankenstein*, despite its otherwise conventional ending; Elizabeth's (Madeline Kahn) breaking out into the melodious "Ah, sweet mystery of life, at last I have found you" as she and the creature engage in an unseen erotic act; the transgressive centrality of Dr. Frank N. Furter's transvestite mad scientist in *The Rocky Horror Picture Show*—all render fuzzy the "safe" borders separating the normal from the monstrous, the natural from the artificial, the sane from the carnivalesque, Dionysus from Baubo. Furthermore, contemporary science-fiction narratives that harken back to primal scenes of birthing effectively rewrite the Frankenstein narrative. For example, Ridley Scott's *Blade Runner* (1982) stages a confrontation between Roy Batty (Rutger Hauer), the best and last of the rebel replicants, "more human than human,"and Tyrell (Joe Turkell), the Frankensteinian "biomechanical god." This time, the creature demands "more life" for itself and its mate and in an elegant game of genetic chess with its father explores all possibilities for prolonging its life. When all such possible moves seem fruitless, Roy Batty becomes a Judas figure, who kisses his father tenderly on the lips (with ambiguous homoerotic tinges) before he crushes his skull. Yet the next sequence aligns him with a howling, avenging beast and a Christlike figure, with his bloodily spiked hand and the white dove that he releases as he expires, granting the gift of life to the stunned Rick Deckart (Harrison Ford), the blade runner assigned to terminate all rebel replicants. *Blade Runner* ends up radically unfixing the categories of the *Frankenstein* narrative. The replicants, rather than the humans, are more genuinely free, committed to life and passion, than their human counterparts. The "heroic" figure, Deckart, is feminized in his fumbling and puny attempts to complete his mission. Significantly he kills off only two of the four replicants, both of whom were women, and one of whom he shot in the back; he is saved from one of the male replicants by a female replicant. In addition there are eventual hints in the narrative that he, too, is a replicant. Despite the persistence of traditional themes (the parthenogenetic birth; the scientist as father-mother), various transgressions, which had not been possible in traditional iterations of the *Frankenstein* myth, now become crucial to the unfolding of the narrative.

A second example of a contemporary science fiction narrative that entails a reenvisaging of the mythic agonism between the stories of Dionysus and Baubo is the *Alien* series, where it is the body of the archaic mother, rather than the parthenogenetic father, that is the site of desire and revulsion, with the films' visual emphases on dark, slimy passages; on teeth dripping blood, acid, and saliva; on exploding stomachs and devouring wombs; and on the "all-incorporating black hole which threatens to reabsorb what it once birthed."[9] The latest in the series, Jean-Pierre Jeunet's *Alien Resurrection* (1997), brings the central character, Ripley (Sigourney Weaver), back to life as a clone whose DNA has been mingled with those of the alien to produce a cold-bloodedly efficient survival machine, whose loyalties to the human race are divided. Despite the strained triumphant note of the patriarchal appropriation of the parthenogenetic birth, hints of Baubo's *anasuromai* resurface, problematizing the politics of gender at the heart of the Frankensteinian myth. But within the traditional filmic iterations of the myth, which has been the topic of this book, the twofold movement of suppressing the three types of shadows and elevating an exaggerated form of the parthenogenetic myth has prevailed, despite its many tensions.

NOTES

1. An earlier version of part of this chapter was published as Caroline Joan ("Kay") S. Picart, "Visualizing the Monstrous in Frankenstein Films," *Pacific Coast Philology* 35 (2000): 17–34.

2. Judith Halberstam, *Skin Shows* (Durham, N.C.: Duke University Press, 1995), 21.

3. Rhona J. Berenstein, *Attack of the Leading Ladies: Gender, Sexuality, and Spectatorship in Classic Horror Cinema* (New York: Columbia University Press, 1996), 202.

4. Barbara Creed, *The Monstrous-Feminine: Film, Feminism, Psychoanalysis* (New York: Routledge, 1993), 1.

5. Mary Russo, *The Female Grotesque* (New York: Routledge, 1995), 278.

6. Marsha Meskimmon, "The Monstrous and Grotesque," *Make: The Magazine of Women's Art* (October 1996): 6–11.

7. Lucy Fischer, *Cinematernity: Film, Motherhood, Genre* (Princeton, N.J.: Princeton University Press, 1996), 79.

8. Creed, 7.

9. Ibid., 30.

Bibliography

"Ask Roy Ashton." *Little Shoppe of Horrors*. (July 1981): 36.

Aycock, Wendell and Michael Schoeneckc. *Film and Literature: A Comparative Approach to Adaptation*. Lubbock: Texas Tech University Press, 1988.

Baldick, Chris. *In Frankenstein's Shadow: Myth, Monstrosity, and Nineteenth Century Writing*. Oxford: Clarendon Press, 1987.

Behrend, Stephen. "Mary Shelley, *Frankenstein*, and the Woman Writer's Fate." In *Romantic Women Writers: Voices and Countervoices*, edited by Paula R. Feldman and Theresa M. Kelley, 69–87. Hanover and London: University Press of New England, 1995.

Behrend, Stephen and Anne Mellor, eds. *Approaches to Teaching Shelley's Frankenstein*. Approaches to Teaching World Literature 33. New York: Modern Language Association of America, 1990.

Benshoff, Harry M. *Monsters in the Closet: Homosexuality and the Horror Film*. Manchester and New York: Manchester University Press, 1997.

Berenstein, Rhona J. *Attack of the Leading Ladies: Gender, Sexuality, and Spectatorship in Classic Horror Cinema*. New York: Columbia University Press, 1996.

Bly, Robert. *Iron John: A Book about Men*. Reading, Mass.: Addison-Wesley, 1990.

Bohls, Elizabeth. *Women Travel Writers and the Language of Aesthetics 1716–1818*. Cambridge, England: Cambridge University Press, 1995.

Branagh, Kenneth. "A Tale for All Time." In *Mary Shelley's Frankenstein*. Screenplay by Steph Lady and Frank Darabont, 9–10. New York: Newmarket Press, 1994.

———. "The Filmmakers and Their Creations." *Mary Shelley's Frankenstein*. Screenplay by Steph Lady and Frank Darabont, 142–178. New York: Newmarket Press, 1994.

———. "Frankenstein Reimagined." *Mary Shelley's Frankenstein*. Screenplay by

Steph Lady and Frank Darabont, 17–29. New York: Newmarket Press, 1994.

"The Bride of Frankenstein." *The Variety Film Reviews 1934–1937*, Vol. 5 May 15, 1935.

"Bride of Frankenstein Review." *New York Times Review*, May 11, 1935.

"Bride of Frankenstein, The" *Variety Film Reviews 1934–1937*, May 15, 1935.

Brooks, Peter. "What Is a Monster? (According to *Frankenstein*)." *Body Work: Objects of Desire in Modern Narrative*. Cambridge, Mass.: Harvard University Press, 1993.

Brunas, Michael, John Brunas, and Tom Weaver. *Universal Horrors: The Studio's Classic Films, 1931–1946*. Jefferson, N.C.: McFarland and Company, 1990.

Burchill, Julie. "Mary Shelley's Frankenstein." *The Sunday Times*, November 6, 1994, 6, 10.

Clover, Carol J. *Men, Women and Chainsaws: Gender in the Modern Horror Film*. Princeton, N.J.: Princeton University Press, 1992.

Cooper, Brenda and David Descutner. " 'It had no voice to it': Sydney Pollack's Film Translation of Isak Dinesen's *Out of Africa*." *Quarterly Journal of Speech* 82 (1996): 228–250.

Creed, Barbara. *The Monstrous-Feminine: Film, Feminism, Psychoanalysis*. New York: Routledge, 1993.

Darling, W. Scott. *Ghost of Frankenstein*, edited by Philip J. Riley. Classic Horror Films, Vol. 4. MagicImage Filmbooks. Atlantic City, Hollywood: Universal Filmscripts Series, 1990.

Denby, David. "What's Up, Docs?" *New York*, November 14, 1994.

Dillard, R.H.W. *Horror Films*. New York: Monarch Press, 1976.

"Durrant's Press Cuttings." *Daily Mirror*, September 29, 1966.

"Durrant's Press Cuttings." *Daily Sketch*, September 29, 1966.

"Durrant's Press Cuttings." *Evening Standard*, September 28, 1966.

Elder, John. *Frankenstein Created Woman*. Unpublished Script. London: Hammer Film Productions, 1966.

The Encyclopedia of Horror Movies. Edited by Phil Hardy, Tom Milne, and Paul Willemen. New York: Harper and Row, 1986.

Erickson, Glenn. "The Bride of Frankenstein." In *Magill's Survey of Cinema*, First Series, Vol. I, edited by Frank Magill, 224. Englewood Cliffs, N.J.: Salem Press, 1980.

Evans, Walter. "Monster Movies: A Sexual Theory." *Journal of Popular Film* 2 (1973): 353–365.

———. "Monster Movies and Rites of Initiation," *Journal of Popular Film* 4 (1975): 124–142.

Everson, William K. *Classics of the Horror Film*. New York: Citadel Press, 1995.

"The Evil of Frankenstein." *The Encyclopedia of Horror Movies*, edited by Phil Hardy, Tom Milne, and Paul Willemen, 161. New York: Harper and Row, 1986.

Fischer, Dennis. *Horror Film Directors, 1931–1990*. Jefferson, N.C.: McFarland and Company, 1991.

Fischer, Lucy. *Cinematernity: Film, Motherhood, Genre*. Princeton, N.J.: Princeton University Press, 1996.

Florescu, Radu. *In Search of Frankenstein*. Boston: New York Graphic Society, 1975.

Forry, Steven Earl. *Hideous Progenies: Dramatizations of Frankenstein from Mary Shelley to the Present*. Philadelphia: University of Pennsylvania Press, 1990.

Fort, Garrett and Francis Edwards Faragoh. *Frankenstein*. Screenplay. Universal Pictures Corporation. August 12, 1931. *Frankenstein*, edited by Philip J. Riley. Universal Filmscripts Series. Classic Horror Films, Vol. 1. Absecon, N.J.: MagicImage Filmbooks, 1989.

Fournier d'Albe, E.E. *The Life of Sir William Crookes*. London: Fisher Unwin, 1923.

Frank, Alan. *The Movie Treasury; Horror Movies, Tales of Terror in the Cinema*. London: Octopus Books, 1974.

Fried, D. "Hollywood's Convention and Film Adaptation." *Theatre Journal* 39 (1987): 294–306.

Giddings, Robert, Keith Selby, and Chris Wensley. *Screening the Novel: The Theory and Practice of Literary Dramatization*. New York: St. Martin's Press, 1990.

Glut, Donald. *The Frankenstein Legend: A Tribute to Mary Shelley and Boris Karloff*. Metuchen, N.J.: Scarecrow Press, 1973.

Halberstam, Judith. *Skin Shows*. Durham, N.C.: Duke University Press, 1995.

Halliwell, Leslie. *The Dead That Walk: Dracula, Frankenstein, the Mummy and Other Famous Monsters*. New York: Continuum, 1988.

Hamilton, Edith. *Mythology: Timeless Tales of Gods and Heroes*. New York: Mentor [Penguin], 1982.

Hanke, Ken. *A Critical Guide to Horror Film Series*. New York: Garland Publishing, 1991.

Hardy, Phil, Tom Milne, and Paul Willemen, eds. *The Encyclopedia of Horror Movies*. New York: Harper and Row, 1986.

Heffernan, James A.W. "Looking at the Monster: Frankenstein and Film." *Critical Inquiry* 24 (1997): 133–158.

Homans, Margaret. *Bearing the Word*. Chicago: University of Chicago Press, 1986.

"House of Dracula Review." *The Hollywood Reporter*, November 29, 1945.

"House of Dracula Review." *Variety*, November 29, 1945.

Hunter, David. "Frankly Lousy Don't Shell Out the Bucks for the Latest Shelley Adaptation." *Los Angeles Village View*, November 4–10, 1994.

Hutchings, Peter. *Hammer and Beyond: The British Horror Film*. Manchester and New York: Manchester University Press, 1993.

Jacques, Bob. "Frankenstein: Creature Feature." *Screen International*, November 4, 1994, 34.

Jensen, Paul M. *Boris Karloff and His Films*. South Brunswick and New York: A.S. Burnes, 1974.

———. *The Men Who Made the Monsters*. New York: Twayne, 1996.

Johnson, Tom and Deborah Del Vecchio. *Hammer Films; An Exhaustive Filmography*. Jefferson, N.C.: McFarland & Company, 1996.

Jones, Stephen. *The Frankenstein Scrapbook; The Complete Movie Guide to the World's Most Famous Monster*. New York: Citadel Press/Carol Publishing Group, 1995.

Kerenyi, Carl. *Dionysos: Archetypal Image of Indestructible Life*. Translated by

Ralph Manheim. Bollingen Series, Vol. 65. Princeton, N.J.: Princeton University Press, 1976.

Klein, Michael and Gillian Parker. *The English Novel and the Movies*. New York: Frederick Ungar Publishing, 1981.

Kofman, Sarah. "Baubo: Theological Perversion and Fetishism." In *Nietzsche's New Seas*, edited by Michael Allen Gillespie and Tracy B. Strong, 175–202. Chicago: University of Chicago Press, 1988.

Lady, Steph and Frank Darabont. *Mary Shelley's Frankenstein*. Screenplay. *Mary Shelley's Frankenstein*. Kenneth Branagh. New York: Newmarket Press, 1994.

Lanza, Joseph. "Frankenstein." In *International Dictionary of Films and Filmmakers—1*, edited by Nicholas Thomas, 2nd ed., 322–324. Chicago and London: St. James Press, 1990.

Lee, Christopher. *Tall, Dark and Gruesome*. London: W.H. Allen, 1977.

Lowe, Edward T. "House of Frankenstein." Screenplay. *House of Frankenstein*. Edited by Philip J. Riley. Universal Filmscripts Series, Classic Horror, Vol. 6. Atlantic City, Hollywood: MagicImage Filmbooks, 1991.

Lubell, Winifred Milius. *The Metamorphosis of Baubo: Myths of Woman's Sexual Energy*. Nashville, Tenn.: Vanderbilt University Press, 1994.

Manguel, Alberto. *Bride of Frankenstein*. London: British Film Institute, 1997.

Mank, Gregory William. *It's Alive! The Classic Cinema Saga of Frankenstein*. San Diego and New York: A.S. Barnes, 1981.

———. "Production Background." In *Frankenstein*, edited by Philip J. Riley, Universal Filmscripts Series, Classic Horror Films, Vol. 1, 20–41. Absecon, N.J.: MagicImage Filmbooks, 1989.

———. "Production Background." In *Frankenstein Meets the Wolfman: The Original Shooting Script*, edited by Philip J. Riley, Universal Filmscripts Series, Classic Horror Films, Vol. 5. Atlantic City, Hollywood: MagicImage Filmbooks, 1990.

Marrero, Robert. *Horrors of Hammer*. Key West, Fla. RGM, 1984.

Masters, Dorothy. "House of Dracula Review," December 22, 1945. Found in University of Southern California Film Archive, file on "Frankenstein Meets the Wolfman."

Maxford, Howard. *Hammer, House of Horror; Behind the Screams*. Woodstock and New York: Overlook Press, 1996.

Mayne, Judith. *Private Novels, Public Films*. Athens: University of Georgia Press, 1988.

McCarty, John. *The Modern Horror Film*. New York and Ontario: Citadel Press, 1990.

———. *Splatter Movies; Breaking the Last Taboo of the Screen*. New York: St. Martin's Press, 1984.

McKay, C.H. "A Novel's Journey into Film: The Case of *Great Expectations*." *Literature/Film Quarterly* 13 (1985): 127–134.

McMullen, Wayne and Martha Solomon. "The Politics of Adaptation: Steven Spielberg's Appropriation of *The Color Purple*." *Text and Performance* 14 (1994): 158–174.

Mellor, Anne K. *Mary Shelley: Her Life, Her Fiction, Her Monsters*. New York: Routledge, 1989.

————. "Possessing Nature: The Female in *Frankenstein*." In *Romanticism and Feminism*, edited by Anne K. Mellor, 220–232. Bloomington and Indianapolis: Indiana University Press, 1988.

Meskimmon, Marsha. "The Monstrous and Grotesque." *Make: The Magazine of Women's Art* (October 1996): 6–11.

Mindell, Arnold. *Dreambody: The Body's Role in Revealing the Self*. Edited by Sisa Sternback-Scott and Becky Goodman. Santa Monica, Calif.: Sigo, 1982.

" 'Monster' Revived on Screens." *Los Angeles Times*, July 18, 1957.

Nash, Jay Robert and Stanley Ralph Ross. *The Motion Picture Guide: E-G, 1927–1983*. Chicago: Cinebooks, 1986.

New York Times Review. May 11, 1935.

Nollen, Scott Allen. *Boris Karloff*. Jefferson, N.C.: American Library Association, 1991.

Palmer, Randy. "Reluctant Monster Maker." *Fangoria* 50 (1986): 48.

Picart, Caroline Joan S. "James Whale's (Mis)Reading of Mary Shelley's *Frankenstein*." *Critical Studies in Mass Communication* 15 (1998): 382–404.

————. *Resentment and the "Feminine" in Nietzsche's Politico-Aesthetics*. State College, Penn.: Pennsylvania State University Press, 1999.

————. "Visualizing the Monstrous in Frankenstein Films." *Pacific Coast Philology* 35 (2000): 17–34.

Pincus, Elizabeth. "Skin Flick: *Mary Shelley's Frankenstein* and the Hideous Beauty of the Beast," *Los Angeles Weekly*, November 4, 1994.

Pirie, David. *A Heritage of Horror; The English Gothic Cinema 1946–1972*. London: Gordon Fraser, 1973.

Polidori, John. *The Diary of Dr. John William Poldori, Relating to Byron, Shelley, etc*. Edited by William Michael Rossetti. London: Elkin Matthews, 1911.

Reinach, Salomon. *Cultes, mythes, religion*, Vol. 4. Paris: Leroux, 1912.

Rossetti, Lucy Madox. *Mrs. Shelley*. Eminent Women Series. London: W.H. Allen, 1890.

Rushing, Janice. "Evolution of 'The New Frontier' in *Alien* and *Aliens*: Patriarchal Co-Optation of the Feminine Archetype," *Quarterly Journal of Speech* 75 (1989): 1–24.

Rushing, Janice H. and Thomas S. Frentz. "The Frankenstein Myth in Contemporary Cinema." *Critical Studies in Mass Communication* 6 (1989): 61–80.

————. *Projecting the Shadow: The Cyborg Hero in American Film*. Chicago: Chicago University Press, 1995.

Russo, Mary. *The Female Grotesque*. New York: Routledge, 1995.

Shelley, Mary. *Frankenstein*. New York: Bantam Books, 1991.

Sinyard, Neil. *Filming Literature: The Art of Screen Adaptation*. London: Croom Helm Limited, 1986.

Siodmak, Curt. "Wolf-Man Meets Frankenstein." In *Frankenstein Meets the Wolfman: The Original Shooting Script*, edited by. Philip J. Riley. Universal Filmscripts Series, Classic Horror Films, Vol. 5. Atlantic City, Hollywood: MagicImage Filmbooks, 1990.

Stock, R.D. *The Flutes of Dionysus; Daemonic Enthrallment in Literature*. Lincoln: University of Nebraska Press, 1989.

Subotsky, Milton. *Frankenstein*. Screenplay. Warner Brothers. ca. 1956.

Sunstein, Emily W. *Mary Shelley: Romance and Reality*. Baltimore, Md.: Johns
    Hopkins University Press, 1991.
Tropp, Martin. *Mary Shelley's Monster*. Boston: Houghton Mifflin, 1976.
Variety. May 15, 1935.
Veeder, William. *Mary Shelley and Frankenstein: The Fate of Androgyny*. Chicago:
    University of Chicago Press, 1986.
Weldon, Michael, Charles Beesley, Bob Martin, and Akira Fitton. *The Psychotronic
    Encyclopedia of Film*. New York: Ballantine Books, 1983.
Whitford, Margaret. "Reading Irigaray in the Nineties." In *Engaging with Irigaray:
    Feminist Philosophy and European Thought*, edited by Carolyn Burke,
    Naomi Schor, and Margaret Whitford, 379–400. New York: Columbia University Press.
Wilson, Deborah. "Technologies of Misogyny: The Transparent Maternal Body
    and Alternate Reproductions in *Frankenstein, Dracula*, and Some Selected
    Media Discourses." In *Bodily Discursions: Genders, Representations, Technologies*, Edited by Deborah Wilson and Christine Moneera Laennec. Albany: State University of New York Press, 1997. 105–133.
Winsten, Archer. " 'Curse of Frankenstein' at Paramount." *New York Post*, August
    7, 1957.

Index

About the Author

CAROLINE JOAN ("KAY") S. PICART is an Assistant Professor of English and Humanities at Florida State University. She is the author of *Resentment and "the Feminine" in Nietzsche's Politico-Aesthetics*, *Thomas Mann and Friedrich Nietzsche: Eroticism, Death, Music, and Laughter*, and, with Jayne Blodgett and Frank Smoot, *The Frankenstein Film Sourcebook* (Greenwood, 2001).